Tyndale Old Testament Commentaries

Volume 24

TOTC

Hosea

T0327233

TYNDALE OLD TESTAMENT COMMENTARIES

VOLUME 24

SERIES EDITOR: DAVID G. FIRTH
CONSULTING EDITOR: TREMPER LONGMAN III

HOSEA
AN INTRODUCTION AND COMMENTARY

ROBIN ROUTLEDGE

Academic
An imprint of InterVarsity Press
Downers Grove, Illinois

Inter-Varsity Press, England
36 Causton Street, London SW1P 4ST, England
Website: www.ivpbooks.com
Email: ivp@ivpbooks.com

InterVarsity Press, USA
P.O. Box 1400, Downers Grove, IL 60515, USA
Website: www.ivpress.com
Email: email@ivpress.com

Inter-Varsity Press, England, publishes Christian books that are true to the Bible and that
communicate the gospel, develop discipleship and strengthen the church for its mission in the world.

IVP originated within the Inter-Varsity Fellowship, now the Universities and Colleges Christian
Fellowship, a student movement connecting Christian Unions in universities and colleges throughout
Great Britain, and a member movement of the International Fellowship of Evangelical Students.
That historic association is maintained, and all senior IVP staff and committee members subscribe
to the UCCF Basis of Faith. Website: www.uccf.org.uk.

InterVarsity Press®, USA, is the book-publishing division of InterVarsity Christian Fellowship/
USA® and a member movement of the International Fellowship of Evangelical Students. Website:
www.intervarsity.org.

Unless otherwise stated, Scripture quotations are from the NIV 2011. For Bible acknowledgments,
see p. xii.

First published 2020

Set in Garamond 11/13pt
Typeset in Great Britain by CRB Associates, Potterhanworth, Lincolnshire
Printed and bound in Great Britain by Ashford Colour Press Ltd, Gosport, Hampshire

Produced on paper from sustainable forests.

UK ISBN: 978-1-78359-964-6 (print)
UK ISBN: 978-1-78359-965-3 (digital)

US ISBN: 978-0-8308-4271-1 (print)
US ISBN: 978-0-8308-4278-0 (digital)

British Library Cataloguing-in-Publication Data
A catalogue record for this book is available from the British Library.

Library of Congress Cataloging-in-Publication Data
A catalog record for this book is available from the Library of Congress.

CONTENTS

GENERAL PREFACE

The decision to completely revise the Tyndale Old Testament Commentaries is an indication of the important role that the series has played since its opening volumes were released in the mid 1960s. They represented at that time, and have continued to represent, commentary writing that was committed to both the importance of the text of the Bible as Scripture and a desire to engage with as full a range of interpretative issues as possible without being lost in the minutiae of scholarly debate. The commentaries aimed to explain the biblical text to a generation of readers confronting models of critical scholarship and new discoveries from the Ancient Near East while remembering that the Old Testament is not simply another text from the ancient world. Although no uniform process of exegesis was required, all the original contributors were united in their conviction that the Old Testament remains the word of God for us today. That the original volumes fulfilled this role is evident from the way in which they continue to be used in so many parts of the world.

A crucial element of the original series was that it should offer an up-to-date reading of the text, and it is precisely for this reason that new volumes are required. The questions confronting readers in the first half of the twenty-first century are not necessarily those from the second half of the twentieth. Discoveries from the Ancient Near East continue to shed new light on the Old Testament, while emphases in exegesis have changed markedly. While remaining true to the goals of the initial volumes, the need for contemporary study of the text requires that the series as a whole be updated. This updating is not simply a matter of commissioning new volumes to replace the old. We have also taken the opportunity to update the format of the series to reflect a key emphasis from linguistics, which is that texts communicate in larger blocks rather than in shorter segments such as individual verses. Because of this, the treatment of each section of the text includes three segments. First, a short note on *Context* is offered, placing the passage under consideration in its literary setting within the book as well as noting any historical issues crucial to interpretation. The *Comment* segment then follows the traditional structure of the commentary, offering exegesis of the various components of a passage. Finally, a brief comment is made on *Meaning*, by which is meant the message that the passage seeks to communicate within the book, highlighting its key theological themes. This section brings together the detail of the *Comment* to show how the passage under consideration seeks to communicate as a whole.

Our prayer is that these new volumes will continue the rich heritage of the Tyndale Old Testament Commentaries and that they will continue to witness to the God who is made known in the text.

David G. Firth, Series Editor
Tremper Longman III, Consulting Editor

AUTHOR'S PREFACE

My fascination with Hosea goes back to university days. A series of inspirational Bible studies at the church I was attending piqued my interest, and it has been my favourite Old Testament book ever since. One reason for that is the intimate portrayal of the relationship between Yahweh and his people – as a husband and as a father – which brings a sense of vulnerability and also highlights aspects of divine love that, in my view, come as close as anything in the Old Testament to the love revealed more fully in Christ. Some recent approaches to the prophecy have focused less on the historical aspects of Hosea's family life. I agree that details are sparse but, nevertheless, view the opening chapters as programmatic for the book as a whole, and have argued that Hosea's marital situation, where it can be reconstructed, and its parallel with Yahweh's 'marriage' to Israel, plays a crucial part in understanding the depth of Yahweh's relationship with his people.

Perhaps in keeping with the relational aspect of the book, the most frequent title for God is YHWH, which appears as 'the LORD' in most English versions. I have rendered the divine name 'Yahweh', whilst translating other terms, *ĕlōhîm* and the less frequent *ēl*, as 'God'.

The commentary was not without its challenges. The text of Hosea is difficult, and I lost count of the number of times commentators described one passage or another as 'among the most difficult in the Old Testament'. Possible reasons for difficulties in translating the text are discussed in the commentary. One result of these challenges is a relatively large number of references to other commentaries and of explanatory footnotes. I hope these are helpful. When comparing differing views, I have sometimes not found it possible to come to a definite conclusion. My aim on those occasions is to note viable alternatives and provide enough information for readers to form their own opinion. Sources for further reading are included in the footnotes. Footnotes are also used to note references to the several recurring themes in the book.

In writing this commentary I am grateful for the help and encouragement of colleagues and friends, and also of students around the world, who have listened to, and given feedback on, some of the ideas expressed here. I am grateful, too, to congregations who have listened, patiently, to numerous sermons on Hosea during the years this volume has been in preparation. It is my hope that this commentary will encourage others to preach and teach on what I consider to be an important book. Thanks, too, to David Firth and Phil Duce, and the team at SPCK, for their hard work, help, encouragement and considerable patience. And thanks to my family: my wife and best friend, Ailsa, my children and my grandchildren, Darcey, Rex, Lucas and Leo, for bearing with me on those occasions when I have pulled out the computer to do 'just a little bit more'. Thanks, finally, to God for his inspired Word, and for the divine love that the book of Hosea gives us insights into.

Robin Routledge

ABBREVIATIONS

JNSL	*Journal of Northwest Semitic Languages*
JSOT	*Journal for the Study of the Old Testament*
JSOTSup	Journal for the Study of the Old Testament Supplement Series
LHB/OTS	Library of Hebrew Bible/Old Testament Studies
LXX	Septuagint
mg.	Marginal reading
MT	Masoretic Text
NICOT	New International Commentary on the Old Testament
NIDOTTE	*New International Dictionary of Old Testament Theology and Exegesis*, ed. W. A. VanGemeren, 5 vols. (Carlisle: Paternoster; Grand Rapids: Zondervan, 1996)
OTE	*Old Testament Essays*
TDOT	*Theological Dictionary of the Old Testament*, ed. G. J. Botterweck, H. Ringgren and H.-J. Fabry, trans. J. T. Willis, G. W. Bromiley, D. E. Green and D. W. Stott, 15 vols. (Grand Rapids: Eerdmans, 1974–2006)
TOTC	Tyndale Old Testament Commentary
TynBul	*Tyndale Bulletin*
VT	*Vetus Testamentum*
WTJ	*Westminster Theological Journal*
ZAW	*Zeitschrift für die alttestamentliche Wissenschaft*

Bible versions

NRSV   From the New Revised Standard Version of the
                Bible, Anglicized Edition, copyright © 1989, 1995
                by the Division of Christian Education of the
                National Council of the Churches of Christ in the
                USA. Used by permission. All rights reserved.

SELECT BIBLIOGRAPHY

Commentaries on Hosea

Achtemeier, E. (1996), *Minor Prophets I*, Understanding the Bible Commentary (Grand Rapids: Baker).

Andersen, F. I. and D. N. Freedman (1980), *Hosea: A New Translation with Introduction and Commentary*, Anchor Bible 24 (New York: Doubleday).

Ben Zvi, E. (2005), *Hosea*, Formation of Old Testament Literature 21A/1 (Grand Rapids/Cambridge: Eerdmans).

Birch, B. C. (1997), *Hosea, Joel, Amos*, Westminster Bible Companion (Louisville: Westminster John Knox).

Davies, G. I. (1992), *Hosea*, New Century Bible (London: Marshall, Morgan & Scott).

Dearman, J. A. (2010), *The Book of Hosea*, NICOT (Grand Rapids/ Cambridge: Eerdmans).

Garrett, D. A. (1997), *Hosea, Joel*, New American Commentary 19A (Nashville: B&H).

Glenny, W. E. (2013), *Hosea: A Commentary Based on Hosea in* Codex Vaticanus (Leiden: Brill).

Gruber, M. I. (2017), *Hosea: A Textual Commentary*, LHB/OTS (London/New York: Bloomsbury T&T Clark).

Harper, W. R. (1905), *Amos and Hosea*, International Critical Commentary (Edinburgh: T&T Clark).

Hubbard, D. A. (1989), *Hosea*, TOTC (Leicester: Inter-Varsity Press).

Keil, C. F. and F. Delitzsch (1980), *Minor Prophets* (Grand Rapids: Eerdmans).

Kidner, D. (1981), *The Message of Hosea: Love to the Loveless*, Bible Speaks Today (Leicester: Inter-Varsity Press; Downers Grove: Inter-Varsity Press).

Knight, G. A. F. (1960), *Hosea*, Torch Bible Commentaries (London: SCM).

Lim, B. H. and D. Castelo (2015), *Hosea*, Two Horizons Old Testament Commentary (Grand Rapids/Cambridge: Eerdmans).

McComiskey, T. E. (1998), 'Hosea', in T. E. McComiskey (ed.), *The Minor Prophets: An Exegetical and Expository Commentary* (Grand Rapids: Baker Academic), pp. 1–237.

Macintosh, A. A. (1997), *A Critical and Exegetical Commentary on Hosea*, International Critical Commentary (Edinburgh: T&T Clark).

Mays, J. L. (1969), *Hosea*, Old Testament Library (London: SCM).

Moon, J. (2018), *Hosea*, AOTC 21 (London: Apollos; Downers Grove: IVP Academic).

Patterson, R. D. (2008), 'Hosea', in R. D. Patterson and A. E. Hill, *Minor Prophets: Hosea–Malachi*, Cornerstone Biblical Commentary 10 (Carol Stream: Tyndale House), pp. 2–96.

Smith, G. V. (2001), *Hosea, Amos, Micah*, New International Version Application Commentary (Grand Rapids: Zondervan).

Stuart, D. (1987), *Hosea–Jonah*, Word Biblical Commentary 31 (Waco: Word).

Sweeney, M. A. (2000), *The Twelve Prophets*, Volume 1, Berit Olam (Collegeville: Liturgical).

Wolff, H. W. (1974), *Hosea*, Hermeneia (Philadelphia: Fortress).

Other works

Abma, R. (1999), *Bonds of Love: Methodic Studies of Prophetic Texts with Marriage Imagery (Isaiah 50:1–3 and 54:1–10, Hosea 1–3, Jeremiah 2–3)* (Assen: van Gorcum).

Ackroyd, P. R. (1963), 'Hosea and Jacob', *VT* 13.3: 245–259.

Adams, K. (2008), 'Metaphor and Dissonance: A Reinterpretation of Hosea 4:13–14', *JBL* 127.2: 291–305.

Albertz, R. (2003), 'Exile as Purification: Reconstructing the "Book of the Four"', in P. L. Redditt and A. Schart (eds.), *Thematic Threads in the Book of the Twelve*, BZAW 325 (Berlin: de Gruyter), pp. 231–251.

Albertz, R., J. D. Nogalski and J. Wöhrle (eds.) (2013), *Perspectives on the Formation of the Book of the Twelve: Methodological Foundations, Redactional Processes, Historical Insights*, BZAW 433 (Berlin: de Gruyter).

Alt, A. (1953), 'Hosea 5,8 – 6,6: Ein Krieg und seine Folgen in prophetischer Beleuchtung', in *Kleine Schriften zur Geschichte des Volkes*, Volume 2 (Munich: C. H. Beck), pp. 163–187.

Anderson, J. S. (2015), *Monotheism and Yahweh's Appropriation of Baal*, LHB/OTS (London/New York: Bloomsbury Academic).

Ansberry, C. B. and J. Hwang (2013), 'No Covenant before the Exile: The Deuteronomic Torah and Israel's Covenant Theology', in C. M. Hays and C. B. Ansberry (eds.), *Evangelical Faith and the Challenge of Historical Criticism* (London: SPCK), pp. 74–94.

Arnold, P. M. (1989), 'Hosea and the Sin of Gibeah', *CBQ* 51.3: 447–460.

—— (1990), *Gibeah: The Search for a Biblical City*, JSOTSup 79 (Sheffield: Sheffield Academic Press).

—— (1992), 'Mizpah', in *ABD* 4.879–881.

Aster, S. Z. (2012), 'The Function of the City of Jezreel and the Symbolism of Jezreel in Hosea 1 – 2', *JNES* 71.1: 31–46.

Baden, J. S. (2012), *The Composition of the Pentateuch: Renewing the Documentary Hypothesis*, Anchor Yale Bible Reference Library (New Haven/London: Yale University Press).

Baker, D. L. (2010), *Two Testaments, One Bible: The Theological Relationship between the Old and New Testaments*, 3rd edn (Nottingham: Apollos).

Barré, M. L. (1978), 'New Light on the Interpretation of Hosea VI 2', *VT* 28.2: 129–141.

Baumann, A. (1974) '*bal*', in *TDOT* 1.44–48.

Baumann, G. (2003), *Love and Violence: Marriage as a Metaphor for the Relationship between YHWH and Israel in the Prophetic Books* (Collegeville: Liturgical).

Beale, G. K. (2012), 'The Use of Hosea 11:1 in Matthew 2:15:
   One More Time', *JETS* 55.4: 697–715.
Bechtel, L. M. (1991), 'Shame as a Sanction of Social Control in
   Biblical Israel: Judicial, Political, and Social Shaming', *JSOT* 49:
   47–76.
Becking, B. (1992), *The Fall of Samaria: An Historical and
   Archaeological Study* (Leiden: Brill).
Ben Zvi, E. (1996), 'Twelve Prophetic Books or "The Twelve":
   A Few Preliminary Considerations', in J. W. Watts and
   P. R. House (eds.), *Forming Prophetic Literature: Essays on Isaiah
   and the Twelve in Honor of John D. W. Watts*, JSOTSup 235
   (Sheffield: Sheffield Academic), pp. 125–156.
—— (2006), 'De-Historicizing and Historicizing Tendencies
   in the Twelve Prophetic Books: A Case Study of the Heuristic
   Value of a Historically Anchored Systematic Approach to
   the Corpus of Prophetic Literature', in B. E. Kelle and
   M. Bishop Moore (eds.), *Israel's Prophets and Israel's Past:
   Essays on the Relationship of Prophetic Texts and Israelite History
   in Honor of John H. Hayes* (London/New York: T&T Clark),
   pp. 37–56.
Bergland, K. (2011–12), 'Analysis and Assessment of
   Chronological Explanations of the Fall of Samaria', *Spes
   Christiana* 22–23: 63–84.
Berlin, A. (1994), *Poetics and Interpretation of Biblical Narrative*
   (Winona Lake: Eisenbrauns; orig. Sheffield: Almond, 1983).
Bird, P. (1989), 'To Play the Harlot', in P. L. Day (ed.), *Gender
   and Difference in Ancient Israel* (Minneapolis: Fortress),
   pp. 75–94.
Blenkinsopp, J. (1996), *A History of Prophecy in Israel*, rev. edn
   (Louisville/London: Westminster John Knox).
Bons, E. (2016), 'Textual Criticism of the Prophetic Corpus', in
   C. J. Sharp (ed.), *The Oxford Handbook of the Prophets* (Oxford/
   New York: Oxford University Press), pp. 117–131.
Bos, J. M. (2013), *Reconsidering the Date and Provenance of the Book of
   Hosea: The Case for Persian Period Yehud*, LHB/OTS (London/
   New York: T&T Clark).
Boshoff, W. (1992), 'Yahweh as God of Nature: Elements of the
   Concepts of God in the Book of Hosea', *JNSL* 18: 13–24.

—— (2004), 'Who Let Grain, Grapes and Olives Grow? Hosea's Polemics Against the Yahwists of Israel', in T. L. Hettma and A. van der Kooij (eds.), *Religious Polemics in Context* (Assen: Koninklijke van Gorcum), pp. 265–275.

Bracke, J. M. (1996), '*ryb*', in *NIDOTTE* 3.1105–1106.

Brenner, A. (1995), 'On Prophetic Propaganda and the Politics of "Love": The Case of Jeremiah', in A. Brenner (ed.), *Feminist Companion to the Latter Prophets* (Sheffield: Sheffield Academic), pp. 256–274.

—— (1996a), 'Pornoprophetics Revisited: Some Additional Reflections', *JSOT* 70: 63–86.

—— (1996b), 'On "Jeremiah" and the Poetics of (Prophetic?) Pornography', in A. Brenner and F. van Dijk-Hemmes (eds.), *On Gendering Texts: Female and Male Voices in the Hebrew Bible* (Leiden/New York: Brill), pp. 177–194.

—— (1997), *The Intercourse of Knowledge: On Gendering Desire and 'Sexuality' in the Hebrew Bible* (Leiden/New York: Brill).

Britt, B. (2003), 'Unexpected Attachments: A Literary Approach to the Term *ḥesed* in the Hebrew Bible', *JSOT* 27.3: 289–307.

Brodsky, H. (1992), 'Bethel', in *ABD* 1.710–712.

Campbell, A. F. and M. A. O'Brien (2000), *Unfolding the Deuteronomistic History: Origins, Upgrades, Present Text* (Minneapolis: Augsburg Fortress).

Carroll, R. P. (1995), 'Desire under the Terebinths: On Pornographic Representation in the Prophets – A Response', in A. Brenner (ed.), *Feminist Companion to the Latter Prophets* (Sheffield: Sheffield Academic), pp. 278–307.

Childs, B. (1979), *Introduction to the Old Testament as Scripture* (Philadelphia: Fortress).

Clark, G. R. (1993), *The Word 'Hesed' in the Hebrew Bible*, JSOTSup 157 (Sheffield: Sheffield Academic).

Clines, D. J. A. (1998), 'Hosea 2: Structure and Interpretation', in D. J. A. Clines, *On the Way to the Postmodern: Old Testament Essays 1967–1998*, Volume 1, JSOTSup 292 (Sheffield: Sheffield Academic), pp. 293–313.

Collins, J. J. (2014), *Introduction to the Hebrew Bible*, 2nd edn (Minneapolis: Fortress).

Cook, S. L. (2004), *The Social Roots of Biblical Yahwism* (Atlanta: SBL).

Coote, R. B. (1971), 'Hosea XII', *VT* 21.4: 389–402.

Craigie, P. C. (1976), *Deuteronomy*, NICOT (Grand Rapids: Eerdmans).

—— (1984), *Twelve Prophets*, Volume 1: *Hosea, Joel, Amos, Obadiah, Jonah*, Daily Study Bible (Louisville/London: Westminster John Knox).

Curtis, B. G. (2009), 'Hosea 6:7 and Covenant-Breaking Like/at Adam', in B. D. Estelle, J. V. Fesko and D. VanDrunen (eds.), *The Law Is Not of Faith* (Phillipsburg: P&R), pp. 170–209.

Curtis, R. I. (2001), *Ancient Food Technology*, Technology and Change in History 5 (Leiden: Brill).

Daniels, D. R. (1987), 'Is There a "Prophetic Lawsuit" Genre?', *ZAW* 99.3: 339–360.

—— (1990), *Hosea and Salvation History*, BZAW 191 (Berlin/New York: Walter de Gruyter).

Davidson, R. M. (2010), 'The Divine Covenant Lawsuit Motif in Canonical Perspective', *Journal of the Adventist Theological Society* 21.1: 45–84.

Davies, G. I. (1993), *Hosea*, Old Testament Guides (Sheffield: JSOT Press).

Day, J. (1985), *God's Conflict with the Dragon and with the Sea: Echoes of a Canaanite Myth in the Old Testament*, University of Cambridge Oriental Publications 35 (Cambridge: University of Cambridge Press).

—— (1986a), 'Pre-Deuteronomic Allusions to the Covenant in Hosea and Psalm LXXVIII', *VT* 36.1: 1–12.

—— (1986b), 'Asherah in the Hebrew Bible and Northwest Semitic Literature', *JBL* 105.3: 385–408.

—— (1992a), 'The Problem of "So, King of Egypt" in 2 Kings XVII 4', *VT* 42.3: 289–301.

—— (1992b), 'Asherah', in *ABD* 1.483–487.

—— (1992c), 'Baal', in *ABD* 1.547–549.

—— (1992d), 'Rahab (Dragon)', in *ABD* 5.610–611.

—— (2000), *Yahweh and the Gods and Goddesses of Canaan*, JSOTSup 265 (London/New York: Sheffield Academic).

—— (2010), 'Hosea and the Baal Cult', in J. Day (ed.), *Prophecy and the Prophets in Ancient Israel: Proceedings of the Oxford Old Testament*

Seminar (New York/London: T&T Clark International), pp. 202–224.

Day, P. L. (1992), 'Anat: Ugarit's "Mistress of Animals"', *JNES* 51.3: 181–190.

—— (1999), 'Anat', in K. van der Toorn, B. Becking and P. W. van der Horst (eds.), *Dictionary of Deities and Demons*, 2nd edn (Grand Rapids/Cambridge: Eerdmans), pp. 36–43.

—— (2006), 'A Prostitute Unlike Women: Whoring as a Metaphoric Vehicle for Foreign Alliances', in B. E. Kelle and M. Bishop Moore (eds.), *Israel's Prophets and Israel's Past: Essays on the Relationship of Prophetic Texts and Israelite History in Honor of John H. Hayes* (New York/London: T&T Clark), pp. 167–173.

Dearman, J. A. (1993), 'Baal in Israel: The Contribution of Some Place Names and Personal Names to an Understanding of Early Israelite Religion', in M. P. Graham, W. P. Brown and J. K. Kuan (eds.), *History and Interpretation: Essays in Honour of John H. Hayes*, JSOTSup 173 (Sheffield: Sheffield Academic), pp. 173–191.

—— (2001), 'Interpreting the Religious Polemics against Baal and the Baalim in the Book of Hosea', *OTE* 14.1: 9–25.

Dempster, S. G. (2014), 'From Slight Peg to Cornerstone to Capstone: The Resurrection of Christ on "the Third Day" According to the Scriptures', *WTJ* 76: 371–409.

Deroche, M. (1981), 'The Reversal of Creation in Hosea', *VT* 31.4: 400–409.

—— (1983a), 'Yahweh's Rîb against Israel: A Reassessment of the So-Called "Prophetic Lawsuit" in the Preexilic Prophets', *JBL* 102.4: 563–574.

—— (1983b), 'Structure, Rhetoric and Meaning in Hosea IV 4–10', *VT* 33.2: 185–198.

Dharamraj, H. (2018), *Altogether Lovely: A Thematic and Intertextual Reading of the Song of Songs* (Minneapolis: Fortress).

Dorn, L. O. (2000), 'Is Gomer the Woman in Hosea 3?', *The Bible Translator* 51.4: 424–440.

Ehrlich, C. S. (1991), 'Coalition Politics in Eighth Century B.C.E. Palestine: The Philistines and the Syro-Ephraimite War', *Zeitschrift des deutschen Palästina-Vereins* 107: 48–58.

—— (1996), *The Philistines in Transition: A History from ca. 1000–730 BCE* (Leiden: Brill).

Eidevall, G. (1996), *Grapes in the Desert: Metaphors, Models and Themes in Hosea 4 – 14,* Coniectanea Biblica, Old Testament 43 (Stockholm: Almqvist and Wiksell).

Els, P. J. J. S. (1996), '*lqḥ*', in *NIDOTTE* 2.812–817.

Emerton, J. A. (1982), 'Leviathan and *ltn*: The Vocalization of the Ugaritic Word for the Dragon', *VT* 32.3: 327–331.

Emmerson, G. I. (1975), 'The Structure and Meaning of Hosea VIII 1–3', *VT* 25.4: 700–710.

—— (1984), *Hosea: An Israelite Prophet in Judean Perspective,* JSOTSup 28 (Sheffield: JSOT Press).

Esler, P. F. (2012), *Sex, Wives and Warriors: Reading Old Testament Narrative with Its Ancient Audience* (Cambridge: James Clarke & Co.).

Fensham, F. C. (1984), 'The Marriage Metaphor in Hosea for the Covenant Relationship between the Lord and His People', *JNSL* 12: 71–78.

Finkelstein, I. (2013), *The Forgotten Kingdom: The Archaeology and History of Northern Israel,* Ancient Near Eastern Monographs 5 (Atlanta: SBL).

Fox, M. V. (1973), 'Jeremiah 2:2 and the "Desert Ideal"', *CBQ* 35: 441–450.

Frankel, R. (1992), 'Tabor', in *ABD* 6.304–305.

Fretheim, T. E. (1996), '*yd*ʿ', in *NIDOTTE* 2.409–414.

Glueck, N. (1967), *Hesed in the Bible* (Cincinnati: Hebrew Union College Press).

Good, E. M. (1966a), 'Hosea 5:8 – 6:6: An Alternative to Alt', *JBL* 85.3: 273–286.

—— (1966b), 'Hosea and the Jacob Tradition', *VT* 16.2: 137–151.

Gordis, R. (1954), 'Hosea's Marriage and Message: A New Approach', *Hebrew Union College Annual* 25: 9–35.

Gordon, R. P. (1996a), 'ʾ*lh*', in *NIDOTTE* 1.403–405.

—— (1996b), '*ʒ'm*', in *NIDOTTE* 1.1129.

Green, Y. (2003), 'Hosea and Gomer Revisited', *Jewish Biblical Quarterly* 31: 84–89.

Gruber, M. I. (1995), 'Marital Fidelity and Intimacy: A View from Hosea 4', in A. Brenner (ed.), *Feminist Companion to the Latter Prophets* (Sheffield: Sheffield Academic), pp. 169–179.

Hadjiev, T. S. (2010), 'Zephaniah and the "Book of the Twelve" Hypothesis', in J. Day (ed.), *Prophecy and the Prophets in Ancient Israel: Proceedings of the Oxford Old Testament Seminar* (New York/ London: T&T Clark International), pp. 325–338.

—— (2012), 'Honor and Shame', in *DOTPr*, pp. 333–338.

—— (2016), 'Adultery, Shame and Sexual Pollution in Ancient Israel and Hosea: A Response to Joshua Moon', *JSOT* 41.2: 221–236.

—— (2020), 'A Prophetic Anthology Rather Than a Book of the Twelve: The Unity of the Minor Prophets Reconsidered', in L.-S. Tiemeyer and J. Wöhrle (eds.), *The Book of the Twelve: Composition, Reception and Interpretation*, Vetus Testamentum Supplement 184 (Leiden: Brill), pp. 90–108.

Hall, G. (1982), 'Origin of the Marriage Metaphor', *Hebrew Studies* 23: 169–171.

Hamilton, J. M., Jr (2008), 'The Virgin Will Conceive: Typological Fulfillment in Matthew 1:18–23', in D. M. Gurtner and J. Nolland (eds.), *Built upon the Rock: Studies in the Gospel of Matthew* (Grand Rapids: Eerdmans), pp. 228–247.

Hanley, R. C. (2017), 'The Background and Purpose of Stripping the Adulteress in Hosea 2', *JETS* 60.1: 89–103.

Harris, R. L. (1961), 'The Meaning of the Word Sheol as Shown by Parallels in Poetic Texts', *Bulletin of the Evangelical Theological Society* 4.4: 129–135.

Hayden, R. E. (1996), '`bal`', in *NIDOTTE* 1.248.

Hayes, K. M. (2002), *The Earth Mourns: Prophetic Metaphor and Oral Aesthetic* (Leiden: Brill).

Hess, R. S. (1994), 'Achan and Achor: Names and Wordplay in Joshua 7', *Hebrew Annual Review* 14: 89–98.

—— (2007), *Israelite Religion: An Archaeological and Biblical Survey* (Grand Rapids: Baker Academic; Nottingham: Apollos).

Hill, A. E. and J. H. Walton (2009), *A Survey of the Old Testament*, 3rd edn (Grand Rapids: Zondervan).

Holladay, W. L. (1966), 'Chiasmus, the Key to Hosea XII 3–6', *VT* 16.1: 53–64.

House, P. R. (1990), *The Unity of the Twelve* (Sheffield: Sheffield Academic).

Hubbard, R. L., Jr (1996a), '*g'l*', in *NIDOTTE* 1.789–794.

—— (1996b), '*pdh*', in *NIDOTTE* 3.578–582.

Huffmon, H. B. (1959), 'The Covenant Lawsuit in the Prophets', *JBL* 78: 285–295.

Hugenberger, G. P. (1994), *Marriage as Covenant: Biblical Law and Ethics as Developed from Malachi* (Eugene: Wipf and Stock).

Hwang, J. (2014), '"My Name Will Be Great among the Nations": The *Missio Dei* in the Book of the Twelve', *TynBul* 65.2: 161–180.

Instone-Brewer, D. (1996), 'Three Weddings and a Divorce: God's Covenant with Israel, Judah and the Church', *TynBul* 47.1: 1–25.

Irvine, S. A. (1990), *Isaiah, Ahaz and the Syro-Ephraimitic Crisis*, Society of Biblical Literature Dissertation Series 123 (Atlanta: Scholars).

—— (1995), 'Politics and Prophetic Commentary in Hosea 8:8–10', *JBL* 114.2: 292–294.

Jenson, P. (1996), '*ēpôd*', in *NIDOTTE* 1.476–477.

Johansen, J. H. (1971), 'The Prophet Hosea: His Marriage and Message', *JETS* 14.3: 179–184.

Johnston, P. S. (2002), *Shades of Sheol: Death and Afterlife in the Old Testament* (Leicester: Apollos; Downers Grove: InterVarsity Press).

—— (2009), 'Faith in Isaiah', in D. G. Firth and H. G. M. Williamson (eds.), *Interpreting Isaiah: Issues and Approaches* (Nottingham: Apollos; Downers Grove: IVP Academic), pp. 104–121.

Kaiser, W. C., Jr (1998), *A History of Israel: From the Bronze Age through the Jewish Wars* (Nashville: B&H).

Kakkanattu, J. P. (2006), *God's Enduring Love in the Book of Hosea*, Forschung zum Alten Testament 2.14 (Tübingen: Mohr Siebeck).

Keefe, A. A. (1995), 'The Female Body, the Body Politic and the Land: A Sociopolitical Reading of Hosea 1 – 2', in A. Brenner (ed.), *Feminist Companion to the Latter Prophets* (Sheffield: Sheffield Academic), pp. 70–100.

—— (2001), *Woman's Body and the Social Body in Hosea 1 – 2*, JSOTSup 338; Gender, Culture, Theory 10 (Sheffield: Sheffield Academic).

—— (2008), 'Family Metaphors and Social Conflict in Hosea', in B. E. Kelle and F. Ritschel Ames (eds.), *Writing and Reading War: Rhetoric, Gender, and Ethics in Biblical and Modern Contexts* (Atlanta: SBL), pp. 113–127.

Kelle, B. E. (2005), *Hosea 2: Metaphor and Rhetoric in Historical Perspective* (Atlanta: SBL).

—— (2009), 'Hosea 1 – 3 in Twentieth-Century Scholarship', *CBR* 7.2: 177–218.

—— (2010), 'Hosea 4 – 14 in Twentieth-Century Scholarship', *CBR* 8.3: 314–375.

Kim, S. (2018), 'Is the Masoretic Text Still a Reliable Primary Source for the Book of Hosea?', *BBR* 28.1: 34–64.

Kirk, J. R. D. (2008), 'Conceptualising Fulfilment in Matthew', *TynBul* 59.1: 77–98.

Kitchen, K. A. (2003), *On the Reliability of the Old Testament* (Grand Rapids/Cambridge: Eerdmans).

Kruger, P. A. (1983), 'Israel, the Harlot (Hos. 2.4–9)', *JNSL* 11: 107–116.

—— (1988a), 'Prophetic Imagery: On Metaphors and Similes in the Book of Hosea', *JNSL* 14: 143–151.

—— (1988b), 'Yahweh's Generous Love: Eschatological Expectations in Hosea 14:2–9', *OTE* 1.1: 27–48.

Kugler, R. A. (1999), 'The Deuteronomists and the Latter Prophets', in L. S. Schearing and S. L. McKenzie, *Those Elusive Deuteronomists: The Phenomenon of Pan-Deuteronomism*, JSOTSup 268 (Sheffield: Sheffield Academic), pp. 127–144.

Kwakkel, G. (2011), '"Out of Egypt I Have Called My Son": Matthew 2:15 and Hosea 11:1 in Dutch and American Evangelical Interpretation', in W. Th. van Peursen and J. W. Dyk (eds.), *Tradition and Innovation in Biblical Interpretation: Studies Presented to Professor Eep Talstra on the Occasion of His Sixty-Fifth Birthday* (Leiden: Koninklijke Brill), pp. 171–188.

Lalleman, H. (2013), *Jeremiah and Lamentations*, TOTC 21 (Nottingham: Inter-Varsity Press; Downers Grove: InterVarsity Press).

Lalleman-de Winkel, H. (2000), *Jeremiah in Prophetic Tradition: An Examination of Jeremiah in the Light of Israel's Prophetic Traditions* (Leuven: Peeters).

Lange, A. (2007), "'They Burn Their Sons and Daughters –
That Was No Command of Mine" (Jer. 7:31): Child Sacrifice
in the Hebrew Bible and in the Deuteronomistic Jeremiah
Redaction', in K. Finsterbusch, A. Lange and K. F. D. Römheld
(eds.), *Human Sacrifice in Jewish and Christian Tradition* (Leiden:
Brill), pp. 109–132.

LaSor, W. S. (1978), 'Prophecy, Inspiration and *Sensus Plenior*',
TynBul 29: 49–60.

Lemche, N. P. (2014), 'Kings and Clients: On Loyalty between
the Ruler and the Ruled in Ancient "Israel"', in N. P. Lemche,
Biblical Studies and the Failure of History: Changing Perspectives 3
(Abingdon: Routledge), pp. 201–211.

Leuchter, M. (2017), *The Levites and the Boundaries of Israelite Identity*
(Oxford: Oxford University Press).

Levenson, J. D. (2006), *Resurrection and the Restoration of Israel: The
Ultimate Victory of the God of Life* (New Haven/London: Yale
University Press).

Lundbom, J. R. (1975), 'Double-Duty Subject in Hosea VIII 5',
VT 25.2: 228–230.

McCartney, D. and P. Enns (2001), 'Matthew and Hosea:
A Response to John Sailhamer', *WTJ* 63: 97–105.

McCasland, S. V. (1961), 'Matthew Twists the Scriptures',
JBL 80.2: 143–148.

McConville, J. G. (1984), *Law and Theology in Deuteronomy*,
JSOTSup 33 (Sheffield: JSOT Press).

—— (1993), *Judgment and Promise: An Interpretation of the Book
of Jeremiah* (Leicester: Apollos).

—— (2002), *Deuteronomy*, AOTC 5 (Leicester: Apollos; Downers
Grove: InterVarsity Press).

McKenzie, S. L. (1979), 'Exodus Typology in Hosea', *Restoration
Quarterly* 22: 100–108.

—— (1986), 'The Jacob Tradition in Hosea XII 4–5', *VT* 36.3:
311–322.

Marsman, H. J. (2003), *Women in Ugarit and Israel: Their Social and
Religious Position in the Context of the Ancient Near East* (Leiden/
Boston: Brill).

Melnyk, J. L. R. (1993), 'When Israel Was a Child: Ancient Near
Eastern Adoption Formulas and the Relationship between

God and Israel', in M. P. Graham, W. P. Brown and J. K. Kuan (eds.), *History and Interpretation: Essays in Honour of John H. Hayes,* JSOTSup 173 (Sheffield: Sheffield Academic), pp. 245–259.

Merrill, E. E. (1996), '*šě'ōl*', in *NIDOTTE* 4.6–7.

Meyers, C. (1992), 'Ephod', in *ABD* 2.550.

Miller, J. M. and J. H. Hayes (2006), *A History of Ancient Israel and Judah,* 2nd edn (Louisville: Westminster John Knox).

Miller, P. D. (2000), *The Religion of Ancient Israel* (London: SPCK; Louisville: Westminster John Knox).

Moberley, R. W. L. (1996), '*'mn*', in NIDOTTE 1.427–433.

Moon, J. (2015), 'Honor and Shame in Hosea's Marriages', *JSOT* 39.3: 335–351.

Morris, G. (1996), *Prophecy, Poetry and Hosea,* JSOTSup 219 (Sheffield: Sheffield Academic).

Motyer, J. A. and M. J. Selman (1980), 'Teraphim', in J. D. Douglas, N. Hillyer et al. (eds.), *The Illustrated Bible Dictionary,* 3 vols. (Leicester: Inter-Varsity Press), 3.1535.

Moughtin-Mumby, S. (2008), *Sexual and Marital Metaphors in Hosea, Jeremiah, Isaiah, and Ezekiel* (Oxford: Oxford University Press).

Na'aman, N. (1990), 'The Historical Background to the Conquest of Samaria (720 BC)', *Bib* 71.2: 206–225.

—— (1993), 'Population Changes in Palestine Following Assyrian Deportations', *Tel Aviv* 20: 104–124.

—— (1997), 'Historical and Literary Notes on the Excavations of Tel Jezreel', *Tel Aviv* 24: 122–128.

—— (2005), 'Forced Participation in Alliances in the Course of Assyrian Campaigns to the West', in N. Na'aman, *Ancient Israel and Its Neighbors: Interaction and Counteraction, Collected Essays 1* (Winona Lake: Eisenbrauns), pp. 16–39.

—— (2015), 'The Book of Hosea as a Source for the Last Days of the Kingdom of Israel', *Biblische Zeitschrift* 59.2: 232–256.

Nelson, R. D. (2004), 'Priestly Purity and Prophetic Lunacy: Hosea 1:2–3 and 9:7', in L. L. Grabbe and A. O. Bellis (eds.), *The Priests in the Prophets: The Portrayal of Priests, Prophets and Other Religious Specialists in the Latter Prophets,* JSOTSup 408 (London: T&T Clark International), pp. 115–133.

Nicholson, E. W. (1966), 'Problems in Hosea VIII 13', *VT* 16.3: 355–358.

—— (1986), *God and His People: Covenant and Theology in the Old Testament* (Oxford: Oxford University Press).

Nielsen, K. (1978), *Yahweh as Prosecutor and Judge: An Investigation of the Prophetic Lawsuit (Rîb-Pattern)*, JSOTSup 9 (Sheffield: JSOT Press).

Nogalski, J. D. (1993a), *Literary Precursors to the Book of the Twelve*, BZAW 217 (Berlin: de Gruyter).

—— (1993b), *Redactional Processes in the Book of the Twelve*, BZAW 218 (Berlin: de Gruyter).

Nogalski, J. D. and M. A. Sweeney (eds.) (2000), *Reading and Hearing the Book of the Twelve* (Atlanta: SBL).

O'Brien, J. M. (2008), *Challenging Prophetic Metaphor: Theology and Ideology in the Prophets* (Louisville/London: Westminster John Knox).

O'Brien, M. A. (2000), *Unfolding the Deuteronomistic History: Origins, Upgrades, Present* (Minneapolis: Augsburg Fortress).

O'Connor, M. (1987), 'The Pseudosorites: A Type of Paradox in Hebrew Verse', in E. R. Follis (ed.), *Direction in Biblical Hebrew Poetry*, JSOTSup 40 (Sheffield: JSOT Press), pp. 161–172.

Oded, B. (1972), 'The Historical Background of the Syro-Ephraimite War Reconsidered', *CBQ* 34: 153–165.

Odell, M. S. (1996), 'Who Were the Prophets in Hosea?', *Horizons in Biblical Theology* 18.1: 78–95.

O'Kennedy, D. F. (2001), 'Healing as/or Forgiveness? The Use of the Term רפא in the Book of Hosea', *OTE* 14.3: 458–474.

Olyan, S. M. (1996), 'Honor, Shame and Covenant Relations in Ancient Israel and Its Environment', *JBL* 115: 201–218.

Park, S. J. (2012), 'A New Historical Reconstruction of the Fall of Samaria', *Bib* 93.1: 98–106.

Patterson, R. D. (2010), 'An Overlooked Scriptural Paradox: The Pseudosorites', *JETS* 53.1: 19–36.

Paul, S. M. (1968), 'The Image of the Oven and the Cake in Hosea VII 4–10', *VT* 18: 114–120.

Petersen, D. L. (2000), 'A Book of the Twelve', in J. D. Nogalski and M. A. Sweeney (eds.), *Reading and Hearing the Book of the Twelve* (Atlanta: SBL), pp. 3–10.

Phillips, A. (2002), *Essays on Biblical Law*, JSOTSup 344 (London: Sheffield Academic).

Pickup, M. (2013), '"On the Third Day": The Time Frame of
    Jesus' Death and Resurrection', *JETS* 56.3: 511–532.
Pitard, W. T. (2002), 'Voices from the Dust: The Tablets from
    Ugarit and the Bible', in M. W. Chavalas and K. L. Younger, Jr
    (eds.), *Mesopotamia and the Bible: Comparative Explorations*,
    JSOTSup 341 (London: Sheffield Academic), pp. 251–275.
Powell, M. A. (1992), 'Weights and Measures', in *ABD* 6.897–908.
Pressler, C. J. (1992), 'Diblaim', in *ABD* 2.193.
Radine, J. (2013), 'Deuteronomistic Redaction of the Book of the
    Four', in R. Albertz, J. D. Nogalski and J. Wöhrle (eds.),
    *Perspectives on the Formation of the Book of the Twelve: Methodological
    Foundations, Redactional Processes, Historical Insights*, BZAW 433
    (Berlin: de Gruyter), pp. 287–302.
Redditt, P. L. (2000), 'The Production and Reading of the Book of
    the Twelve', in J. D. Nogalski and M. A. Sweeney (eds.), *Reading
    and Hearing the Book of the Twelve* (Atlanta: SBL), pp. 11–33.
Redditt, P. L. and A. Schart (eds.) (2003), *Thematic Threads in the
    Book of the Twelve*, BZAW 325 (Berlin: Walter de Gruyter).
Reimer, D. J. (1996), '*ṣdq*', in *NIDOTTE* 3.744–769.
Rendtorff, R. (1998), *The Covenant Formula: An Exegetical and
    Theological Investigation* (Edinburgh: T&T Clark).
Ringgren, H. (2003), '*qdš*', in *TDOT* 12.521–545.
——— (2004), '*rîb*', in *TDOT* 13.473–479.
Robson, J. (2012), 'The Literary Composition of Deuteronomy',
    in D. G. Firth and P. S. Johnston (eds.), *Interpreting Deuteronomy:
    Issues and Approaches* (Nottingham: Apollos), pp. 19–59.
Rooker, M. E. (1993), 'The Use of the Old Testament in the Book
    of Hosea', *Criswell Theological Review* 7.1: 51–66.
Ross, A. P. (1996), 'Baking, Boiling, Cooking, Roasting', in
    NIDOTTE 4.433–436.
Routledge, R. (1992), 'Siege and Deliverance of the City of David
    in Isaiah 29:1–8', *TynBul* 43.1: 181–190.
——— (1995), '*Ḥesed* as Obligation: A Re-Examination', *TynBul* 46.1:
    179–196.
——— (2008a), *Old Testament Theology: A Thematic Approach*
    (Nottingham: Apollos; Downers Grove: IVP Academic).
——— (2008b), 'Death and Afterlife in the Old Testament', *Journal
    of European Baptist Studies* 9.1: 21–39.

—— (2009), 'Prayer, Sacrifice and Forgiveness', *European Journal of Theology* 18.1: 17–28.

—— (2010), 'Did God Create Chaos? Unresolved Tension in Genesis 1:1–2', *TynBul* 61.1: 69–88.

—— (2012), 'Blessings and Curses', in *DOTPr*, pp. 60–64.

—— (2013), 'Replacement or Fulfillment? Re-applying Old Testament Designations of Israel to the Church', *Southeastern Theological Review* 4.2: 137–154.

—— (2014a), 'The Exodus and Biblical Theology', in R. M. Fox (ed.), *Reverberations of the Exodus* (Eugene: Pickwick), pp. 187–209.

—— (2014b), 'Cursing and Chaos: The Impact of Human Sin on the Environment in the Old Testament', in J. Moo and R. Routledge (eds.), *As Long as the Earth Endures: The Bible, Creation and the Environment* (Nottingham: Apollos), pp. 70–91.

—— (2016), *Old Testament Introduction: Text, Interpretation, Structure, Themes* (London: Apollos).

—— (2018), 'Hosea's Marriage Revisited', *TynBul* 69.1: 25–42.

Rowley, H. H. (1956), 'The Marriage of Hosea', *Bulletin of the John Rylands Library* 39: 200–233.

Russell, M. (2008), 'On the Third Day, According to the Scriptures', *Reformed Theological Review* 67.1: 1–17.

Sailhamer, J. H. (2001), 'Hosea 11:1 and Matthew 2:15', *WTJ* 63: 87–96.

Sakenfeld, K. D. (1978), *The Meaning of Hesed in the Hebrew Bible: A New Inquiry* (Missoula: Scholars).

Satterthwaite, P. E., R. S. Hess and G. J. Wenham (eds.) (1995), *The Lord's Anointed: Interpretation of Old Testament Messianic Texts* (Carlisle: Paternoster).

Scharbert, J. (1974), '*ālâ*', in *TDOT* 1.261–266.

Schart, A. (2000), 'Reconstructing the Redaction History of the Twelve Prophets: Problems and Models', in J. D. Nogalski and M. A. Sweeney (eds.), *Reading and Hearing the Book of the Twelve* (Atlanta: SBL), pp. 34–48.

Schüngel-Straumann, H. (1995), 'God as Mother in Hosea 11', in A. Brenner (ed.), *Feminist Companion to the Latter Prophets* (Sheffield: Sheffield Academic), pp. 194–218.

Schunk, K.-D. (1992), 'Benjamin', in *ABD* 1.671–673.

Sechelea, C. (2009), 'The Relationship between God's Covenant with His People and Marriage in the Old Testament', *Studia Theologica* 8.4: 250–273.

Seebass, H. (1997), '*lqḥ*', in *TDOT* 8.16–21.

Seitz, C. R. (2007), *Prophecy and Hermeneutics: Towards a New Introduction to the Prophets* (Grand Rapids: Baker Academic).

Seow, C. L. (1982), 'Hosea 14:10 and the Foolish People Motif ', *CBQ* 44.2: 212–224

——— (1992a), 'Hosea, Book of', in *ABD* 3.291–297.

——— (1992b), 'Hosts, Lord of', in *ABD* 3.304–307.

Setel, T. D. (1985), 'Prophets and Pornography: Female Sexual Imagery in Hosea 1 – 3', in L. M. Russell (ed.), *Feminist Interpretation of the Bible* (Louisville: Westminster John Knox), pp. 86–95.

Sherwood, Y. M. (2004), *The Prostitute and the Prophet: Hosea's Marriage in Literary-Theoretical Perspective*, JSOTSup 212 (Sheffield: Sheffield Academic Press, 1996); reprinted as *The Prostitute and the Prophet: Reading Hosea in the Late Twentieth Century* (London: T&T Clark).

Sloane, A. (2008), 'Aberrant Textuality? The Case of Ezekiel the (Porno) Prophet', *TynBul* 59.1: 53–76.

Smith, C. (2018), 'The "Wilderness" in Hosea and Deuteronomy: A Case of Thematic Reappropriation', *BBR* 28.2: 240–260.

Smith, M. S. (2001), *The Origins of Biblical Monotheism: Israel's Polytheistic Background and the Ugaritic Texts* (Oxford: Oxford University Press).

——— (2002), *The Early History of God: Yahweh and Other Deities in Ancient Israel*, 2nd edn (Grand Rapids/Cambridge: Eerdmans).

Smolarz, S. R. (2011), *Covenant and the Metaphor of Divine Marriage in Biblical Thought: A Study with Special Reference to the Book of Revelation* (Eugene: Wipf and Stock).

Stovell, B. M. (2015), '"I Will Make Her Like a Desert": Intertextual Allusion and Feminine and Agricultural Metaphors in the Book of the Twelve', in M. J. Boda, M. H. Floyd and C. M. Toffelmire (eds.), *The Book of the Twelve and the New Form Criticism*, Ancient Near East Monographs 10 (Atlanta: SBL), pp. 37–61.

Thiele, E. R. (1994), *The Mysterious Numbers of the Hebrew Kings*, rev. edn (Grand Rapids: Kregel Academic).

Thompson, J. A. (1980), *The Book of Jeremiah*, NICOT (Grand Rapids: Eerdmans).

Thompson, M. E. W. (1982), *Situation and Theology: Old Testament Interpretations of the Syro-Ephraimite War* (Sheffield: Almond).

Tomes, R. (1993), 'The Reason for the Syro-Ephraimite War', *JSOT* 59: 55–71.

Trotter, J. M. (2001), *Reading Hosea in Achaemenid Yehud*, JSOTSup 328 (Sheffield: Sheffield Academic).

van Dam, C. (1966), '*prṣ*', in *NIDOTTE* 3.691–694.

van der Toorn, K. (1989), 'Female Prostitution in Payment of Vows in Ancient Israel', *JBL* 108.2: 183–205.

van der Woude, A. S. (1982), 'Three Classical Prophets: Amos, Hosea, Micah', in R. Coggins, A. Phillips and M. Knibb (eds.), *Israel's Prophetic Tradition: Essays in Honour of Peter R. Ackroyd* (Cambridge: Cambridge University Press), pp. 32–57.

van Dijk-Hemmes, F. (1996), 'The Metaphorization of Woman in Prophetic Speech: An Analysis of Ezekiel 23', in A. Brenner and F. van Dijk-Hemmes (eds.), *On Gendering Texts: Female and Male Voices in the Hebrew Bible* (Leiden/New York: Brill), pp. 167–176.

Vang, C. (2011), 'God's Love according to Hosea and Deuteronomy: A Prophetic Reworking of a Deuteronomic Concept', *TynBul* 62:2: 173–194.

VanGemeren, W. A. (1990), *Interpreting the Prophetic Word: An Introduction to the Prophetic Literature of the Old Testament* (Grand Rapids: Zondervan).

Vielhauer, R. (2013), 'Hosea in the Book of the Twelve', in R. Albertz, J. D. Nogalski and J. Wöhrle (eds.), *Perspectives on the Formation of the Book of the Twelve: Methodological Foundations, Redactional Processes, Historical Insights*, BZAW 433 (Berlin: de Gruyter), pp. 55–75.

Vogels, W. (1988), 'Hosea's Gift to Gomer (Hos 3,2)', *Bib* 69.3: 412–421.

Wacker, M.-T. (2012), 'Father-God, Mother-God – and Beyond: Exegetical Constructions and Deconstructions of Hosea 11', *Lectio Difficilior* 2, <http://www.lectio.unibe.ch/12_2/inhalt_e.htm>.

Walton, J. H., V. H. Matthews and M. W. Chavalas (2000), *IVP Bible Background Commentary: Old Testament* (Downers Grove: IVP Academic).

Watts, J. D. W. (2000), 'A Frame for the Book of the Twelve: Hosea 1 – 3 and Malachi', in J. D. Nogalski and M. A. Sweeney (eds.), *Reading and Hearing the Book of the Twelve* (Atlanta: SBL), pp. 209–217.

Weems, R. J. (1989), 'Gomer: Victim of Violence or Victim of Metaphor?', *Semeia* 47: 87–104.

—— (1995), *Battered Love: Marriage, Sex, and Violence in the Hebrew Prophets*, Overtures to Biblical Theology (Minneapolis: Fortress).

Wenham, G. (1985a), 'The Date of Deuteronomy: Linch-pin of Old Testament Criticism; Part One', *Themelios* 10.3: 15–20.

—— (1985b), 'The Date of Deuteronomy: Linch-pin of Old Testament Criticism; Part Two', *Themelios* 11.1: 15–18.

Wenzel, H. (2018), *The Book of the Twelve: An Anthology of Prophetic Books or the Result of Complex Redactional Processes?* (Göttingen: Y&R Academic).

Westbrook, R. (2005), 'Patronage in the Ancient Near East', *Journal of the Economic and Social History of the Orient*, 48.2: 210–233.

Westenholz, J. G. (1989), 'Tamar, Qědēšā, Qadištu, and Sacred Prostitution in Mesopotamia', *Harvard Theological Review* 82.3: 245–265.

Whitt, W. D. (1991), 'The Jacob Traditions in Hosea and Their Relation to Genesis', *ZAW* 103.1: 18–43.

Wilson, R. R. (1980), *Prophecy and Society in Ancient Israel* (Philadelphia: Fortress).

Wyatt, N. (2002), *Religious Texts from Ugarit*, 2nd edn (London/ New York: Sheffield Academic).

Yee, G. A. (1987), *Composition and Tradition in the Book of Hosea: A Redaction Critical Investigation*, Society of Biblical Literature Dissertation Series 102 (Atlanta: Scholars).

—— (2001), '"She Is Not My Wife and I Am Not Her Husband": A Materialist Analysis of Hosea 1 – 2', *Biblical Interpretation* 9.4: 345–383.

—— (2003), *Poor Banished Children of Eve: Women as Evil in the Hebrew Bible* (Minneapolis: Fortress).

—— (2012), 'Hosea', in C. A. Newsom, S. H. Ringe and
J. E. Lapsley (eds.), *Women's Bible Commentary*, rev. edn
(Louisville: Westminster John Knox), pp. 207–215.

Yoo, Y. J. (1999), 'Israelian Hebrew in the Book of Hosea'
(PhD thesis, Cornell University).

Younger, K. L., Jr (1998), 'The Deportations of the Israelites',
JBL 117.2: 201–227.

—— (1999), 'The Fall of Samaria in Light of Recent Research',
CBQ 61.3: 461–482.

—— (2002), 'Recent Study on Sargon II, King of Assyria:
Implications for Biblical Studies', in M. W. Chavalas and
K. L. Younger, Jr (eds.), *Mesopotamia and the Bible*, JSOTSup 341
(Sheffield: Sheffield Academic), pp. 288–329.

Zobel, H. (1986), '*ḥesed*', in *TDOT* 5.44–64.

INTRODUCTION

1. Context

a. Date and historical context

Hosea prophesied in the northern kingdom, and his oracles are directed primarily against Israel (e.g. 1:4–6; 3:1; 4:1; 5:1; 6:10; 9:1; 10:1; 11:1; 14:1), against Samaria, the northern capital (7:1; 8:5–6; 10:5, 7; 13:16), and against northern shrines, particularly Bethel (e.g. 10:15; cf. 4:15; 10:5).

The opening verse sets his ministry in the eighth century BC, *during the reigns of Uzziah, Jotham, Ahaz and Hezekiah, kings of Judah, and during the reign of Jeroboam [II] son of Joash king of Israel* (1:1). Jeroboam II was, effectively, the last king of the dynasty that began when Jehu killed Ahab's son Joram and usurped the throne of Israel (2 Kgs 9 – 10). Jeroboam's son Zechariah did come to the throne, but was assassinated after only six months (2 Kgs 15:8–12). *I will soon punish the house of Jehu for the massacre at Jezreel* (1:4) indicates that Jehu's dynasty is about to come to an end, suggesting that the early part of Hosea's ministry coincided with the closing years of

Jeroboam's reign, in the middle of the eighth century BC (Thiele 1994: 12; Kitchen 2003: 31; Miller and Hayes 2006: 222). Hezekiah is the latest king mentioned. He probably began to reign as co-regent with his father, Ahaz, in around 727 BC, became sole ruler in 715 BC (Kitchen 2003: 31; see also Thiele 1994: 174; Miller and Hayes 2006: 403–404; cf. Becking 1992: 54–55) and died in the early seventh century BC. Hosea warns of impending judgment and exile at the hands of the Assyrians (e.g. 10:6; 11:5–7; cf. 13:15–16), who were becoming increasingly powerful. That judgment, though, does not yet appear to have taken place, suggesting that most of the material in the book dates to around 725 BC, at or near the start of the chain of events that led to the fall of the northern kingdom.

Hosea's prophecy is thus set against the background of Assyrian expansion, and the chaos in Israel that followed Jeroboam's death and which culminated in the fall of the northern capital, Samaria. And, while it is possible that some of the text has been edited, there is no compelling reason why most, if not all, of the material may not have originated in that setting (see Andersen and Freedman 1980: 57–59, 317; Dearman 2010: 4–8; Moon 2018: 7–8; see also J. Day 2010: 202–224).[1]

Assyria's most recent resurgence began with the accession of Tiglath-Pileser III (744–727 BC), also known as Pul (2 Kgs 15:19), and continued under Shalmaneser V (726–722 BC), Sargon II (721–705 BC) and Sennacherib (704–681 BC). During the relatively long reigns of Jeroboam II in Israel and Uzziah in Judah both kingdoms enjoyed prosperity and stability. That changed with Jeroboam's death, and in Israel a series of kings vied for power. Jeroboam's son, Zechariah, was assassinated by Shallum, who was, in turn, killed by Menahem. Biblical and non-biblical sources show that Menahem paid tribute to Assyria (2 Kgs 15:19; *COS* 2.285, 287). This may have been enforced, though it is also possible that Menahem elicited Assyrian support for his coup, and alliances with Assyria are suggested in 5:13; 7:11; 8:9; 12:1. Menahem reigned for about ten years and was succeeded by his son Pekahiah. After two years,

1. See further below, pp. 16–21.

Pekahiah was killed by Pekah,[2] who rebelled against Assyria. The assassination of Pekahiah may be alluded to in 7:3–7 (Macintosh 1997: 255–261).[3] Pekah formed an alliance with the Syrian king, Rezin, and, in the so-called 'Syro-Ephraimite war', invaded Judah (cf. 2 Kgs 15:37; 16:5; Isa. 7:1–9).[4] This is commonly viewed as an attempt to draw Judah into the rebellion and replace its king, Ahaz, with someone more compliant (Isa. 7:6) (M. E. W. Thompson 1982; Irvine 1990; Kelle 2005: 181–200; Na'aman 2005: 28–30). Another view is that this was a local conflict over territory (Oded 1972; Tomes 1993). The rebellion of Pekah and Rezin against Assyria would not be served by engaging in a potentially debilitating war with Judah (Oded 1972: 153; Tomes 1993: 70), and if there was a significant anti-Assyrian coalition, it is likely to have been more prominent in Tiglath-Pileser's annals (Tomes 1993: 64–66). However, there are records of action by Tiglath-Pileser against several nations (*COS* 2.287–288; cf. Dearman 2010: 25), suggesting possible coordinated opposition against Assyria. Ehrlich (1991: 55; 1996: 88–94) suggests that what may have started as a coalition against Judah over the control of land developed into an anti-Assyrian league in the light of the growing threat from Assyria. Following Alt (1953), several commentators see a reference to the Syro-Ephraimite war in 5:8.[5]

---

2. Pekah's twenty-year reign (2 Kgs 15:27) may include a period of rule only over Gilead (Thiele 1994: 53); cf. Dearman 2010: 23–24. Reference to Israel and Ephraim alongside Judah (5:5) may reflect division in the northern kingdom.

3. Wolff (1974: 111, 124) links it with Hoshea's assassination of Pekah. See comments below.

4. The northern kingdom is frequently referred to as 'Ephraim', the name of its largest tribe.

5. Alt relates 5:8 – 6:6 to a Judean incursion into Israel during the Syro-Ephraimite war. See also Mays 1969: 86–88; Wolff 1974: 111–113; M. E. W. Thompson 1982: 63–78; Stuart 1987: 101; Hubbard 1989: 118–121; Macintosh 1997: 194–198. Arnold (1989: 447–460) sees, instead, a reference to the Syro-Ephraimite advance towards Jerusalem. Dearman (2010: 179–181) also suggests a Syro-Ephraimite background

Ahaz, against the advice of the prophet Isaiah (Isa. 7), appealed
to Assyria for help, with the result that Judah became an Assyrian
vassal. Tiglath-Pileser III seems to have responded to Ahaz's
plea (2 Kgs 16:9) and campaigned against Syria and Israel (734–
732/1 BC),[6] though he would probably have acted anyway in his own
political interests. During this time, Hoshea appears to have killed
Pekah, seized the throne in Samaria (2 Kgs 15:30) and come to
terms with Assyria.[7] Later, Hoshea rebelled, probably with the
promise of Egyptian support (cf. 2 Kgs 17:4).[8] This vacillating
between Assyria and Egypt is noted in 7:11. Hoshea's rebellion
prompted the then king of Assyria, Shalmaneser V, to invade, and
following a lengthy siege Samaria fell around 722 BC (Kaiser 1998:
363–365; Younger 1999: 465, 482; cf. Becking 1992: 56). According
to the Babylonian Chronicle, Shalmaneser 'shattered' Samaria (*COS*
1.467; cf. Younger 1999: 466–468, 479), suggesting that he captured
the city (cf. 2 Kgs 17:3–6; 18:9–12). His successor, Sargon II, also
claims to have conquered the city (*COS* 2.296).[9] This may refer to a
subsequent attack in 720 BC (Becking 1992: 39–40; Younger 1999:
482); it may have been propaganda by Sargon, to support his claim
to the throne (Kitchen 2003: 39–40; Younger 2002: 291); or, possibly, Shalmaneser died before the siege ended, and it was Sargon
who took the city (Na'aman 1990: 206–225). Sargon also claims to
have deported 27,290 people from Samaria (*COS* 2.296), thus
completing the subjugation of Israel begun by Shalmaneser. As a

---

(note 5 *cont.*) but does not specify the direction of attack. See also Good
  1966a; Garrett 1997: 148–149; Sweeney 2000: 60–65; Ben Zvi 2005:
  140–142; Bos 2013: 85–87; Moon 2018: 108–109.

6. Though this may not have been his only, or primary, motive (Ehrlich
  1996: 93; Na'aman 2005: 30–31).

7. Tiglath-Pileser records the death of Pekah and his installation of
  Hoshea as king (*COS* 2.288, 291); cf. 2 Kgs 17:3.

8. King So of Egypt (2 Kgs 17:4) may refer to Pharaoh Osorkon (Kitchen
  2003: 15–16); though see J. Day 1992a: 289–301.

9. On the fall of Samaria, see Na'aman 1990; 1993; Becking 1992; Younger
  1998: 201–227; 1999; Bergland 2011–12; Park 2012. Cf. Dearman 2010:
  27–29.

result, by 720 BC, and maybe a few years earlier, Israel was an Assyrian province (see Becking 1992: 56; Younger 2002: 288–289). The suggested dates of Hosea's ministry (750–725 BC) make him a later contemporary of Amos, who also prophesied in the northern kingdom, probably around 765–745 BC. Though their periods of ministry may have overlapped by a few years, there is no indication of direct contact between them. The books have different emphases, but they address similar issues. Hosea's dates also coincide with the ministry of Isaiah in the south, which probably began around 740 BC.[10] Again, though, there is no indication of contact between them.

b. Religious context

There are several references in the book of Hosea to *Baal* (*ba'al*) or *the Baals* (*bĕ'ālîm*) (2:8, 13, 16, 17; 11:2; 13:1). The Hebrew word means 'lord' or 'master' and may sometimes be a generic reference: 'lord of . . .'. In the Old Testament, the terms frequently refer to Canaanite gods,[11] including deities associated with particular places. Discoveries at Ugarit have shed further light on the Canaanite understanding of Baal. The epic *Baal and the Sea* describes the victory of the storm god Baal, also referred to as Hadad (*COS* 1.247, 253, 261, 263, 265, 266), over the sea god Yam, and Baal's subsequent elevation to a chief god of the Canaanite pantheon. Baal's victory results in 'well-being on the earth', primarily in the form of rain (*COS* 1.253). The role of the goddess Anat in this,[12] together with texts that suggest a sexual relationship between Anat and Baal (see

---

10. 'In the year that King Uzziah died' (Isa. 6:1); see Thiele 1994: 12. This is often understood as a reference to Isaiah's call.

11. There are frequent references to 'Baal' (e.g. Judg. 2:13; 6:25–32; 1 Kgs 16:31–32; 18:19; 2 Kgs 17:16; 21:3; Jer. 2:8; 7:9; 11:17; 12:16; Zeph. 1:4) and 'the Baals' (e.g. Judg. 2:11; 3:7; 8:33; 10:6; 1 Kgs 18:18; 2 Chr. 24:7; 28:2; Jer. 2:23; 9:14), as well as specific references to 'Baal of Peor' (Num. 25:3, 5; Deut. 4:3; Ps. 106:28; cf. Hos. 9:10), 'Baal-Berith' (Judg. 8:33; 9:4) and 'Baal-Zebub' (2 Kgs 1:2–6, 16).

12. The request for Anat to 'pour well-being out into the earth' is a frequent refrain in *Baal and the Sea*.

J. Day 2000: 142–143; Wyatt 2002: 155–161; Yee 2012: 208), led to the common view that Baal worship was characterized by fertility rites and cult prostitution. In recent years, though, the view of the relationship between Baal and Anat has been challenged (P. L. Day 1992: 183–186; 1999: 36–43; M. S. Smith 2001: 57; Pitard 2002: 257–258), along with the understanding of what may have been involved in the Baal cult in Israel. In the Ugaritic epic, Baal's pride following his victory led to him falling victim to Mot (death), but he was revived, and his prosperity restored (*COS* 1.271). Baal's dying and rising is often taken to reflect the cycle of the seasons in the agricultural year (J. Day 2000: 117–118; cf. M. S. Smith 2001: 104–131). The association of Baal with fertility is alluded to in 2:5. The imagery of dying and rising may be reflected in 6:2; 13:14.

Since the discoveries of the Ugaritic texts, Baal (singular) in the Old Testament has generally been understood as a reference to the Canaanite god (J. Day 1992c; 2000: 68–90). However, Ancient Near Eastern texts refer to other names with the appellative 'Baal' (see Dearman 1993: 173–191; 2001: 12), including the Phoenician Baal-Shamem, 'Lord of the Heavens' (*COS* 2.146). One view is that these are 'different manifestations of the one god, Baal' (e.g. J. Day 2000: 68–69). Others suggest that they are distinct deities (see Dearman 1993; 2001: 13), though maybe with local manifestations.[13] It is possible that distinctive characteristics were attributed to these different manifestations. So, for example, Baal-Zebub of Ekron seems to have been associated with healing (2 Kgs 1:2–6, 16). Old Testament references to 'the Baals' probably reflect this multiplicity of these deities (e.g. Mays 1969: 43; Wolff 1974: 39; Davies 1992: 77). References in the singular, 'Baal', may indicate that a particular deity is in mind, though it is not certain which one, or even if it is the same god in all cases. Hosea, though, appears concerned less about the specific details of 'the Baals', and more about what the worship of false gods represents: spiritual adultery away from Yahweh.

---

13. Hess (2007: 14–15) suggests that Baal may refer to 'the chief male spirit of a region'; cf. M. S. Smith 2002: 79.

Kelle argues that Israel's 'lovers' in Hosea are not other gods, but foreign powers with which Israel formed alliances. He claims that there is little evidence for a continuing Baal cult in Israel in the eighth century BC, and argues that references to 'Baal' and 'the Baals' should also be understood in the context of political treaties with these foreign 'lords' (2005: 17–20, 111–166; see also Keefe 1995: 70–100; 2001; 2008: 113–127; Yee 2001: 354–357). Nations with which Israel formed improper alliances are sometimes described as Israel's 'lovers' (e.g. Jer. 4:30; 22:20, 22 [NRSV]; Ezek. 16:33–37; 23:5, 9, 22; cf. Hos. 8:9) (see also P. L. Day 2006: 167–173). However, there is little to suggest that references to Baal in Hosea should be understood in this way (P. L. Day 2006: 167 n. 2; Dearman 2010: 351). Also, while there may be few references to Baal worship in other texts relating to this period, by the time of Jeremiah it seems to have been a significant problem in Judah (e.g. Jer. 2:8; 7:9; 9:14; 11:13; 12:16; 19:5; 23:13). Jehu had made an important move towards eradicating Baal worship in the northern kingdom (2 Kgs 10:18–28), but his was not a thoroughgoing reform. In particular, Jehu continued in the ways of Jeroboam (2 Kgs 10:29), who had set up golden calves in Dan and Bethel (1 Kgs 12:28–29; cf. Hos. 8:5–6; 10:5). These were easily confused with the bull-like representations of Baal and are associated with Baal in the list of reasons for the fall of Samaria (2 Kgs 17:16). This suggests that aspects of Baal worship did survive in Israel within the official cult, up to, and beyond, the time of Hosea.

Hosea prophesied, then, at a time of significant religious apostasy; the people worshipped Canaanite gods and participated in the religious practices associated with them. What those practices were, though, is unclear. They included illicit sacrifice (e.g. 4:13, 14; 11:2), which was unacceptable to Yahweh (e.g. 8:13; 9:4; 12:11). Other features commonly associated with this false worship may, though, be questionable.

Baal worship has frequently been associated with cult prostitution, whereby temple servants, both men and women, engaged in sexual acts as part of fertility rituals (e.g. Mays 1969: 75; Andersen and Freedman 1980: 370; Hubbard 1989: 81–82; Birch 1997: 32–33; cf. J. Day 2010). This is related to the idea of *hieros gamos* ('sacred

marriage'),[14] which linked agricultural fertility with the sexual
union between a god, primarily Baal in this context, and the earth,
represented by an earth goddess, possibly Anat (cf. Wolff 1974: 15;
Davies 1992: 126–127). However, the view that 'sacred marriage'
and rituals associated with it, including cult prostitution, were part
of Israel's syncretistic worship has been questioned. The terms
qādēš and *qĕdēšâ*, which are frequently translated 'shrine/temple
prostitute' (Deut. 23:17; 1 Kgs 14:24; Hos. 4:14), are related to *qādôš*
('holy, set apart') and probably refer to individuals in the service of
the cult.[15] And, in the Old Testament, the feminine forms, *qĕdēšâ*
and *qĕdēšôt*, appear only in close association with *zônâ*,[16] the usual
term for 'prostitute'. This suggests a link between the two and
implies that these temple servants did engage in sexual activity (e.g.
Bird 1989: 87; van der Toorn 1989: 203; Dearman 2010: 166, 364).
This seems to be confirmed in Hosea 4:14, where *zônâ* and *qĕdēšôt*
again appear in parallel. It is less certain that this was their primary
role and had specific cultic significance.[17] In the context of Hosea's
indictment of Israel, though, whether or not it was connected with
specific religious rituals, illicit sex does have associations with the
Baal cult, and parallels Israel's spiritual adultery.

---

14. Associated with *hieros gamos* was the view that women were required to
    have sexual relations with a stranger, usually before marriage, as part
    of a ritual ensuring fertility (Wolff 1974: 14–15, 86–87), though this was
    almost certainly not part of Israel's worship; cf. Westenholz 1989: 261;
    Macintosh 1997: 123–125; Abma 1999: 14–15; Marsman 2003: 497–498;
    Kelle 2005: 132–135.

15. Some suggest that *qĕdēšâ* does not necessarily suggest sexual activity;
    see Westenholz 1989: 248; Keefe 1995: 81 n. 6; Miller 2000: 205–206;
    Marsman 2003: 497–498; Ringgren 2003: 542–543; Kelle 2005: 123–132;
    Yee 2012: 209; Lim and Castelo 2015: 123.

16. Tamar is described as a *zônâ* and a *qĕdēšâ* (Gen. 38:15, 21–22), and the
    terms appear together in Deut. 23:17–18 where both seem related to
    prostitution (see Craigie 1976: 301; van der Toorn 1989: 203).

17. Some see little or no formal connection to the cult (van der Toorn
    1989: 203; Gruber 1995: 176–177), though van der Toorn suggests that
    qĕdēšîm may have engaged in prostitution as a source of temple funds.

One aspect of Israel's apostasy is highlighted in 2:16: 'On that day, says the LORD, you will call me, "My husband", and no longer will you call me, "My Baal"' (NRSV). The term 'my Baal' (*baʿlî*) could be translated 'my master' (as NIV),[18] though it is probable that the term here refers to the Canaanite god (cf. 2:17), indicating that Yahweh and Baal had become confused in the minds and worship of the people. In the period of the settlement and early monarchy a number of personal names were compounded with 'baal' (cf. Dearman 1993: 187–190). Saul and David gave such names to their children,[19] suggesting that 'baal' might have been used as an epithet for Yahweh (cf. Wolff 1974: 49–50). Also, the related verb, *bāʿal* ('to rule over, marry'), has Yahweh as subject in Isaiah 54:5; Jeremiah 3:14; 31:32. Some mythological language associated with Baal also appears in the Old Testament, where it is applied to Yahweh. In Ancient Near Eastern literature Baal is referred to as 'cloud-rider' (*COS* 1.248–258; see also J. Day 1985: 30–32; M. S. Smith 2002: 81–82; Anderson 2015: 86–88), and similar expressions are used of Yahweh (Ps. 68:4; Isa. 19:1; cf. Dan. 7:13). Lotan, a monster overcome by Baal, is described in a similar way to Leviathan, who is defeated by Yahweh.[20] This may not have been a problem initially. However, Hosea's language suggests the development, by his day, of a religious syncretism, whereby Yahweh was worshipped, not as Israel's unique God, but alongside other Canaanite deities, as just one more of them (contra Stuart 1987: 57–58). And worship practices associated with Baal were incorporated into the worship of Yahweh. This might not constitute an explicit rejection of Yahweh,

---

18. It could also mean 'my husband', though that does not fit in this context.

19. 2 Sam. 2:8 (cf. 1 Chr. 8:33); 1 Chr. 8:34 (cf. 2 Sam. 4:4); 1 Chr. 14:7 (cf. 2 Sam. 5:16).

20. *Baal and the Sea* describes Lotan as 'the fleeing serpent . . . the twisting serpent, the close coiling one with seven heads' (*COS* 1.265). In Isa. 27:1, Leviathan is referred to as 'the fleeing serpent . . . the twisting serpent' (NRSV). Ps. 74:14 further refers to Leviathan's several heads. See Emerton 1982; J. Day 1985: 4–5; M. S. Smith 2002: 86; Anderson 2015: 93.

but it was equally unacceptable, and Hosea's prophecy looks forward to a time when false worship in all its aspects will be removed, and Yahweh will be known and worshipped as he should be.

2. Hosea and the Old Testament

a. Hosea and the 'Book of the Twelve'

The book of Hosea is the first of the twelve so-called 'Minor Prophets', a designation that is more indicative of their size, relative to the much longer prophetic books of Isaiah, Jeremiah and Ezekiel, than their significance. In the Hebrew Old Testament the collection appears as a single book, traditionally known as '(The Book of) The Twelve'. It is possible that the individual prophetic books were brought together primarily to fill a scroll (Childs 1979: 309), or maybe to prevent some of the smaller books from being lost,[21] and in the past they have been treated separately. However, the collection is referred to as one book from early in the development of the Old Testament canon,[22] and some recent discussion suggests that the collection should be read in its final form as a unified work.[23] Others suggest that the unity of The Twelve has been exaggerated, and continue to argue that the individual books should be read primarily as distinct units.[24]

The Book of the Twelve has possible unifying elements. There are common themes, including the 'Day of the LORD', which

---

21. *Baba Batra* notes that Hosea's 'scroll is so small that if copied on its own it might get lost' (*b. B. Bat.* 14b).

22. Sirach 49:10 refers to 'the Twelve Prophets'. *Baba Batra*'s list of canonical texts also includes 'the twelve prophets' (*b. B. Bat.* 14b).

23. E.g. House 1990; Nogalski 1993a; 1993b; Nogalski and Sweeney 2000; Redditt and Schart 2003; Kakkanattu 2006: 181–183; Albertz, Nogalski and Wöhrle 2013; see also Lim and Castelo 2015: 27–30; Wenzel 2018. Seitz (2007: 189–247) argues that interpretation needs to take into account the individual books' historical context and place within the canon.

24. E.g. Ben Zvi 1996: 125–156; 2005: 6–7; Petersen 2000: 3–10; Hadjiev 2010: 325–338; 2020: 90–108.

appear in most of the individual books.[25] And Malachi's hope of a new world order serves as an appropriate conclusion to the collection. Yahweh's love for his people, which is set in the context of a marriage in Hosea, is also reflected in Malachi 1:2. Both books also point to the relationship between father and son (Hos. 11:1–4; Mal. 2:10).[26] In Watts's view, this continuing love of God, which has not changed (cf. Mal. 3:6) despite the changing circumstances between the eighth and fifth centuries BC, provides a frame for the Book of the Twelve (Watts 2000: 209–217; cf. Lim and Castelo 2015: 39–40). Within The Twelve, there are a number of repeated catchwords and phrases (cf. Nogalski 1993a: 21–57; Redditt 2000: 14–15).[27] And some of the smaller books, such as Nahum and Obadiah, which are limited in scope, might be seen to take on additional significance when read as part of a wider group. House (1990: 63–109), for example, suggests that the Book of the Twelve has a structural and literary unity with three main sections: Hosea–Micah focuses on sin;[28] Nahum–Zephaniah sets out the consequences of sin; Haggai–Malachi points to future restoration. Hwang (2014) sees the *Missio Dei* as a unifying theme.

The process by which the Book of the Twelve was compiled is not clear. It is possible that Hosea may have been joined to other texts to form a smaller group, maybe of four books, Hosea, Amos,

---

25. E.g. Joel 1:15; 2:1; Amos 5:18; Obad. 15; Zeph. 1:7, 14; Mal. 4:5; see also Mic. 2:4; 4:6; 5:10–15; Hag. 2:21–23; Zech. 2:10–12; 12:1–9.

26. There is a suggestion that the picture in Hos. 11:1–4 may point instead to God as mother (Schüngel-Straumann 1995), though this seems unlikely; see on 11:4 below.

27. Examples include 'the LORD will roar from Zion and thunder from Jerusalem' (Joel 3:16; Amos 1:2), being 'cast' (*šālak*) into the 'depths' (*měṣûlâ*) of the 'sea' (*yām*) (Jon. 2:3; Mic. 7:19) and the use of Exod. 34:6–7 in Joel 2:13; Jon. 4:2; cf. Mic. 7:18–19; Nah. 1:3.

28. The MT and LXX order the books differently. Hosea is first in both and the last six are in the same order. This does not affect House's overall structure.

Micah and Zephaniah,[29] sometimes referred to as the 'Book of the Four', which was then added to, in further stages, to form the final collection (e.g. Nogalski 1993a: 278–280; 1993b: 274–275; Schart 2000: 41–45; Albertz 2003: 231–251).

It is important to look at how texts function, both in their immediate context and within the wider canon. If it is possible to speak of a 'Book of the Twelve', rather than an anthology of twelve independent prophetic books, reading the book of Hosea as part of a larger collection might give an insight into the theological context in which it was transmitted. A key issue here, though, is whether existing texts have simply been ordered in a particular way, or whether their content has been edited so as to give greater coherence to the final work. In my view, arguments for unifying redactions of the Book of the Twelve are not convincing. Individual prophecies may have been put together in such a way as to give the collection an overall structure (e.g. House 1990), but this would primarily have involved ordering previously existing material rather than changing its content. It is also possible that the collection has no clear pattern and the order is broadly chronological, or grouped around common expressions and ideas. Hosea's position at the beginning of the collection may, nevertheless, be significant. The first three chapters, in particular, introduce the theme of Israel's unfaithfulness, which will result in punishment but which does not, ultimately, affect Yahweh's love for them. This provides an appropriate introduction to the collection (House 1990: 74–76; Watts 2000),[30] which ends with the hope of final restoration. There is little, though, to suggest that the text of Hosea has been adapted to fit into that context, and while its place within, and relationship to, the Minor Prophets as a whole may have some

---

29. The same expression 'the word of the LORD came to' (*děbar yhwh 'ăšer hāyāh 'el*) introduces Hosea, Micah and Zephaniah (though also appears in Joel 1:1). Amos and Hosea both refer to northern and southern kings (Uzziah and Jeroboam). See also Lim and Castelo 2015: 43–44.

30. Albertz (2003: 250) suggests that Hosea served as 'the model that shaped the concept and the structure of the Book of the Four'.

significance in providing a context for interpretation, it does not affect discussion of it also, and primarily, as an independent book.

b. Hosea and Deuteronomy

Several commentators and scholars note that the book of Hosea has elements in common with Deuteronomy.[31] There is significant emphasis on the covenant relationship between Yahweh and Israel (8:1; cf. 2:18; 6:7), and on the possibility of a return to the wilderness (*midbār*) (cf. C. Smith 2018), where that covenant relationship began (2:14–15). Both books liken breaking the covenant to prostitution (e.g. 1:2; 4:10, 12; 9:1; cf. Deut. 31:16). Hosea's criticism of false worship recalls Deuteronomic regulations. In particular, the expression in 3:1 – *pānâ ʾel ʾĕlōhîm ʾăḥērîm* (*turn to other gods*) – occurs in that form only here and in Deuteronomy 31:18, 20 (cf. 30:17). Hosea 14:9 also echoes the language of Deuteronomy 32:29. As already noted, in Hosea the basis for Yahweh's commitment to, and forgiveness of, his people is his love, and in that context the noun *ʾăhăbâ* occurs in 3:1; 11:4, and the related verb, *ʾāhab*, in 11:1; 14:4. The verb also points to Yahweh's commitment to his people in Deuteronomy 4:37; 7:8, 13; 10:15; 23:5 (see further, Vang 2011). The threefold reference to *grain* (*dāgān*), *new wine* (*tîrôš*) and *oil* (*yiṣhār*) (2:8, 22) appears in a very similar form in Deuteronomy (7:13; 11:14; 12:17; 14:23; 18:4; 28:51). This suggests a possible link, though similar expressions occur in other passages.[32]

Links with Deuteronomy have led some scholars to conclude that the book of Hosea underwent a 'Deuteronomistic' redaction, maybe around the time of the Babylonian exile (e.g. Yee 1987: 308–313;[33] Nogalski 1993a: 278–279; 1993b: 274–275; Radine 2013). The term 'Deuteronomistic' is generally used to describe writings

---

31. Andersen and Freedman 1980: 75; J. Day 1986a: 1–12; Dearman 2010: 39; Robson 2012: 48–49; see also Nogalski 1993a: 278–279; 1993b: 274–275; Albertz 2003; Radine 2013: 287–302; Vielhauer 2013: 55–75.

32. E.g. 2 Chr. 31:5; 32:28; Neh. 5:11; 10:39; 13:5; Jer. 31:12; Joel 2:19; Hag. 1:11; cf. Gruber 2017: 128.

33. Yee suggests a double redaction: during the reign of Josiah and again during the Babylonian exile.

associated with a so-called 'Deuteronomic movement'[34] which reflects the theology of Deuteronomy and is linked with reforms from around the time of Josiah, at the end of the seventh century BC and into the early exilic period.[35] However, there seems little need to date the final version of Hosea later than the early seventh century BC. Consequently, it seems better to suggest that Hosea was aware of the book of Deuteronomy,[36] or that he was influenced by the same theology that also influenced the Deuteronomic reformers (Dearman 2010: 19–20, 39).[37] Another possibility is that the message of prophets like Hosea had an impact on later movements (e.g. Wolff 1974: xxxi;[38] Kugler 1999: 138–139). Some scholars point to the possible link between Deuteronomic traditions and Levites, and suggest, too, a close connection between those levitical reform circles and prophets such as Hosea (e.g. Wolff 1974: xxii–xxiii; Achtemeier 1996: 5; Cook 2004: 61–62, 231–266; Leuchter 2017: 142–154).

c. Hosea and Jeremiah

It is widely recognized that there are links between the prophecies of Hosea and Jeremiah (e.g. J. A. Thompson 1980: 81–85; Dearman

---

34. This is most commonly associated with the so-called 'Deuteronomistic History', comprising the historical books Joshua–2 Kings. See further, Routledge 2016: 253–257; see also Campbell and O'Brien 2000: 1–37.

35. Some also date the idea of God's relationship with Israel as a covenant from this period. See, however, J. Day 1986a; Nicholson 1986: 179–189; Routledge 2008a: 160–163; 2016: 120–123; Ansberry and Hwang 2013: 77.

36. Most recent scholars date Deuteronomy in the late seventh century BC. However, see Craigie 1976: 22–24; McConville 1984; 2002: 21–38; Wenham 1985a; 1985b. See also Vang 2011.

37. It has also been suggested that, while sharing Deuteronomic ideas, Hosea's conclusions are not the same as those of the 'Deuteronomistic history' (Albertz 2003: 247–251; Vielhauer 2013: 60). Wilson (1980: 227–228) links Hosea with an Ephraimite tradition with affinities with Deuteronomy and Jeremiah.

38. Wolff suggests that the book was put into its final form by Deuteronomistic redactors.

2010: 7, 19–20, 143–144; Lalleman 2013: 57–58). Both view the unfaithfulness of the people in going after *the Baals* (*habbĕʿālîm*, 2:13,
17; 11:2; Jer. 2:23; 9:14)[39] as prostitution (*zānâ*) (e.g. 1:2; 4:10; Jer. 2:20;
3:1) and, uniquely, describe Israel's sin as something *horrible* (*šaʿărûr*)
(6:10; Jer. 18:13; cf. Jer. 5:30; 23:14). In both, the covenant relationship between Yahweh and his people is likened to a marriage
characterized by steadfast love (*ḥesed*),[40] with idealized beginnings
in the desert in the days of Israel's youth (*nĕʿûrîm*) (2:14–20; Jer. 2:2).
And, following the people's failure, both point to a new, restored
covenant relationship which will recapture that early faithfulness
(2:18–19; Jer. 31:31–34). Both liken the relationship between Yahweh
and Israel to that between father and son (11:1–4; Jer. 31:9, 20).
Further common ideas include the call to return (*šûb*) to Yahweh
(e.g. 6:1; 7:10; 14:1; Jer. 3:10, 14; 4:1)[41] and the importance of knowing
or acknowledging (*yādaʿ*) Yahweh (2:20; 5:4; 6:3; 13:4; cf. Jer. 9:3, 6,
24; 24:7; 31:34).[42]

Some explain the similarities between Hosea and Jeremiah by
suggesting that both were edited by Deuteronomists. However, as
noted already, that implies an unnecessarily late date for Hosea.[43]
It is probable, though, that the prophecy of Hosea was taken to
Judah, perhaps at the end of the eighth century BC, and Jeremiah
may have become aware of it there.

---

39. This expression does not occur in other prophetic books.
40. See the discussion of *ḥesed* below, pp. 31–32.
41. On *šûb*, see also below, p. 24. Lalleman (Lalleman-de Winkel 2000:
    91–115; Lalleman 2013: 37–40) notes that for Jeremiah *šûb* relates to
    a return to the land, while Hosea focuses primarily on the restoration
    of the relationship. This reflects their respective historical contexts.
42. The verb *yādaʿ* occurs several times through Hosea. It may refer, as
    here, to the knowledge of Yahweh. It is also linked with Israel's failure
    to acknowledge the source of their blessings (2:8; 11:3) or their own
    weakness (7:9). The related term *daʿat*, also referring to the knowledge
    of Yahweh, occurs in 4:1, 6; 6:6. See Fretheim 1996.
43. There are also questions about the Deuteronomistic editing of
    Jeremiah. See Routledge 2016: 294–295; see further, McConville 1993:
    12–23; Lalleman 2013: 28–37.

3. Unity, composition, structure

While many commentators attribute much, if not all, of the content of the book of Hosea to the eighth-century prophet or to his followers, there have been suggestions that some of the material is the result of later redactions.

In the past it was argued that the original message of Hosea focused predominantly on judgment, and so did not contain elements of hope (Harper 1905: clix–clxi). Passages pointing to future hope were, therefore, viewed as later additions. However, scholars now generally allow that messages of hope and of judgment may appear alongside one another (Wolff 1974: xxviii–xxix; Emmerson 1984: 9–16; Macintosh 1997: xcii–xcvii; Sweeney 2000: 7; Gruber 2017: 30–31), and it is not necessary to regard passages that refer to future salvation as secondary.

It is commonly held that some references to Judah may be attributable to one or more redactions in the southern kingdom, after the fall of Samaria (Wolff 1974: xxxi–xxxii; Childs 1979: 378–381; Emmerson 1984; Macintosh 1997: lxx–lxxiv; Collins 2014: 323). Hosea's ministry is dated primarily with reference to kings of Judah (1:1), which is more relevant to a southern audience, and suggests that the book may have been preserved and transmitted in a Judean context (Hubbard 1989: 57; Macintosh 1997: lxx; Dearman 2010: 79). It is also argued that there are more references to Judah than might be expected in a prophecy addressed primarily to the north (Emmerson 1984: 4), and that several appear inconsistent with the immediate context, where the main focus is on Israel. The reference to the Davidic king (3:5) is also seen as a later addition. Among the references to Judah, some contrast Judah and Israel (1:6–7; 4:15; 11:12 [NRSV]),[44] while some indict both (5:5; 6:10–11a; 10:11; 11:12 [NIV]; 12:2). This has been taken to suggest a double redaction: one favourable towards Judah, maybe viewing Judah and the Davidic monarchy as a possible source of hope for the whole nation; the other negative, anticipating that Judah would share Israel's

---

44. The reference to Judah in 11:12 is interpreted both positively (NRSV, ESV) and negatively (NIV). See discussion in the commentary.

judgment. There is no agreement, though, on the order of the redactions.[45]

Some references to Judah are accepted by critical scholars as original (1:11; 5:10–14; 6:4; 8:14). Some of these (5:10–14; 6:4) probably relate to the Syro-Ephraimite war, when Judah was likely to be a matter of concern.[46] In those cases, Judah is indicted alongside Israel. Emmerson (1984: 77) argues that the prophet saw hostility between Israel and Judah as a sin, and war between them leads to judgment on both. However, that is not the only issue. While 5:10 relates specifically to Judah's hostility, 6:4, which uses the same Ephraim–Judah pairing, challenges their faithfulness to Yahweh, not their hostility towards one another.[47] The reference to fortifications in 8:14 may also suggest hostility between Israel and Judah (Emmerson 1984: 76–77), though may also point to the wider concern that the people rely on themselves and their own resources rather than on Yahweh (Mays 1969: 124; Wolff 1974: 146; Macintosh 1997: 333–334). The expression of future hope in terms of the reunification of Israel and Judah in 1:11 may also fit a situation where those two kingdoms are at odds with one another.[48]

---

45. Wolff (1974: xxxi) suggests that the positive view of Judah arose in Hosea's later ministry, and the threat of judgment on Judah is part of the Judean redaction; see also Emmerson 1984: 88–95. Childs (1979: 379–380, 381) considers that the message of judgment on Judah came first, and the more positive view emerged later.

46. However, Gruber (2017: 268–269), following Ginsberg, argues that in all of the texts which parallel Ephraim with Judah (5:5, 12, 13, 14; 6:4; 10:11), 'Judah' replaces an original 'Israel'. Ephraim–Israel is the usual word pairing and has been changed by a Judean redactor after the fall of Samaria.

47. Emmerson (1984: 68–74, 77) takes references to Judah in 5:10–14 as original, though sees 6:4 as part of a Judean redaction. Most commentators, though, interpret 6:4 in its present context; cf. Mays 1969: 96–97; Wolff 1974: 119; Macintosh 1997: 228–229; Lim and Castelo 2015: 134.

48. Some regard this as original (Wolff 1974: 24–29; Emmerson 1984: 95–98); others take it to reflect Hosea's thought, but come short of direct attribution (e.g. Mays 1969: 31; Macintosh 1997: 33–35).

The distinction between suggested primary and secondary references to Judah, though, is not decisive. Several references generally regarded as secondary do appear in passages which focus primarily on Israel (e.g. 5:5; 6:10–11; 10:11), but that is also the case with 8:14. And it is reasonable to suppose that, while bringing charges against Israel, Hosea might also have included a warning to Judah. All the more so if, as seems likely, Hosea considered that Israel's future hope lay in union with Judah (Wolff 1974: xxxi; Emmerson 1984: 88–95; Gruber 2017: 30–31). This would also explain texts that seem more favourable towards Judah (1:7; 11:12 [NRSV]), or which urge Judah not to follow the path Israel has taken (4:15). The reference to *one leader* in 1:11 also raises doubt over the view that 3:5 is secondary. Hosea is likely to see a single head of a united nation coming not from the failed northern dynasties (cf. 1:4), but from the line of David (see Stuart 1987: 67–68; Hubbard 1989: 31; see also Emmerson 1984: 101–113; Dearman 2010: 140). A more debatable text is 12:2:

> *The LORD has a charge to bring against Judah;*
> *he will punish Jacob according to his ways.*

(NIV)

It seems strange, in a prophecy directed primarily towards Israel, to address Judah first (though this also happens in 1:11), and the pairing Judah–Jacob is also unusual.[49] It is commonly held, therefore, that a later redactor has replaced an original 'Israel' with 'Judah' (Mays 1969: 161–162; Wolff 1974: 206, 211; Emmerson 1984: 63–65; Macintosh 1997: 479–480). This gives a more natural reading. And in the play on words in 12:3, where the name 'Jacob' (*ya'ăqōb*) is linked with the verb *'āqab* ('to cheat, supplant'; cf. Gen. 25:26; 27:36), we might expect the verb 'to strive, struggle' (*śārâ*) to correspond to the name 'Israel', as in Genesis 32:28. There is, though, no textual evidence for the change, and no clear

---

49. It occurs in later texts where both terms refer to the surviving southern kingdom (Isa. 65:9; Jer. 5:20); see, however, Hos. 10:11; Mic. 1:5.

explanation for why it was necessary, since a text referring to Jacob could be applied to Judah as it stands.[50] It is possible that *śārâ* is not part of the wordplay, but highlights another instance in Jacob's life of contention with God. The verse begins with a conjunction which Dearman (2010: 299–301) translates 'also' ('the LORD *also* has a charge to bring against Judah'). This links the judgment on Judah with that on Ephraim in 12:1, and brings the text into line with other passages which are directed primarily against Israel, but which also make reference to Judah.

Its superscript (1:1) suggests that the book of Hosea did circulate in Judah after the fall of Samaria and may have been reapplied to the situation there. It is not impossible that this may have led to the inclusion of what some see as a disproportionate number of references to Judah. There is, though, no compelling reason to suggest that this later reapplication resulted in any significant additions or changes to the prophet's original message.[51] The postscript (14:9) is also regarded as editorial. However, its language and thought are typically Hosean, and it may have been added by Hosea himself, or by a close follower.[52]

It is also, therefore, unnecessary to accept the view that the book was compiled even later, for an audience in post-exilic Judah, during the Persian period.[53] Ben Zvi (2005: 13–16) argues that the idea of the return from exile as a second exodus, and the hope of the reunification of Israel and Judah under a Davidic king, best fits a post-monarchic situation. However, as noted, Hosea appears to

---

50. Emmerson (1984: 64–65) notes that the change is unnecessary, though still regards the evidence for it as conclusive.

51. For a defence of Hosean authorship of references to Judah, see Moon 2018: 13–18.

52. See the discussion below, p. 175.

53. Ben Zvi (2005: 6–16; 2006: 42–45) attributes the book to literati living in Yehud (Judah) during the Persian period. In his view Hosea exists only within the book but has been integrated into a reconstruction of Israel's past. See also Bos 2013; Trotter 2001. Lim and Castelo (2015: 32) suggest 'significant redactional additions' to the original material during this period.

have viewed union with Judah as a basis for Israel's hope, and it seems natural to link that with the Davidic monarchy. Similarly, hope for the future occupation of the land (1:11) fits the context of Assyrian control over the region in the eighth century BC. And, while national restoration is linked with a second exodus in later texts (e.g. Isa. 40 – 55), that idea is not developed in Hosea, and it seems reasonable to suppose that it, like the marriage imagery in Jeremiah, builds on Hosea's original message.

The process by which the book of Hosea has come to be in its present written form is unclear. The book is usually divided into two or three sections. Chapters 1–3 focus on the prophet's personal circumstances, in particular his marriage and family. Chapters 4–14 contain Hosea's prophetic messages. These chapters are frequently divided into two (4:1 – 11:11; 11:12 – 14:9). Wolff (1974: xxxi) notes that the sections have parallel structures, moving from accusation, to the threat of judgment, to the hope of salvation (see also Hubbard 1989: 34; Dearman 2010: 7–18; Lim and Castelo 2015: 33–34). The relatively small number of prophetic formulae may indicate that the material has been removed from its original setting of prophetic proclamation and arranged, possibly chrono-logically or topically. It is also possible that some of the text may have originated in a literary, rather than an oral, form (Dearman 2010: 4, 16). The superscript (1:1), postscript (14:9), inclusion of the third-person narrative in chapter 1 and the overall structure suggest that the book was put into its present form by an editor, though some of that arrangement may be attributable to Hosea himself (Macintosh 1997: lxxii–lxxiv). There seems no good reason to question the historicity of the narrative in chapter 1, and the content suggests a writer who was familiar with the prophet and his family circumstances. He would also have been acquainted with Hosea's message, and it is reasonable to assume that the biographical detail complements the content of chapters 2 and 3.[54] Similarly, though chapters 4–14 may contain only 'samplings of Hosea's total repertoire' (Hubbard 1989: 33), they may be taken to reflect the message and theological emphasis of the prophet. And any editing

---

54. Yee (1987: 112–115) suggests a much more intrusive editorial role.

of the final text is likely to have been limited primarily to arranging, rather than adding to or changing, original Hosean material.

Within the general pattern of accusation, threat and restoration, chapters 1–3 are programmatic for the prophecy as a whole (Garrett 1997: 34–35; Abma 1999: 262). They highlight the nature of Israel's unfaithfulness to the covenant as spiritual adultery or prostitution (cf. 4:10–15; 5:3; 6:10; 7:4; 9:1). They also point to Yahweh's love for a wayward people, and his willingness to restore and renew his relationship with them. Chapters 4–14 then relate to more specific aspects of the nation's apostasy. Twice in these chapters Yahweh is described as bringing a *charge* (*rîb*) against his people (4:1; 12:2).[55] This reinforces the idea of a tripartite structure. The promise of restoration in 11:8–11 ends with the expression *declares the* LORD, suggesting that the third section begins with the accusation in 11:12.

4. Text and literary features

It has been widely recognized that the Hebrew text of Hosea is among the most difficult in the Old Testament (see Andersen and Freedman 1980: 66–68; Macintosh 1997: lxxiv–lxxvi). A traditional view suggests that the text has become corrupt in transmission, and uses the LXX, which differs from the MT in several places, to arrive at a correct version (Harper 1905: clxxiii–clxxiv; cf. Stuart 1987: 13). A more recent view is that the problem may lie with Hosea's peculiar dialect, language or writing style (Macintosh 1997: liii–lxi; Dearman 2010: 9–11).[56] This would have been unfamiliar to those who translated the book into Greek, and may have resulted in some of the text being emended, thus accounting, at least in part, for differences between the MT and LXX (Macintosh 1997: lxxvi–lxxviii; Lim and Castelo 2015: 30–31). Peculiarities of language and

---

55. See the further discussion below, p. 22.

56. It is widely held that Hosea used a northern regional dialect (Seow 1992a: 292; Yoo 1999; Lim and Castelo 2015: 31; Kim 2018: 55–63); though see Andersen and Freedman 1980: 67–68; Macintosh 1997: liv. For a survey, see Kelle 2010: 317–321.

style might also have affected the transmission of the Hebrew text, and the possibility of corruption cannot be ruled out (Andersen and Freedman 1980: 66; Dearman 2010: 9). Nevertheless, despite its difficulty, the consonantal MT is still generally preferred; and it seems better to start there, and take each variation on its merits (cf. Bons 2016: 129; Moon 2018: 18–19).[57] Particular problems in Hosea include the frequent occurrence of *hapax legomena*, terms which appear only here in the Old Testament, and the unusual use or form of what appear to be standard Hebrew terms (see Macintosh 1997: lvi–lix). These will be discussed as they arise in the commentary.

The prophecy has several distinctive aspects. Much of it is made up of divine speeches, which include messages of judgment and salvation. The speaker frequently alternates between the prophet and Yahweh. Also, speeches often speak *about* Israel rather than addressing the people directly. As noted above, some judgment speeches use the term *rîb*.[58] This is sometimes taken to suggest a legal setting, possibly a covenant lawsuit, in which Yahweh indicts the people for their failure to meet their covenant obligations (e.g. Mays 1969: 61; Wolff 1974: 65–66; Andersen and Freedman 1980: 332; Stuart 1987: 45, 73; Gruber 2017: 186–187). There is some debate about whether *rîb* does indicate a judicial framework (Deroche 1981; 1983a; Daniels 1987: 360). But even if that is the case elsewhere, Hosea's use of the term does not fit the normal pattern (Hubbard 1989: 96; Garrett 1997: 109; Lim and Castelo 2015: 116–117; cf. Huffmon 1959: 294).

Like other prophets, Hosea uses a mixture of poetry and prose. Here too, though, his style is distinctive. His poetry appears to have a pattern (see Dearman 2010: 14–16), but it does not always

---

57. Kim (2018) gives a detailed defence of the MT. For commentary on the LXX text, see Glenny 2013.

58. The noun *rîb*, translated *charge* (NIV) or 'indictment' (NRSV), occurs twice (4:1; 12:2); the associated verb appears in two pairs. In 2:2 it is translated 'to rebuke' (NIV), 'to plead with' (NRSV); and in 4:4, 'to bring a charge' (NIV), 'to contend' (NRSV). See further, Bracke 1996; Ringgren 2004. On covenant lawsuit, see Huffmon 1959; Nielsen 1978; VanGemeren 1990: 108, 400–402; Davidson 2010.

follow convention. Andersen and Freedman suggest that 'for the most part Hosea goes off on his own bent, a kind of free verse, or unregulated rhythm pattern' (1980: 65; cf. Hubbard 1989: 37). The relatively small number of prophetic formulae and transitional phrases can also sometimes make the text appear disjointed, as the subject matter jumps from one topic or image to another. The book also includes several literary features. Some of these are mentioned here. Others will be noted in comments on the particular passages where they appear.

One significant feature of the book of Hosea is the frequent use of similes and metaphors (Wolff 1974: xxiv; Kruger 1988a; Hubbard 1989: 37–38; Eidevall 1996; Macintosh 1997: lxiii; Dearman 2010: 10–13; Stovell 2015). Chapters 1–3 contain the key metaphor of Israel as Yahweh's adulterous wife; and the metaphor of adultery or prostitution continues into the rest of the book (e.g. 4:13–14; 5:3; 7:4). Chapter 11 employs another familial metaphor, with Israel as Yahweh's ungrateful son. Metaphors and similes use a variety of images, including from domestic life, from the animal kingdom, from agriculture and from nature. As well as Israel's husband and father, God is like a lion (5:14; 13:7), a leopard (13:7) and a bear (13:8). Israel is likened to a *stubborn heifer* (4:16), a *wild donkey* (8:9), a *trained heifer* (10:11) and a senseless dove (7:11). The leaders are like a heated oven (7:4, 6), and the nation, a part-baked cake (7:8). They *sow the wind and reap the whirlwind* (8:7); their love (*ḥesed*), and the nation itself, is like a transient morning mist (6:4; 13:3).

Hosea also makes considerable use of wordplay (see Hubbard 1989: 38; Morris 1996; Macintosh 1997: lxiv; Dearman 2010: 13–14). There are several plays on the name Ephraim (*ʾeprayim*). As noted above, Ephraim is likened to a heifer (*pārâ*, 4:16) and a wild donkey (*pereʾ*, 8:9). And Ephraim is also related to fruitfulness (*pārāʾ*, 13:15; *pĕrî*, 9:16; 14:8). As we have also seen, 12:3 links the name Jacob (*yaʿăqōb*) with the verb *ʿāqab* ('to cheat, supplant'). There is, too, alliteration and assonance. So, for example, 4:16 includes the phrase *sōrērâ sārar yiśrāʾēl* – '(like a) stubborn (heifer) Israel is stubborn'. Similar-sounding words also occur in 9:15, where Israel's 'leaders' (*śārîm*) are described as 'rebels' (*sōrĕrîm*), and in 7:14–15, where the people have turned against (*sûr*) God, even though God has instructed (*yāsar*) them. Similarly, there is a link between Jezreel (*yizrĕʿeʾl*) and Israel (*yiśrāʾēl*), which look and sound similar (e.g. 1:4–5).

There is also wordplay around the verb *šûb* ('to return'). Most references are linked with returning to Yahweh. Some are indictments because of the people's unwillingness or inability to do so (5:4; 7:10; 11:5); others appear to be genuine calls to repentance (6:1; 12:6; 14:1–2). Some express the possibility of a restored relationship (2:7; 3:5; 14:7), and the term is also used in the context of turning away divine anger (14:4) and the restoration of the fortunes of the nation (6:11). The term is thus associated with hope for the future. The same word, though, is also used to refer to the 'turning away' of God's people to other things (7:16) and to the threat that Yahweh will 'return to [his] place' (5:15, NRSV), suggesting that he will 'turn away' from them. As well as referring to the 'giving back' of fortunes (6:11), *šûb* is used when Yahweh threatens to 'take back' blessings already given (2:9), and to *repay* the people for their sin (4:9; 12:2, 14). This demonstrates a symmetry between the action of the people and the action of Yahweh. Divine judgment is also expressed in the threat that the people will *return* to Egypt (8:13; 9:3; 11:5). The play on words that is implicit elsewhere is made explicit in 11:5: the failure of the people to return to Yahweh will result in their return to captivity, indicating a direct correspondence between the punishment and the crime.

Linked with wordplay, Hosea also includes repetition (see Morris 1996: 45–73; Macintosh 1997: lxiv; Ben Zvi 2005: 66–67). Sometimes this appears to be for emphasis, for example: *I will answer . . . I will answer* (2:21, NRSV). The repetition of the same verb several times in the verses that follow may also be for rhetorical effect. The same may be true of the threefold repetition of *I will betroth you to me* (2:19–20). *I have been the LORD your God ever since you came out of Egypt*, which translates more literally as 'I am your God from the land of Egypt', is repeated (12:9; 13:4). And the expression *like the morning mist, like the early dew that disappears* describes both Israel's transient love (6:4) and the nation itself (13:3). This again suggests a correspondence between sin and divine judgment. Ephraim is also twice referred to as a *dove*: turning to Assyria (7:11) and returning from Assyria (11:11).

5. Theology and message

a. Sin, judgment and hope

A key part of Hosea's message is to challenge the apostasy, idolatry and syncretistic religious practices of the nation. The people do not know (*yāda'*) Yahweh (e.g. 5:4; 11:3),[59] and offer unacceptable sacrifices (4:13–14; 6:6; 8:13; 9:4; 11:2; 12:11; 13:2). And, though the message is directed primarily at the northern kingdom, Judah does not escape criticism. Israel's priests, who lead the people into sin, face particular condemnation (4:4–11; 5:1; 6:9; 10:5). False worship results in a breakdown of right relationships within society and, though not as prominent as in Amos, condemnation of social sins is also a feature of Hosea's prophecy. The people, badly led by the priests, disobey God's law (4:6; 8:1, 12; 9:17); there is a lack of righteousness (cf. 2:19; 10:12) and justice (cf. 2:19; 12:6); evildoers break into houses or rob in the streets (6:8–9; 7:1); there is drunkenness (7:5), sexual misconduct (4:2, 14, 18), dishonesty (4:2; 7:3; 10:4, 13; 12:7), bloodshed and murder (4:2; 6:9; 12:14). Related to idolatry is the nation's failure to rely on Yahweh. Hosea condemns the arrogance of those who trust in their own strength (7:10; 10:13; see also 8:14; 12:8; 13:6), turn to other gods (2:5; 3:1) or look to Egypt and Assyria for help (5:13; 7:11; 12:1; cf. 14:3). He condemns, too, the people's ingratitude and failure to appreciate the blessings Yahweh has given them (2:8; 7:15; 11:2–4; 13:5–6).

Israel's sin and stubborn rebellion (4:16; 7:14; 9:15) results in judgment.[60] This includes a breakdown in the relationship with Yahweh (e.g. 1:9; 2:2; 5:6, 15; 9:12) and the withdrawal of blessings associated with it (e.g. 2:9; 9:2–3). Judgment will take the form of defeat, and exile in Assyria (9:3; 10:5–6; 11:5–6; cf. 8:13). Hosea also gives an insight into Yahweh's care for Israel, which leads to frustration (e.g. 6:4; 7:13), and his unwillingness to destroy them completely (11:8–9). Consequently, indictments and pronouncements of judgment are also accompanied by messages of hope for

---

59. See above, p. 15 n. 42.

60. E.g. 1:4–5; 2:9–13; 4:3, 10; 7:12–13; 8:13–14; 9:7–9, 15–17; 10:14–15; 11:5–7; 12:2; 13:7–9, 15–16.

the future.[61] These parallel the judgments: the broken relationship will be restored (e.g. 1:10; 2:14–23), along with its associated blessings (e.g. 2:15); and those exiled to Assyria will return (11:10–11).

b. Covenant and marriage

The idea of Yahweh's covenant relationship with Israel is important to Hosea.[62] There is a specific reference in 8:1; and it is further alluded to in 2:23 (cf. 1:9), which uses a characteristic covenant formula.[63] The prophet's condemnation of false worship practices is closely related to his particular understanding of this covenant as a marriage. Elsewhere in the Old Testament, false worship is sometimes referred to as *prostitution* (Exod. 34:15–16; Deut. 31:16), and Hosea also uses that language. However, he appears to be the first to make explicit the link between covenant and marriage (Hall 1982; Kruger 1983: 107; Hugenberger 1994: 294–296; Baumann 2003: 85; Sechelea 2009; Smolarz 2011: 61) and, more specifically, between covenant unfaithfulness and spiritual adultery. This is probably related to his own unhappy marital situation.[64]

---

61. As noted above (pp. 20–21), each of the book's three main sections ends with a message of hope.

62. See also discussion of *ḥesed* (below, pp. 31–32) and allusions to the exodus (below, pp. 33–34).

63. This formula comprises variations of 'I will take you as my people, and I will be your God' (Exod. 6:7); e.g. Lev. 26:12; Jer. 11:4; 24:7; 31:1, 33; 32:38; Ezek. 11:20; 37:23, 27; Zech. 13:9. See Rendtorff 1998.

64. Another suggestion (Davies 1993: 87–92; Moughtin-Mumby 2008: 215–224) is that Hosea became involved with a prostitute and their illicit relationship reflects Israel's prostitution to Baal. However, the expression in 1:2, where *lāqaḥ* ('to take'), *lĕ* ('to') and *'iššâ* ('wife, woman') appear together, usually relates to legitimate marriage (e.g. Gen. 24:3–4; 27:46; 28:2; Exod. 6:20, 23, 25; Deut. 21:11; Judg. 3:6). See also Kruger 1983: 107; Fensham 1984: 72; Els 1996: 814; Seebass 1997: 19; Routledge 2018: 32.

i. Hosea's marriage

There is considerable debate over the precise circumstances of Hosea's marriage to Gomer (1:2–3).[65] One issue is the meaning of *'ēšet zĕnûnîm* (1:2), an expression that occurs only here. The term *zĕnûnîm* is related to the verb *zānâ* ('to commit fornication, to be a prostitute') and the noun *zônâ* ('prostitute'), and a literal translation might be 'woman/wife of prostitutions' (cf. NRSV: 'wife of whoredom'; NIV: *promiscuous woman*). This suggests promiscuous tendencies. Gomer may have been a prostitute, though in that case she would more likely have been described as a *zônâ*. However, there is debate about when those tendencies became evident. Was Hosea commanded to marry a woman already known to be promiscuous, or did her adulterous behaviour become apparent only later?

Another view is that *'ēšet zĕnûnîm* relates more generally to the sinful state of the nation as a whole. Gomer is an *adulterous wife* because she is part of a nation that has committed spiritual adultery by turning to other gods (Stuart 1987: 11–12, 26–27; see also Gordis 1954: 15). However, Hosea's action is widely understood as a prophetic sign-act, and it is difficult to see how marriage to a typical Israelite woman would serve that function. Related to this is the suggestion that she, like other women of her day, had taken part in sexual initiation rites associated with the Baal cult (Wolff 1974: 14–15; cf. Craigie 1984: 9; Fensham 1984: 71). Recent discussion questions the nature and extent of such ritual sexual practices (Macintosh 1997: 123–125; Dearman 2010: 366–367; Lim and Castelo 2015: 52).[66] And, again, if this was common, it is difficult to see how Hosea's marriage to her serves as a sign-act.

It seems more likely that *'ēšet zĕnûnîm* relates to Gomer's promiscuous character. If this was evident earlier, marrying such a woman would be part of the sign-act (Kidner 1981: 19; Garrett 1997: 49; McComiskey 1998: 11–17; Nelson 2004: 125; Moon 2018: 36, 40–44). However, in Hosea and Jeremiah, Israel's relationship with Yahweh is portrayed as beginning well. Jeremiah 2:2 suggests an idyllic start

---

65. For a recent overview of the debate, see Routledge 2018; see also Rowley 1956; Macintosh 1997: 113–126; Kelle 2009: 179; Dearman 2010: 80–88.
66. See above, pp. 7–8.

to the relationship, and Hosea, too, views Israel's restoration as a
return to that desert idyll (2:14–15).[67] The parallel with Hosea's
marriage fits better with the view that *ʾēšet zĕnûnîm* relates to
Gomer's subsequent marital infidelity. On this understanding, the
call to *marry a promiscuous woman* (1:2) is proleptic (Knight 1960: 28;
Johansen 1971: 183; Andersen and Freedman 1980: 116; Hubbard
1989: 54–55; Macintosh 1997: 8; Patterson 2008: 12; Routledge 2018:
33–35). Gomer's tendencies resulted in adultery, and Hosea recognized in hindsight that this was part of Yahweh's intention when
he gave the command to marry. Hosea's response to his wife's unfaithfulness then mirrors Yahweh's relationship with Israel.

Another issue relates to the identity of the woman in 3:1. Some
argue that she is not necessarily Gomer (Stuart 1987: 64–66; Davies
1993: 90–91; Moughtin-Mumby 2008: 232–236; Moon 2018: 70).[68] The
rhetorical purpose of Hosea's action in showing love to this unnamed
adulterous woman is to reflect Yahweh's response to his adulterous
people, and the identity of the woman or her previous husband is not
directly relevant.[69] It seems better, though, to see chapter 3 as a continuation of the narrative begun in chapter 1, and to take 3:1 as a
reference to Gomer, who appears to have left Hosea and has found

---

67. Moughtin-Mumby (2008: 95–96) argues that Israel's idyllic past is
    contrasted with her current unfaithfulness; see also J. A. Thompson 1980:
    163; Sherwood 2004: 207–208; Lalleman 2013: 76. Fox (1973) argues that
    ḥesed is not shown by people to God and, in Jer. 2:2, must refer to God's
    love for Israel. However, see Routledge 1995: 193–195. Ezek. 23 suggests
    that Israel's promiscuity began in Egypt, though this is different from the
    picture in Hosea and Jeremiah and has a different rhetorical purpose.

68. See also van der Woude 1982: 44–45; Dorn 2000; Sweeney 2000: 15;
    Lim and Castelo 2015: 80.

69. Moon (2015; 2018: 70–71) argues that the primary rhetorical factor
    here, and in 1:2, is the disgrace attached to the man who marries such
    a woman. Yahweh willingly accepts that disgrace because of his
    continuing commitment to his people. See also Yee 2003: 46–48. The
    emphasis here, though, is on the sin and the shame of the unfaithful
    wife (2:5; 2:10; cf. 2:3). See Hadjiev 2012; 2016. For further discussion
    of honour–shame, see Bechtel 1991; Olyan 1996.

herself in trouble, necessitating a payment to secure her restoration (3:2) (Andersen and Freedman 1980: 294–295; Garrett 1997: 98–99; Macintosh 1997: 95–97; McComiskey 1998: 50–51; Dearman 2010: 131–132; Routledge 2018: 38–41). This fits better with the symbolism of the narrative: the bride that Yahweh seeks to restore is the one he first married and who has committed adultery against *him*. Here, too, we see the extent of Yahweh's commitment to his people, and the love, grace and forgiveness extended to them, despite their sin. Yahweh's willingness to restore his bride is evident in 2:14–23. He will bring his people back into the desert (2:14), to where the relationship began, and, in that place of new beginnings, he will establish with them a new and everlasting covenant (2:18–20).

In line with this understanding of the relationship between Yahweh and Israel as a marriage, Hosea frequently describes the nation's unfaithfulness as adultery or prostitution (e.g. 4:10–15; 5:3; 6:10; 7:4; 9:1). This includes spiritual adultery, though actual adulterous behaviour and sexual promiscuity were probably further consequences of apostasy and religious syncretism.

ii. Criticism of the marriage metaphor
There has, though, been some criticism of the marriage metaphor. The man representing Yahweh and the woman representing sinful Israel appear to reflect and sanction patriarchal gender stereotyping.[70] And for the metaphor to work, it might be assumed that the level of control and potential sexual violence and humiliation in Hosea 2 was not unknown within the context of marriage in the Old Testament. The language here, and in other similar passages,[71] has been described as 'pornographic' (Setel 1985; see also Brenner 1995; 1996a; 1996b), reflecting a culture of misogyny. J. M. O'Brien (2008: 33–34) goes so far as to suggest that the treatment of the woman in Hosea 2 has the

---

70. E.g. Setel 1985; Weems 1989; 1995; van Dijk-Hemmes 1996; Brenner 1996a; 1996b; 1997; Baumann 2003; Yee 2003; 2012; J. M. O'Brien 2008. See also Castelo (Lim and Castelo 2015: 229–233). For a response, particularly to Brenner and van Dijk-Hemmes, see Sloane 2008; cf. Garrett 1997: 124–133.

71. Other texts discussed in this context include Jer. 2 – 4; Ezek. 16; 23.

characteristics of domestic abuse. This is particularly significant because the prophets are widely thought to represent the high point of ethical monotheism, and there is concern that their message reinforces and justifies controlling and abusive patriarchal attitudes and practices.[72]

Patriarchal ideology is evident in much of the Old Testament, and some practices appear questionable to a modern eye, though, in my view, it is going too far to describe the culture as misogynistic (cf. Carroll 1995; Sloane 2008: 66–68). It is important to recognize the particular historical and cultural context of the prophets. But it is reasonable, too, to examine the underlying ideology and be aware of current attitudes that might be influenced by it, and claim support from it. However, this does not necessarily undermine the relevance of other aspects of the prophets' message (Sloane 2008: 53–54).

The primary purpose of the marriage metaphor is to describe Yahweh's relationship with Israel, not to set out a continuing pattern for marriage. In its original context, the metaphor emphasizes God's sovereignty over his people. And the punishment imposed on unfaithful Israel, while not appropriate within marriage today, nevertheless warns the nation of the disastrous consequences of violating its covenant relationship. The metaphor need not, though, be taken wholly negatively. Some approaches seem to start from the premise that the relationship is abusive: God's dealings with Israel are primarily about power, and even expressions of tenderness are manipulative and reflect that desire to control (J. M. O'Brien 2008: 47). That is too cynical. The Old Testament does emphasize divine sovereignty and the consequences of disobedience. But it also indicates Yahweh's love, and even his vulnerability.[73] The marriage metaphor in Hosea, despite some weaknesses when viewed in a modern context, expresses divine love, compassion, faithful commitment, and God's willingness to forgive and restore an unfaithful nation (cf. Weems 1989: 100). As

---

72. Setel (1985: 95) suggests that some 'pornographic' texts should not be described as 'God's Word' in a public setting; Baumann (2003: 104) argues for the need to 'confront the marriage imagery and its problems' and 'seek counter images'.

73. See e.g. Routledge 2008a: 102–103, 108–112.

such, it continues to be important in understanding the relationship between God and his people.

c. Ḥesed

The term *ḥesed* occurs six times in Hosea (2:19; 4:1; 6:4, 6; 10:12; 12:6): more times, in proportion to its size, than in any other prophetic book.[74] *Ḥesed* is a characteristically Hebrew term that is difficult to convey adequately in English. In these six passages it is translated in different ways: in the NRSV as 'steadfast love' (2:19; 6:6; 10:12), 'loyalty' (4:1) and 'love' (6:4; 12:6); in the NIV as *love* (2:19; 4:1; 6:4; 12:6), *mercy* (6:6) and *unfailing love* (10:12).

In the wider Old Testament context, *ḥesed* occurs predominantly in the context of relationships, notably those involving a covenant (*běrît*).[75] It relates to an inward disposition of goodwill, together with its outward expression in dutiful and compassionate action. Some link it primarily with kindness or benevolence, but that is too limiting (Routledge 1995: 194–195). The term includes a mutual and reciprocal element: there is an obligation on those who have been shown *ḥesed* to show it in return. And while this may, in some cases, be expressed in acts of kindness, the specific action corresponding to *ḥesed* will be determined by the relationship. This element of mutuality has been linked with the relationship between patron and client (Westbrook 2005; Esler 2012: 305–316; Lemche 2014: 205–207). With patronage, though, the relationship is primarily asymmetrical, and while that is usually the case with *ḥesed*,[76] it is not necessarily so.[77]

---

74. It occurs proportionately more times only in Psalms and 2 Samuel.

75. For further discussion of *ḥesed*, see Routledge 1995; see also Glueck 1967; Sakenfeld 1978; Zobel 1986; Clark 1993; Britt 2003.

76. Clark's analysis indicates that in around two-thirds of its occurrences, *ḥesed* is shown by God to human beings (1993: 49). *Ḥesed* is also linked with the relationship between king and subject (2 Sam. 3:8; Prov. 20:28; Isa. 16:5), between host and guest (Gen. 19:19; 21:23; Josh. 2:12) and between powerful and weaker members of society (Ps. 109:16).

77. *Ḥesed* may also be shown in the context of friendship (2 Sam. 3:8; Job 6:14), between relatives (Gen. 24:49) and between members of the covenant community (Mic. 6:8; Zech. 7:9).

In the majority of its occurrences in the Old Testament, *ḥesed* is shown by God, and expresses his faithful love for his people. This is also linked to covenant. In Exodus 34:6–7, which describes the renewal of the Sinaitic covenant following the incident with the golden calf, *ḥesed* is listed twice among the divine attributes. In addition, there are several couplets where *ḥesed* and *běrît* appear as parallel elements (e.g. Pss 89:28; 106:45; Isa. 54:10). The close connection between *ḥesed* and *běrît* is associated with Deuteronomic theology (Zobel 1986: 50–61), and it seems reasonable to suppose that Hosea was familiar with it. Another aspect of divine *ḥesed* is as that characteristic of God which seeks to maintain the covenant relationship despite the failure of his covenant partner (Routledge 1995: 191–193), and this corresponds to God's action in restoring his wayward bride.

In the book of Hosea, *ḥesed* relates primarily to human conduct. This includes the right behaviour of those within the covenant community towards one another, and also the proper response of the people to God. In this context, Israel's response is faithful obedience and devotion (cf. Jer. 2:2). However, in the light of the prophet's emphasis on covenant, it seems likely that he was fully aware of the mutuality of the relationship. The new covenant relationship between Yahweh and his people will include *ḥesed* (2:18–19).[78] This is one of the bridal gifts bestowed on Israel and refers to the endowment of a quality previously lacking (cf. 4:1; 6:4). It points, too, to a restored relationship characterized, on both sides, by *ḥesed*.

d. Allusions to Israel's past

The book of Hosea makes several references to Israel's past. Some note instances from the life of Jacob (12:3–4, 12). Many are related to the exodus, including coming out of Egypt and the time in the desert. These narratives point back to the nation's beginnings and indicate an important link between story and theology (Dearman

---

78. *Compassion* (*raḥămîm*), here, may suggest divine activity, though may indicate an important aspect of the people's renewed relationship with one another.

2010: 29–44; see also McKenzie 1979; Daniels 1990; Rooker 1993; Bos 2013: 154–162; Routledge 2014a).

Jacob grasping his brother's heel (Gen. 25:22–26; cf. Hos. 12:3) foreshadows his future priority over Esau, and his place with Abraham and Isaac as a founding patriarch of the nation. His encounter with a 'man' at Jabbok (Gen. 32:24–29; cf. Hos. 12:4) results in him being renamed Israel. His earlier flight to Aram and subsequent marriage(s) (cf. 12:12) also play a significant part in the nation's beginnings. But these also point to Jacob's competitive and contentious character; something that is shared by the people descended from him. Internecine rivalry is all too evident in the current fighting between Israel and Judah. And the state of the nation's worship reveals a people at odds with God. Nevertheless, just as God met Jacob at Bethel, there is hope, too, for his contentious and rebellious descendants.

Allusions to the exodus point to several things. First, they emphasize the uniqueness of the God who redeemed Israel from Egypt. *I have been the LORD your God ever since you came out of Egypt*, which, as already noted, reads more literally as 'I am the LORD your God from the land of Egypt' (12:9; 13:4a), echoes Exodus 20:2 and Deuteronomy 5:6 – 'I am the LORD your God, who brought you out of Egypt' – both of which go on to say, 'You shall have no other gods before me' (Exod. 20:3; Deut. 5:7; cf. Hos. 13:4b). This is a key emphasis for Hosea and underlies the description of Israel's idolatry as prostitution or adultery. The people have forsaken their one true covenant partner and turned to other gods. Second, they highlight Israel's ingratitude. Yahweh brought the people out of Egypt, took them as his own, entered into an intimate relationship with them, and fed and sustained them, yet still they rejected him (9:10; 11:1–4; 13:5–6). Particularly poignant here is the reference to Israel as Yahweh's son (11:1; cf. Exod. 4:23). Like the marriage metaphor, this emphasizes Yahweh's deep, personal commitment to the relationship. Third, they point to coming judgment. Because they have rejected Yahweh, who brought them out of Egypt, they *will return to Egypt* (8:13; 9:3; 11:5): they will again experience exile in a foreign land. Judgment is also portrayed as a forfeiture of divine blessings and a return to the wilderness (e.g. 12:9; cf. 2:9–12). Fourth, whether viewed in terms of the relationship between father and son or husband and wife, the escape from Egypt, the covenant at Sinai and the wilderness wanderings are viewed as an idealized period in the Yahweh–Israel relationship (e.g. 2:15; 9:10; 11:1; cf. Jer. 2:2). That gives greater pathos to the description of Israel's subsequent failure. However, while a return to Egypt represents judgment, it also takes the people back to where things began and offers the possibility of a new start in the relationship. Hosea anticipates a second exodus, in which Yahweh will again bring his people out of Egypt (11:11) and establish a new covenant relationship with them (2:14–20), which, as noted above, includes a restatement of the traditional covenant formula (2:23; cf. Exod. 6:7).[79] And in place of failure, represented by Israel's disobedience in the Valley of Achor at the entrance to the Promised Land (Josh. 7), this restored relationship will bring renewed hope (2:15).

79. See above, p. 26 n. 63.

ANALYSIS

As noted above, the book is usually divided into two or three sections. Chapters 1–3 describe Hosea's marriage(s). These are followed by a series of prophetic speeches in chapters 4–14 in which Yahweh twice makes a *charge* (*rîb*) against his people (4:1; 12:2), suggesting a further twofold division. There is, though, no clear order to the way the oracles are presented, and the outline here aims to note areas covered by the oracles, rather than to identify their structure.

1. HOSEA'S MARRIAGE: ISRAEL AS YAHWEH'S UNFAITHFUL WIFE (1:1 – 3:5)
   A. Superscript (1:1)
   B. Hosea's call and marriage; naming of children as symbols of judgment (1:2–9)
   C. Restoration: reversal of judgment (1:10 – 2:1)
   D. Judgment on an unfaithful wife (2:2–13)
   E. Restoration and reconciliation; a new beginning (2:14–23)
   F. Hosea's love and Yahweh's love (3:1–5)

2. ORACLES RELATING TO SINFUL ISRAEL (4:1 – 11:11)

    A. Yahweh's case against the people (4:1 – 5:7)
        i. General charge against the people of the land (4:1–3)
        ii. Israel's spiritual prostitution (4:4 – 5:7)
            a. Judgment on priests and people (4:4–19)
            b. Judgment on leaders and people (5:1–7)
    B. Divine wrath on Israel and Judah (5:8–15)
    C. Failure to repent (6:1 – 7:2)
        i. Call to repentance (6:1–3)
        ii. A fickle and unfaithful people (6:4 – 7:2)
    D. Internal and international politics (7:3–16)
        i. Israel and its kings (7:3–7)
        ii. Israel and the nations (7:8–16)
    E. False confidence, and impending judgment (8:1 – 9:9)
        i. A broken covenant (8:1–3)
        ii. Kings and idols (8:4–6)
        iii. Trust in foreign alliances (8:7–10)
        iv. Empty sacrifices (8:11–14)
        v. The end of festivals (9:1–9)
    F. Unfulfilled promise (9:10 – 10:15)
        i. Fruit becoming unfruitful (9:10–17)
        ii. A vine overrun by thorns and thistles (10:1–10)
        iii. A trained heifer ploughing wickedness (10:11–15)
    G. Divine commitment to a beloved but ungrateful child (11:1–11)

3. PAST INGRATITUDE AND FUTURE HOPE (11:12 – 14:9)

    A. Yahweh's case against the people (11:12 – 12:14)
        i. Deceit and false confidence (11:12 – 12:1)
        ii. Jacob: past and present (12:2–14)
    B. Ephraim's exaltation, sin and judgment (13:1–16)
    C. Call to return to Yahweh; healing and restoration (14:1–9)

COMMENTARY

1. HOSEA'S MARRIAGE: ISRAEL AS YAHWEH'S UNFAITHFUL WIFE (1:1 – 3:5)

A. Superscript (1:1)

Context
Hosea's prophetic role is indicated by the expression *the word of the LORD that came to*. This appears in the openings of several prophetic books (Joel 1:1; Mic. 1:1; Zeph. 1:1), and similar wording is associated with the prophetic ministries of Ezekiel (1:3), Jonah (1:1; 3:1), Haggai (1:1) and Zechariah (1:1). The call to prophetic ministry was initiated by God: his word came to the prophet, who proclaimed it to the people.

Comment
The prophet's name, which comes from the Hebrew *yāša'* ('to help, deliver'), reflects God's ultimate goal for his people. It is shared by four other figures in the Old Testament: it was the former name of Joshua (Num. 13:8, 16); it was also the name of Israel's last king (Hoshea), of an official who signed Ezra and Nehemiah's renewed

covenant (Neh. 10:23) and of one of the leaders of the tribe of Ephraim (1 Chr. 27:20).[1]

We know nothing of Hosea's father, *Beeri*.[2] The name means 'my well', suggesting an expression of joy at the birth of a child. It may have had significance to the original audience, though the reference to Beeri may have been included to distinguish the prophet, particularly from King Hoshea, who was contemporary with Hosea and presided over Israel's downfall.

As noted, Hosea's ministry is set *during the reigns of Uzziah, Jotham, Ahaz and Hezekiah, kings of Judah, and during the reign of Jeroboam son of Joash king of Israel*,[3] placing it in the eighth century BC, during the most recent Assyrian resurgence. Similar lists of Judean kings are noted by the southern prophets Isaiah (1:1) and Micah (1:1), though they do not refer to northern rulers. Amos 1:1 refers to Uzziah and Jeroboam, but that is not unexpected since Amos was a southerner who prophesied in the north. It is surprising for a northern prophet to list the names of southern kings, and, particularly, to list them first. This has strengthened the view that Hosea's message was redacted in a Judean context, and that the superscript was part of that redaction.[4] It is also a little surprising that only Jeroboam is mentioned, since allusions to the chaotic situation prior to the fall of Samaria indicate that Hosea's ministry extended into the reigns of other Israelite kings. One suggestion is that the superscription was originally linked to chapters 1–3 and refers to the beginning of Hosea's ministry (Mays 1969: 21; Wolff 1974: 3–4; Emmerson 1984: 2; Macintosh 1997: 1–4). Alternatively, if the superscription was given its present form by Judean editors, references to further Israelite kings, during what may well have appeared to be a confusing period of history, would not have been directly relevant to the new audience, and so might not have been included (Stuart

---

1. EVV render these other names 'Hoshea', though the Hebrew term (*hôšēaʿ*) is the same. Two (Num. 13:8; 1 Chr. 27:20) are from Ephraim, furthering speculation that Hosea was an Ephraimite. See Wolff 1974: 5.

2. It is unlikely that Beeri is a place in Ephraim.

3. See above, pp. 1–5.

4. See above, pp. 16–19.

1987: 1). Another possibility is that Jeroboam was viewed as the last significant king of Israel, and his death was seen as the prelude to the end of the northern kingdom (Andersen and Freedman 1980: 148; Garrett 1997: 42; McComiskey 1998: 10–11).

Meaning

Whatever the history of its composition, the superscript now stands as the title for the whole book. Key to that is the opening expression *The word of the LORD*. Through the course of the book, Yahweh speaks through his prophet. That may be through the sign-act of Hosea's marriage, or through prophetic oracles. In each case, though, it is the word of Yahweh that first confronts the prophet and is then brought before the people.

The superscript also sets the prophecy against a particular historical background. While the word of God has relevance to a much wider audience, and Hosea's message may have been applied to a southern as well as a northern context, that word also comes at a particular point in time and space. Yahweh remains intimately involved in the affairs of his people and speaks both through his continuing activity in their history and into their historical situation.

B. Hosea's call and marriage; naming of children as symbols of judgment (1:2–9)

Context

These verses are written in the third person. While it is not impossible that Hosea is the author, it seems more likely that they were written by someone else, who was familiar with the prophet's family circumstances.

The section comprises a series of sign-acts: symbolic outworkings of the divine word in the prophet's life which are evident to his audience and which reinforce the message. These take the form of divine commands, each followed by an explanation. The first is to marry *a promiscuous woman* (1:2), which Hosea obeys by marrying Gomer (1:3). Central to this sign-act is the idea that the covenant relationship between Yahweh and his people, established at Sinai, is likened to a marriage and that breaking the covenant

represents spiritual adultery. Gomer's unfaithfulness to Hosea thus
reflects Israel's unfaithfulness to Yahweh, and that idea is programmatic for the whole book. The result of unfaithfulness is judgment
on the nation, and that is reflected in further sign-acts associated
with the symbolic naming of Gomer's three children (1:4, 6, 9).
National judgment is also linked with judgment on the house of
Jehu, who had killed Ahab's son Joram (2 Kgs 9:24) and made himself king in a bloodthirsty coup, marked by the murder of seventy
other sons of Ahab (2 Kgs 10:6–7) and the massacre of those in
Jezreel who had supported Ahab (2 Kgs 10:11), and of the rest of
his family in Samaria (2 Kgs 10:17). Jehu was also responsible for
the deaths of Ahaziah, king of Judah, also a descendant of Ahab
(2 Kgs 8:18, 26), and forty-two members of his family (2 Kgs 9:27;
10:13–14). Both judgments were effected through the death of
Jeroboam II, who was the last significant member of Jehu's dynasty,
and whose demise led to the sequence of chaotic events that
culminated in the fall of Samaria.

Comment

2. The opening could be understood as a temporal clause: *When
the LORD began to speak through Hosea*; or, possibly, as a heading for
the sequence of commands that follow: 'the beginning of the
LORD's speaking through Hosea' (see LXX). The call of a prophet
was generally seen as important, giving validity and authority to the
message (e.g. Isa. 6:8–9; Jer. 1:4–10; Amos 7:14–15; Jon. 1:1–2).
While there is no reference to a specific call, this appears to
mark the start of Hosea's ministry. There is debate as to whether
the Hebrew preposition *bĕ* should be translated 'through' (cf. Num.
12:2; 2 Sam. 23:2; 1 Kgs 22:28)[5] or 'to' (cf. Num. 12:6; Hab. 2:1)
(Andersen and Freedman 1980: 154–155; Macintosh 1997: 7–8).
Both indicate Hosea's prophetic status. The latter is possible in that
Yahweh gives instructions relating specifically to Hosea. However,
the prophet's response to those divine commands results in public
actions by which Yahweh speaks *through* him to the nation. Given

---

5. This is the more widely accepted translation; see NIV, NRSV, ESV and
many recent commentaries.

that the prophetic role is, primarily, to communicate God's word, there is, perhaps, not too much difference between them. A key point is that the message communicated to the people, however mediated, is essentially from God.

Go, marry a promiscuous woman is the first of four commands. The term translated *marry* is, literally, 'take to you a woman/wife', which is a standard expression relating to marriage.[6] As already noted, there is debate about whether this statement should be understood literally, as a command to marry a woman whom Hosea knew to be promiscuous, or proleptically, as a reinterpretation of the divine command in the light of Hosea's later discovery that his wife, whom he married in good faith, was unfaithful. In my view, primarily because Hosea portrays the relationship between Yahweh and Israel as having an idealized beginning (2:14–15; cf. Jer. 2:2), the latter understanding is more likely.

Hosea is commanded to marry an *'ēšet zĕnûnîm* (*promiscuous woman*),[7] and *zĕnûnîm* is also applied to the children (*yaldê zĕnûnîm*; nrsv: 'children of whoredom') who are to be born. This may suggest that the children, who also represent the nation, share the same tendency towards unfaithfulness (Wolff 1974: 13; see also Bird 1989: 80–81). When related to Hosea's family life, it may suggest that some of the children were born as the result of adulterous relationships (Knight 1960: 40; Routledge 2018: 36), or, more straightforwardly, that they are the children born in the context of Hosea's relationship with a promiscuous woman.

With each command, Hosea is also given an explanation of the significance of the symbolic action. In this case, Gomer's unfaithfulness mirrors the unfaithfulness of Israel and emphasizes, both to Hosea and to his audience, the extent and seriousness of that sin. The *land*, here, may be a reference to the northern kingdom. However, in view of the prophet's interest in Judah as well as Israel, it may refer to both kingdoms. Their unfaithfulness includes worship of the 'Baals', and making alliances with other nations, which involved allying, too, with their gods and so was also a form of idolatry.

---

6. See above, p. 26 n. 64.

7. See above, pp. 27–28.

3. Hosea demonstrated his obedience to the divine command by marrying Gomer. The Hebrew text here says, simply, 'he took' Gomer, and that expression could suggest a sexual relationship outside marriage. However, following on from verse 2, where the extended expression does refer to marriage, this should be understood in the same way.

Some have tried to attach symbolism to the names *Gomer* and *Diblaim*,[8] but that seems unlikely. If they were symbolic, we would expect their significance to be explained, as is the case with the names of Gomer's children. It has also been suggested that *Diblaim* might be a reference to Gomer's home town, Diblathaim, in Moab (cf. Jer. 48:22). This too seems unlikely. It is better to take these simply as the names of the figures involved.

Following the marriage, Gomer bore Hosea a son. Despite her possible adultery, the first child is specifically described as being his, literally 'to him' (*lô*).

4–5. The name of Hosea's first child points to judgment on the dynasty of Jehu. Jezreel was the scene of some of the massacres that marked Jehu's overthrow of the family of Ahab. It was located in a relatively flat valley, the Valley of Jezreel, which was suitable for chariots and was the scene of some significant confrontations (e.g. Judg. 6:33; 1 Sam. 29:1). The city, and surrounding region, was politically and militarily strategic, and Ahab had a palace there (1 Kgs 21:1) (Aster 2012).

Commentators differ over the significance of the references to Jehu and the *massacre at* [literally, 'bloods of'] *Jezreel*. Translations appear to suggest that Yahweh will punish Jehu's dynasty for the blood that Jehu shed at Jezreel. However, despite the negative appraisal in 2 Kings 10:31, that particular action had divine sanction and approval (2 Kgs 9:6–10; 10:17, 30), and it seems odd to make it,

---

8. *Gomer* is sometimes linked with *gāmar* ('to complete, bring to an end, fail'). *Diblaim* (*diblāyim*) has been taken as the dual form of *dĕbēlâ*, indicating a pressed-together fruit cake, and, based on the reference to *raisin cakes* (3:1), which are assumed to be part of Baal worship, to suggest Gomer's involvement in the Baal cult (Keil and Delitzsch 1980: 38–39). See also Pressler 1992.

so much later, a basis for judgment. It may be that Jehu's action was excessive. Or maybe, by killing Azariah of Judah and massacring his family, he went beyond God's purpose; though, as a member of Ahab's family, Azariah might be regarded as a legitimate target. But if Jehu had overstepped the mark, why was he initially commended, and why has judgment been delayed for so long?

The construction here, the verb *pāqad* with the preposition *'al* ('on, upon'), has the sense of 'to bring . . . upon'. That can mean 'to punish . . . for' (e.g. Exod. 20:5; 32:34), but that formula is not always appropriate (e.g. Lev. 26:16; Jer. 15:3). Here it may mean, not that the house of Jehu is being punished for the bloodshed at Jezreel, but that the judgment visited on Ahab's dynasty through Jehu will now be visited on Jehu's own house (Moon 2018: 34). While Jehu's actions against Ahab's family may have been sanctioned, his subsequent disobedience was not (2 Kgs 10:29–31). By the time of Jeroboam II, the sin of Jehu's dynasty and of Israel has reached a crisis point, and the result is divine judgment on both.

Breaking *Israel's bow* points to military defeat. This anticipates the fall of the nation to Assyria. The reference to the Valley of Jezreel continues the play on the name Jezreel. This was a place of important battles, including military defeats. The Israelites had camped at Jezreel (1 Sam. 29:1; cf. 2 Sam. 4:4) before the battle at Gilboa, in which Saul and Jonathan were killed. The city is also likely to have been destroyed by the Syrians under Hazael, in the ninth century BC (cf. 2 Kgs 13:3, 7, 22) (Na'aman 1997: 122–128; Finkelstein 2013: 119–128). It may, therefore, have been associated with significant past defeats (though see Judg. 6:33). That will again be Israel's fate. It is possible, too, that Jezreel was a significant military centre, and symbolized Israel's dependence on its own strength and ability to control its own fortunes (Aster 2012). That false confidence will be ended.

The wordplay around the similar-sounding Jezreel (*yizrĕ'e'l*) and Israel (*yiśrā'ēl*) has already been noted.[9] The two terms are also linked by the chiastic structure of verses 4b–5: Jezreel–Israel–Israel–Jezreel. *Jezreel* means 'God sows'. 'Sowing' is generally

---

9. See above, pp. 23–24.

associated with fertility, and the reference here, which foreshadows judgment on Israel, may be ironic: the nation that has been so blessed by God has, nevertheless, failed to produce. However, since sowing also involves scattering seed, there may be an allusion, too, to the coming exile. Other references to 'sowing' in Hosea link Israel's actions with their consequences, both negative (8:7) and positive (10:12) (Dearman 2010: 95–96), and something of that too may be implied by the name.

6. The name given to Gomer's second child, *Lō' Ruḥāmâ*,[10] also speaks of Yahweh's judgment on his people. *Ruḥāmâ* is linked to the term *raḥămîm* ('pity, compassion'), and to *reḥem* ('womb'), suggesting tenderness and affection (cf. NIV, *love*). The name means 'not shown compassion' and is thus a stark reference to the withdrawal of those feelings that would normally be associated with family relationships (cf. 11:8). The people have turned away from him, and now he will turn away from them. This judgment is real and will result in the Assyrian exile. However, it is intended not to destroy, but to refine and lead to repentance, as later verses show.

There is no specific reference to this child being Hosea's. The term *lô* ('to him') is absent. It may be that it can be assumed, and the omission is not significant. However, the expressions 'she conceived' and 'she gave birth to a son/daughter' are otherwise identical to those in verse 3, and through this repetition with variation the narrator may be drawing attention to what is omitted, and so hinting at the child's questionable parentage.

The term *nāśā'* means 'to lift, bear, take away', and may be translated 'to forgive' in the sense of bearing or taking away sins (cf. 14:2; see also, e.g., Gen. 18:26; Exod. 34:7; Isa. 2:9; 33:24). It is repeated here for emphasis (cf. NIV, *I will [not] . . . at all forgive them*). The link here between compassion and forgiveness recalls Exodus 34:6–7: 'The LORD, the LORD, the compassionate [*raḥûm*] and gracious God . . . forgiving [*nāśā'*] wickedness, rebellion and sin.' This picks up a recurring theme: the people have rejected Yahweh

---

10. The names of Gomer's second and third children relate to specific Hebrew terms and in the first instance are transliterated. Subsequent references take them as proper names (cf. NRSV).

and turned to other gods, and in so doing have rejected Yahweh's blessings, including his readiness to forgive. Alongside his love, Yahweh 'does not leave the guilty unpunished' (Exod. 34:7), and Israel cannot presume on their relationship with him to escape the consequences of unfaithfulness.

7. The contrast here between Israel and Judah has been seen as part of the Judean redaction,[11] possibly in the light of the fact that Jerusalem was delivered from the Assyrians, in 701 BC, and so did not share the fate of the northern kingdom. It is unlikely to relate to the deliverance of Jerusalem from the Syro-Ephraimite coalition, which was the result of an appeal to Assyria, contrary to prophetic advice, and is presented as the antithesis of relying on God (Isa. 7:9). The deliverance in 701 BC was accomplished by God, without human agency (2 Kgs 18 – 19; Isa. 37), and emphasizes the importance of trusting him alone (cf. Routledge 1992; 2016: 100–101). Judgment on Israel includes breaking its military power (1:5). Judah may fare better, but only by resisting the temptation to trust in the traditional sources of national strength and security (cf. Isa. 31:1). If so, this verse could have been inserted at an early stage, by a follower of Hosea, or maybe even by the prophet himself.

8–9. Again, it is unclear whether the absence of a specific reference to Hosea being the father of Gomer's third child, *Lō' 'Ammî* ('not my people'), is significant; the implications of the name, however, are very significant. When Israel came out of Egypt, a key part of Yahweh's covenant commitment to them at Sinai was that he would take them as his people and he would be their God (cf. Exod. 6:7).[12] Now that relationship has been annulled. This might express divine judgment: because of their unfaithfulness, Yahweh has rejected them as his people. However, the text seems, rather, to be stating a grim reality: the people have turned to worship other gods and that has negated their covenant bond with Yahweh. The expression *I am not your God* reads, literally, 'I (am) not I am [*'eyeh*] to you' (cf. NIV mg.). The same term, *'eyeh*, appears in Exodus

---

11. See above, pp. 16–19.

12. See above, p. 26 n. 63.

3:14 in the context of the revelation of the divine name, Yahweh, to Moses – 'I AM [*'eyeh*] has sent me to you' (Achtemeier 1996: 18). Israel's worship of other gods has undermined the special relationship implicit in the divine name. And this is the result, not of God's vindictiveness, but of Israel's choice: the people have brought it on themselves. The statement of the breakdown of the relationship is made all the more poignant in that it is addressed directly to Israel. In the earlier part of the chapter, statements are made *about* Israel. Here, the message is directly *to* Israel: '*you* are not my people, and I am not *your* God'.

Meaning

A key factor in Hosea's ministry is his obedience to Yahweh's voice. On four occasions in these verses we see divine commands: first, to marry, and then in the naming of the three children. Whether or not Hosea knew about Gomer's promiscuous tendency before their marriage, his obedience came at a price, both socially and emotionally.

In contrast to Hosea's obedience, we see Israel's unfaithfulness. Like Gomer, Israel has committed adultery, by turning to other gods. And the symbolic namings of Jezreel, Lo-Ruhamah and Lo-Ammi point to the consequences of their actions: judgment on the nation and the annulment of the covenant bond between Yahweh and his people. Israel prided themselves on their relationship with Yahweh and appear to have taken the blessings associated with it for granted, irrespective of their behaviour towards him. That relationship, though, must be two-sided, and the book begins by announcing that things cannot continue as they are. Israel's attitude towards Yahweh is not consistent with the nation's unique calling as God's people, so that privileged position has been withdrawn. That is not Yahweh's last word. But if there is to be restoration, the people must first be brought to their senses.

For the moment, Judah is spared the same fate as Israel. Following the repentance of the more godly king, Hezekiah, the immediate Assyrian threat to Judah (in 701 BC) was removed, and this may have suggested a model for future hope. A key factor in that hope, though, is dependence on God alone, rather than on

anything else the nation might be tempted to rely on,[13] including
military power. The reference to the Valley of Jezreel points to the
loss of Israel's military strength. Removing that source of false
confidence opens the way for restoration through renewed dependence on God.

C. Restoration: reversal of judgment (1:10 – 2:1) [MT 2:1–3]

Context
The theme of these verses is the reversal of the judgment associated
with the children's names in 1:2–9. The suddenness of the change,
together with the reference to the reunion of the northern and
southern kingdoms, has led to the suggestion that this is the work
of a redactor.[14] The idea of God ultimately showing mercy to his
people, though, is consistent with Hosea's overall message, and
with the judgment–salvation pattern running through the book.
The reference to Israel and Judah coming together is also consistent
with other parts of the prophecy (Emmerson 1984: 95–101; Moon
2018: 45). Consequently, there seems little reason not to regard this
as original.

The final verse (2:1) begins with a second person imperative
plural (*Say*) and is sometimes attached to the next section, which
begins with the same imperative form (*Rebuke*). The positive
reference to the children's names, though, suggests that it might fit
better with the previous salvation section, rather than with the
judgment oracle in 2:2–13. It should possibly be viewed as a transitional text, linking the two sections closely together.

Comment
    10. *Like the sand on the seashore* indicates a measureless amount
(e.g. Gen. 41:49; Josh. 11:4; Judg. 7:12; 1 Sam. 13:5; 1 Kgs 4:29). In
particular, when linked with the number of Israelites, it recalls
God's promises to the patriarchs about the future size of the nation

---

13. This is also a major emphasis in Isa. 1 – 39; see e.g. Isa. 22:8b–11;
    30:1–2; 31:1; cf. 7:9; 25:9; 28:16; 30:15. See also Johnston 2009: 104–121.
14. See Macintosh 1997: 33–35.

(Gen. 22:17; 32:12; cf. Isa. 10:22; Jer. 33:22). The expression here is most similar to the promise to Jacob: 'I . . . will make your descendants like the sand of the sea, which cannot be counted' (Gen. 32:12). This suggests a further link with the Jacob narrative,[15] and points to the future revival of the nation's fortunes. Despite their present unfaithfulness, and in the face of its current historical improbability,[16] they will become what God intended them to be.

Future restoration includes reversing the breakdown of the covenant relationship. Those who have been called *not my people* will be brought back into the family and accepted as *children of the living God*. This new designation as *children of the living God* (*běnê 'ēl ḥāy*) contrasts with the description *yaldê zěnûnîm* ('children of whoredom', NRSV) in 1:2 (Dearman 2010: 104)[17] and reflects the complete rehabilitation of an unfaithful nation. The expression *in the place* may refer to a particular location,[18] though may simply mean 'instead' (Wolff 1974: 27; Garrett 1997: 72), emphasizing Israel's transformed status.

The expression *living God* frequently occurs in contexts which emphasize the reality of Israel's God:[19] acting on behalf of his people (Josh. 3:10), challenging those who underestimate his power (1 Sam. 17:36; 2 Kgs 19:4, 16) or contrasting him with other gods (Jer. 10:10; cf. Dan. 6:20, 26). The term may also point to God as the one who brings life to his people (Mays 1969: 32; Garrett 1997: 72).

---

15. See above, p. 33.

16. Wolff (1974: 26) notes Israel's relative insignificance on the world stage at this time.

17. The terms for *children* are different, though *běnê zěnûnîm* ('children of whoredom', NRSV) is used in 2:4.

18. Andersen and Freedman (1980: 203) take it as the desert, where Israel was first described as God's children (cf. Deut. 14:1). Mays (1969: 32) and Kelle (2005: 111–112) suggest Jezreel. For Moon (2018: 46) it is the land where they have been unfaithful but where they will be given an honourable name.

19. The expression in 1:10, *'ēl ḥāy*, also occurs in Josh. 3:10; Pss 42:2; 84:2. Expressions using *'ĕlōhîm* instead of *'ēl* occur in Deut. 5:26; 1 Sam. 17:26, 36; 2 Kgs 19:4, 16; Jer. 10:10; 23:36; Dan. 6:20, 26. A related expression, 'as the LORD lives' (*ḥay yhwh*), appears in Hos. 4:15.

11. Hosea regards the division between Israel and Judah as sinful (cf. Emmerson 1984: 77) and, in the future, these two kingdoms will be reunited under a single 'head' (NRSV; *rōʾš*). This anticipates the restoration of the Davidic monarchy (cf. 3:5) and has possible messianic overtones, though the reference on this occasion is not specific.

The reference to coming *up out of the land* could refer to return from exile, in which case *the land* would be Assyria or Babylon, though it seems more likely that it refers to Israel. It may be linked with the meaning of Jezreel ('God sows') and refer to the future flourishing of the nation, growing up out of the earth (Garrett 1997: 73; Dearman 2010: 105–106). Another possibility, particularly if it is set around the time of the Assyrian incursions of 732/1 BC, is that 'go up' has military connotations and refers to Israel and Judah taking possession of the land (cf. NRSV) (Mays 1969: 33; Wolff 1974: 28; Moon 2018: 46–47). As noted already, Jezreel is associated with Israel's military might. Judgment results in the loss of that strength and the call to trust in God alone. However, in the future, a kingdom united under a single leader will rise up and recover the land.[20] *Great will be the day of Jezreel* indicates that the future glory of the nation will reverse the earlier judgment (1:5).

2:1. This continues the theme of reversal. It picks up on the names of Gomer's children, though *brothers* and *sisters* are plural, indicating a wider significance for the nation as a whole. *Say* is also plural, suggesting that here the nation is invited to address itself. However, though there may be logical inconsistencies, the content is clear: God will act decisively to restore the broken relationship with his people symbolized by the names Lo-Ammi and Lo-Ruhamah.

---

20. Aster (2012: 43–44) understands Jezreel geographically. By analogy with 'the day of Midian' (Isa. 9:4), *the day of Jezreel* points to the destruction of Jezreel and the self-reliance it represents, opening the way for restoration. The rhetorical link between Jezreel and Israel, though, makes it more likely that this is a positive expression analogous to the 'day of the LORD' (cf. 7:5).

Meaning

There is nothing in the text to prepare the reader for this oracle of salvation, which follows immediately after the threat of judgment. We might expect a reference to the conditions for receiving salvation – for example, repentance and turning back to God. Those things are present elsewhere in the book (e.g. 6:1–3; 14:1–3). Here, though, we see only the promise.[21] Israel's sin has serious consequences, but God will not give up on those who belong to him, and judgment is not the last word. It is this divine grace that allows judgment and the hope of salvation to stand side by side.

That salvation results in the reversal of the threatened judgment, including Israel's acceptance and the bestowal of a new name and status. Beyond that, it results in the renewal of the covenant promises made to Abraham and Jacob, and the restoration of the people to what they were meant to be. In spite of Israel's unfaithfulness, God's purpose for his people will be fulfilled. That purpose includes the unity of Israel and Judah and its future prosperity under a single leader. That leader is later identified with David (3:5), suggesting messianic significance, and Christians further identify the one through whom the people of God will be restored, united and blessed, despite their sin, with Jesus Christ.

In the New Testament, Paul relates the transformation in status here to the Gentiles, who may now be described as God's people and be included in the promise of salvation (Rom. 9:24–26). Peter also notes the changed names, which he applies to the body of believers, who, through Christ, have become God's people (1 Pet. 2:10) (Hubbard 1989: 71; G. V. Smith 2001: 55).[22] These express the same principle of divine grace: that those who have no right to it may, nevertheless, be incorporated into the people and purposes of God.

---

21. The hope of salvation also immediately follows the threat of judgment in 11:5–11.

22. On the relationship between the church and Israel as the people of God, see Routledge 2013.

D. Judgment on an unfaithful wife (2:2–13) [MT 2:4–15]

Context
This section is primarily directed towards Israel. Continuing the marriage metaphor, it describes the punitive action that Yahweh will take against his unfaithful covenant partner. It remains, though, closely related to the narrative of Hosea's marriage, and should not be viewed in isolation from it. Thus, the initial accusation (v. 2) is delivered by the children, who without the details in the previous chapter would be unknown. The idea of the children, who represent Israel, indicting their mother, who also represents Israel, makes most sense if it is derived from an actual family context, since otherwise we have Israel indicting Israel (for a summary of views, see Ben Zvi 2005: 62–63; Kelle 2005: 82–94). There is, though, a transition, early in the passage, from Hosea's domestic situation to the relationship between Yahweh and Israel.

There is debate about the structure of this section. Clines (1998: 294–299) includes 2:14–15, because of the threefold repetition of *Therefore* (vv. 6, 9, 14) (see also Mays 1969: 34–35; Wolff 1974: 41). In the first two cases, however, *Therefore* introduces a message of judgment. In the third it introduces a message of hope, and that fits better in the next section, which elaborates on the hopeful theme (Hubbard 1989: 49; Macintosh 1997: xiii; Dearman 2010: 107–108).

Comment
2. It has been suggested that the statement *she is not my wife, and I am not her husband* reflects an Ancient Near Eastern divorce formula (Wolff 1974: 33; Instone-Brewer 1996: 4; Phillips 2002: 89–90), and that Yahweh (and Hosea) brings the marriage to an end. This may also include the formal shaming of the guilty party, and possibly reflects a custom whereby members of the family are called as witnesses to the wife's unfaithfulness and become part of the shaming process, though the Old Testament provides no evidence of this. When applied to Israel, the detailed analogy breaks down. However, references to mother and children both fit with the more general metaphor of family (Dearman 2010: 111). Ben Zvi (2005: 70) and Macintosh (1997: 41) suggest the context of a 'family quarrel'.

Rebuke translates the imperative of the Hebrew verb *rîb*, which, like the corresponding noun, may suggest a judicial setting.[23] However, though the statement is similar to some found in the Ancient Near East in connection with formal divorce proceedings, there is little evidence that this was used in Israel (Mays 1969: 37–38; Macintosh 1997: 41; Kelle 2005: 54–55; Dearman 2010: 109–110[24]). Also, because the intention of the accusation here appears to be to open the way for reconciliation, an actual divorce seems unlikely. However, echoing the name of Gomer's third child, Lo-Ammi, this does signal a significant breakdown in the marriage and in the covenant relationship between Yahweh and his people.

The verb translated *remove* (*sûr*) might relate to something physical, and references to *face* and *breasts* have led some to suggest that this might refer to objects worn by participants in the Baal fertility cult (Mays 1969: 38; Wolff 1974: 33–34; Andersen and Freedman 1980: 224),[25] or by prostitutes more generally (Kruger 1983: 109–111; Hubbard 1989: 73). It may be better, though, to take this metaphorically (Kelle 2005: 95–97; Dearman 2010: 110): the children urge their mother to turn aside from everything associated with her former adulterous behaviour, so that reconciliation may be possible.

3. *Otherwise* leaves open the possibility of reconciliation, but indicates, too, the disastrous consequences of Gomer/Israel not leaving behind her adulterous ways. Exposing nakedness (see also 2:10) was associated with shame (e.g. Isa. 20:4; 47:3; Nah. 3:5–6), and Ancient Near Eastern texts suggest that this was a punishment for an unfaithful wife (Andersen and Freedman 1980: 225; Kruger 1983: 111–113; Macintosh 1997: 43; Phillips 2002: 89–90; Dearman 2010: 111).[26] Hanley (2017) questions the Ancient Near Eastern background and takes this instead as a reference to removing

---

23. See above, p. 22.

24. Dearman regards the situation as unclear, though notes the absence of legal elements that might be expected to be present in divorce.

25. Though see above, pp. 7–8.

26. For discussion of what some see as the sexually abusive content of the verse, see above, pp. 29–30.

covenant blessings. The imagery is also associated with the humiliation of the nation through defeat and exile (e.g. Lam. 1:8; Ezek.
16:36–39; 23:10). There may, too, be an economic aspect associated
with divorce proceedings, whereby an adulterous wife was dis-
owned, and expelled from her husband's house with none of the
things he had provided for her, including clothes (Mays 1969: 38;
Wolff 1974: 34; Kelle 2005: 60–62; Moon 2018: 53–54). While this
might not refer to a formal divorce, there is a clear breakdown of
the relationship, including withdrawal of the husband's provision.
For Israel, a key part of divine provision was rain and corresponding fruitfulness (e.g. Deut. 11:10–17). Without it, the land will
become a parched, lifeless desert.

The day she was born (v. 3) could refer to Gomer, though the further
reference to 'wilderness' (NRSV; cf. v. 14) also suggests the exodus,
which marked the birth of the nation. Israel will be taken back to
the kind of experience that marked their desert wanderings
(Andersen and Freedman 1980: 225–227). This appears to mark
the transition to an oracle focused primarily on Israel (Hubbard
1989: 74).

4–5. This reiterates the judgment in chapter 1. *I will not show my
love* recalls the name of Gomer's second child, Lo-Ruhamah (1:6),
and *children of adultery* (*běnê zěnûnîm*) corresponds to *yaldê zěnûnîm*
(1:2). If this reflects Hosea's relationship with Gomer, it may
support the view that some of the children were not his. More
likely, it indicates that the children are implicated in the disgrace
of the mother. From this point Hosea's marriage fades from view,
and the focus shifts to the relationship between Yahweh and Israel.
Some suggest that the *mother* here represents Israel's capital, Samaria
(Kelle 2005: 86–90; Lim and Castelo 2015: 64). The primary application, though, is to the nation as a whole (Dearman 2010: 112).

Though *lovers* may refer to foreign nations with which Israel has
established treaties,[27] the reference to physical provision suggests
that the primary reference here is to false gods. It was common
to associate local gods with the fertility and prosperity of the land,
and Israel had turned from Yahweh, the true source of blessing

27. See above, p. 7.

(e.g. 2:8), to these 'Baals'. The commodities listed, 'bread' (NRSV), *water, wool, linen, oil* and *drink*, may be intended to represent the standard necessities of life (Andersen and Freedman 1980: 233), though some suggest that the final two are luxuries (Mays 1969: 39; Wolff 1974: 35), thus widening the scope of the provision. Lim notes, further, that in the Ancient Near East these were expected to be supplied by the wife's husband, and seeking them from lovers emphasizes her willing marital unfaithfulness (Lim and Castelo 2015: 69–90). The rhythmical nature of the expression has led to the suggestion that Hosea may be quoting ironically part of a hymn connected with the Baal fertility cult (Garrett 1997: 80; cf. Andersen and Freedman 1980: 232; Hubbard 1989: 75).

6–7. These verses continue the theme of judgment on an unfaithful nation. Part of that judgment is that the people who have wrongly attributed material blessings to false gods will be frustrated in their search for those things. But the remedial aspect of judgment is also evident. Yahweh will limit the ability of Israel to turn to her *lovers* as part of his ultimate goal of bringing her back to himself.

Some see Israel's decision to *go back* [*šûb*] *to* [*her*] *husband* as prompted by mere self-interest. There is no reference to remorse, and Israel's return to Yahweh appears to be primarily because of the fruitlessness of turning to other gods (Macintosh 1997: 53; Clines 1998: 298–299; Dearman 2010: 123–115; Dharamraj 2018: 64; Moon 2018: 55). However, *šûb* in this context indicates the possibility of a restored relationship, and so suggests some level of repentance (Mays 1969: 40; Andersen and Freedman 1980: 239; Hubbard 1989: 76; see also Lalleman 2013: 37–39).[28] The expression *ʾāmrâ ʾēlkâ* (*she will say, 'I will go'*, v. 7b) is the same as in verse 5b, where it relates to going after *my lovers*. This suggests a deliberate contrast between Israel's desire to return to her first husband and her current idolatry, and indicates, for whatever reason, a change in attitude. There are clear similarities here with Jesus' parable of the prodigal son, who also recognized that his previous life was better than the situation he found himself in, and chose to return home.

---

28. On *šûb*, see above, p. 24.

It has been noted that, according to Deuteronomy 24:1–4, a wife who has been divorced and has then remarried may not return to her first husband. This would not apply here if no formal divorce had taken place. However, Jeremiah 3:1–5, which may have been influenced by Hosea, applies the law in a similar way, and goes on to mention divorce specifically (3:8). The purpose is to highlight how unlikely reconciliation is in the light of the people's sin. Ultimately, though, however impossible it might seem, the people may be forgiven and restored (cf. Jer. 3:12–14). And when Israel comes to its senses, even though prompted, at least initially, by selfish motives, there is the hope of a renewed relationship with Yahweh.

8–13. This elaborates on the judgment in 2:6–7. There is the hope of return and restoration, but first the nation needs to understand the nature of its sin. The section begins and ends on a similar note: the people's failure to recognize Yahweh as the source of the blessings they have received.

The people have not *acknowledged* (*yāda'*) Yahweh as the one who has provided for them (v. 8).[29] *Grain, the new wine and oil* may echo divine provision in Deuteronomy.[30] The same expression occurs as part of God's restored blessings in 2:22 (cf. Joel 2:19). *Silver* and *gold* were precious commodities, and not only has their true source not been recognized, but they have been used in the worship of Baal, possibly including the manufacture of idols (e.g. 8:4; 13:2; cf. Ps. 115:4; Isa. 31:7; 40:19).

Because Israel has not acknowledged Yahweh's provision, he will take it back (v. 9), in order to make the nation's dependence on him clear. *I will take back* reads, literally, 'I will return [*šûb*] and take'. This again plays on the word *šûb*. Yahweh's 'return' in judgment is intended to bring about Israel's 'return' in repentance. The repeated *my* emphasizes the divine source, and the reference to *my wool and my linen* contrasts with 2:5, where the same expressions are linked with gifts from Israel's *lovers*. These were intended to cover Israel's nakedness; withdrawing them will expose the nation to public shame (v. 10; cf. 2:3).

---

29. On *yāda'*, see above, p. 15 n. 42.

30. See above, p. 13.

Cultic practices will also be ended (v. 11). Among the *celebrations* are annual feasts, monthly festivals[31] and the weekly Sabbath. These may have included events dedicated to Baal (v. 13). The terms are also used to refer to Israel's traditional festivals,[32] though they, too, have become corrupted, with Yahweh worshipped as just one more 'baal' (2:16).[33] Within the Baal cult, worship and festivals were associated with the fertility of the land. *Vines* and *fig trees* are examples of Yahweh's provision (Deut. 8:8; cf. Joel 2:22) and also are linked with future security (e.g. 1 Kgs 4:25; Mic. 4:4). Israel sees them as gifts from Baal, though Hosea's more disparaging assessment is they are payment for prostitution (*'etnâ*).[34] However, provision and security come from Yahweh alone, and to make the people aware of their dependence on him, and of the futility of serving the Baals, their vines and fig trees will be ruined.[35] They will become thickets, providing shelter and food only for wild animals.

Verse 13 points again to Israel's false worship. The description of a woman adorning herself with jewellery to make herself more attractive to her lovers might suggest the reappearance of Gomer, though the charge of burning incense *to the Baals*, and the final statement '*but me she forgot* [*šākaḥ*)],' *declares the* LORD, make it clear that Israel is still in view. This picks up the reference to going after her lovers in 2:5. *Her lovers* are referred to several times (2:5, 7, 10, 12). Here they are paralleled explicitly with *the Baals. Punish . . . for* is

---

31. The New Moon festival is noted in Num. 29:6; 1 Sam. 20:24; Ezek. 46:6.

32. Similar lists relating to legitimate festivals occur in 1 Chr. 23:31; 2 Chr. 8:13; 31:3; Neh. 10:33; Ezek. 45:17. *Yearly festivals* translates *ḥag*, which usually refers to Israel's pilgrim festivals: Passover/Unleavened Bread, Weeks and Tabernacles (see e.g. Exod. 23:14–17; Deut. 16:1–17).

33. See above, pp. 9–10.

34. The term translated *pay* (*'etnâ*) occurs only here. It is generally viewed as a variation of *'etnan*, which refers to a prostitute's pay in Deut. 23:18; Ezek. 16:31; Hos. 9:1.

35. Ruining vines and fig trees symbolizes divine judgment in Ps. 105:33; Jer. 5:17; Joel 1:7; cf. Hab. 3:17.

the same expression as in 1:4. Yahweh will deal with his people in accordance with their actions in worshipping the Baals. *The days she burned incense to the Baals* reads, more literally, 'the days of the Baals, when she made smoke go up to them'. This could refer to offering sacrifices, though more probably refers to burning incense. In all of this, Israel acknowledges other gods, while forgetting the true source of her well-being.

Meaning
This passage begins within a family context, with the children rebuking their mother. However, the emphasis soon switches. Yahweh is the wronged husband, and Israel the unfaithful wife, who has committed spiritual adultery by worshipping the *Baals*, here described as her *lovers*.

A key indictment is that the people have failed to recognize that what they have comes from Yahweh. He is their provider, but they have not acknowledged him (v. 8); they have forgotten him (v. 13) and, instead, give credit to Baal. As a result, Yahweh will take it all back! But his action is educative, not vindictive. This is a judgment oracle and there is no reference to Yahweh's love for his wayward bride – that will come later. However, removing his provision is intended to emphasize the people's dependence on him and bring them to a place where, like the prodigal son in Jesus' parable, they come to their senses and realize that they were better off at home – in this case, with their first 'husband' (v. 7).

Yahweh's willingness to wait for his bride to return highlights his patience. Sin has serious consequences, including the breakdown of relationship with God. But that breakdown is not final, and the possibility of return and reconciliation remains open. Yahweh's commitment to restoring the relationship is evident in what follows.

E. Restoration and reconciliation; a new beginning (2:14–23) [MT 2:16–25]

Context
The theme of divine judgment ends abruptly with 2:13. Following the condemnation of the previous verses, *Therefore* (*lākēn*) at the

beginning of verse 14 might be expected, as in verses 6 and 9, to introduce a further announcement of judgment. Instead, it introduces a series of divine promises, each introduced by *I will*. The repetition of *lākēn* links this to the previous section, though the emphasis now is on Israel's salvation and restoration.

At its heart is a new exodus experience:[36] Yahweh will take his people back to the wilderness, to where the relationship began, and there he will renew his commitment to them. He promises, too, the restoration of the blessings that have been removed and, again, the reversal of the judgment associated with the names of Gomer's children. This calls attention back to the relationship between Hosea and his wife, which, while never far from the surface, has given way to a more specific focus on Yahweh's relationship with Israel. And that leads to the further reference to Hosea's relationship with his wife in chapter 3.

Verses 16–23 may be divided into three sections, each including the expression *In that day* (vv. 16, 18, 21). This is generally understood as an eschatological term, maybe referring to the 'Day of the Lord' (Mays 1969: 47; Andersen and Freedman 1980: 277–278; Lim and Castelo 2015: 74), which is a frequent theme in the Book of the Twelve.[37] It points to a new era of restoration and peace as a result of Yahweh's intervention.

Comment

14. The use of *lākēn* in this context may be a quirk of Hosea's language. However, given that the term has been used twice already in its usual sense of 'therefore', it seems unlikely that it is meant to be taken differently here. One way of understanding this is that, because Israel has forgotten Yahweh, the only hope for true reconciliation lies with God taking the initiative and winning her back. There is the idea of return in 2:7, and while that may indicate partial repentance, it is for selfish reasons and more needs to happen. But Israel's condition is such that the people are incapable of responding as they need to, and only Yahweh's direct action can open the way

---

36. See above, pp. 33–34.
37. See above, pp. 10–11.

for that to happen. This may be further indicated by the interjection *hinnēh*. Here it is translated *now* but is more commonly translated 'behold'. It usually emphasizes the next word, and, in narrative, frequently indicates a change in perspective.[38] Here it does both. The first part of verse 14 could be translated, 'Therefore, behold me alluring her', changing the focus from Israel's waywardness to Yahweh and his intervention. It is an indication of Yahweh's love and patience that his response to Israel, who has turned to the Baals and forgotten him, is to seek to win her back, rather than to announce further judgment, however deserved that judgment might be.

The first part of Yahweh winning back his bride is to *allure* (*pātâ*) her. The term here refers to enticing or persuading. It may suggest deception (e.g. 1 Kgs 22:20; Jer. 20:7; cf. Hos. 7:11) or seduction (Exod. 22:16; Deut. 11:16; Job 31:9). In this case, while no less intense, it is more positive. It emphasizes Yahweh's commitment to doing whatever is needed to restore his relationship with Israel.

The reference to the *wilderness* recalls 2:3, which points to the privations associated with Yahweh withholding his blessings, and which will play a significant part in bringing Israel back to himself. In this context, though, it relates primarily to the exodus, which is significant for Hosea's understanding of the relationship between God and Israel. It was in the desert that the relationship began, and now Yahweh will take Israel back to the desert, to the place of new beginnings, to renew the relationship.

Speak tenderly to her translates literally as 'speak to her heart [*lēb*]'.[39] This points to the warmth and intimacy of Yahweh's feelings for Israel. Emphasis on the heart also indicates that Yahweh is looking for an inward response from Israel (cf. 1 Sam. 16:7), rather than the more superficial reason for returning in 2:7. The heart in ancient Israel was the seat of the will, and as Yahweh seeks to renew his relationship with his bride, he calls Israel to make a willing

---

38. On the use of *hinnēh* in biblical narrative, see Berlin 1994: 62–63; Routledge 2016: 166.

39. Similar expressions occur in Gen. 34:3; 50:21; Judg. 19:3; Ruth 2:13; 2 Chr. 30:22; Isa. 40:2.

commitment to that renewal.[40] And, as we see elsewhere, Yahweh will himself enable that heart response. He promises, through Jeremiah, a new covenant in which his law will be written on human hearts (Jer. 31:31–33), and, through Ezekiel, a heart of flesh that will also facilitate a new obedience (Ezek. 36:26–28).[41]

15. Having brought Israel back into the desert, to where the relationship began, Yahweh will give back the vineyards that were among the blessings associated with the occupation of Canaan (cf. Deut. 6:11), but which had previously been laid waste (2:12; cf. Deut. 28:30, 39). The people have associated these signs of prosperity with the Baals, but Yahweh will sever that relationship (2:6–7; cf. v. 17), so that Israel will recognize the true source of blessings.

The *Valley of Achor* recalls events following Israel's entry into the Promised Land. After the victory at Jericho, the people were instructed not to keep any of the spoil: it was all to be devoted to God (Josh. 6:17–19). However, Achan disobeyed and kept some for himself (Josh. 7:1). This brought judgment on the whole nation, which suffered an unexpected defeat at the next city, Ai (Josh. 7:2–5, 11–12). After Achan was discovered and executed, Yahweh's anger turned away, and the place of his burial was named 'the Valley of Achor' (Josh. 7:16–26). 'Achor' (*ākôr*) means 'trouble' and there is wordplay between it and the name 'Achan' (*ākān*).[42] Israel's entrance into the Promised Land should have been associated with opportunity. Instead, sin made it a place of trouble. This also reflects Israel's present experience: because of sin they have forfeited the blessings of the land. But Yahweh offers a new beginning, in which the Valley of Achor can become what it always should have been: a *door of hope* [*tiqwâ*]; a gateway into all that he has

---

40. 'Speak to her heart', corresponding to *pātâ*, may also include the sense of persuasion.

41. The covenant formula 'you will be my people, and I will be your God' (Ezek. 36:28) (see above, p. 26 n. 63) indicates that Ezekiel also anticipates a new covenant relationship (cf. Hos. 2:18).

42. 'Achan' is probably original, though appears as 'Achar' in 1 Chr. 2:7 and the LXX of Josh. 7, making the link with 'trouble' clearer. For further discussion see Hess 1994.

prepared for his people. The same term (*tiqwâ*) appears in Jeremiah's vision of the future (29:11; 31:17). There may also be a further allusion to Jericho. Rahab the prostitute sheltered Israelite spies and was promised protection if she tied a crimson 'cord' (*tiqwâ*) in her window (Josh. 2:18, 21). Here, Hosea offers hope to another 'prostitute', Israel (Andersen and Freedman 1980: 276; Garrett 1997: 91; Dearman 2010: 123).

The link with the exodus period is seen, too, in the reference to Israel's *youth*, which is paralleled with coming *up out of Egypt*. Yahweh seeks to elicit from Israel the response that marked the early days of the relationship, which were later idealized as a kind of 'honeymoon period'.[43] Similar language is used by Jeremiah, who refers to 'the devotion of [Israel's] youth' in the wilderness (Jer. 2:2).

16–17. In previous verses Israel has been referred to in the third person singular (*she, her*). In the first part of verse 16 the address is in the second person, *you will call me*, before going back to the third person: *her lips* (v. 17). This variation may be for rhetoric effect.

The first *In that day* points to the removal of all aspects of Baal worship. At one level, there is little difference between the Hebrew words translated, respectively, *husband* ('*îš*) and *master* ('Baal', NRSV; *ba'al*). Both can mean 'husband' or 'lord'. However, when set in the context of Israel's unfaithfulness, the difference is significant. There appears to have been confusion over what constituted true worship of Yahweh.[44] In the coming era of salvation, though, all mention of Baal will be removed, and with it the possibility of worshipping anyone other than Yahweh. In the new, restored relationship, Yahweh will have no rival.

18. *In that day*, too, Yahweh promises to establish a covenant, one which focuses on Israel's security, and also notes the prospect of a new marital relationship (vv. 19–20). A covenant constitutes a binding agreement between two or more parties. In a secular context it might include treaties and alliances. We have noted

---

43. See above, pp. 33–34.

44. See above, pp. 9–10.

already the significance of the idea for Hosea.[45] Here the personal
pronoun changes again to refer to the people in the third person:
I will make a covenant for them . . . so that [they] may lie down in safety.

Reference to *the beasts of the field, the birds in the sky and the creatures
that move along the ground* recalls the creation account (Gen. 1:30) and
the list of creatures that came out of the ark with Noah (Gen. 9:2)
and which were party to the covenant made then with 'every living
creature' (Gen. 9:9–10). The main emphasis here seems to be on the
reversal of the threat posed by wild beasts (cf. v. 12).[46] However,
the possible allusion to creation and to the Noahic covenant
suggests a wider restoration, which includes bringing peace and
harmony to the whole created order (cf. Isa. 11:6–9).

In that future consummation, all threat of war will also be
removed. 'Abolishing' (or 'breaking') the bow repeats the terms
used in 1:5. There it points to Israel's impending defeat and loss of
military strength at the hands of the Assyrians. Here it envisages a
time when military threats to Israel will be brought to an end. This
is further emphasized by references to *sword* and *battle*. As a result,
the people, here referred to in the third person ('they'), will know
true security, even when lying down and so at their most vulnerable
(cf. Ps. 4:8). Ezekiel expresses a similar idea when referring to a
'covenant of peace' that offers safety and security from wild animals
and military threats (Ezek. 34:25, 28).

19–20. In these verses, which resume the marriage metaphor,
Israel is addressed by Yahweh directly, in the second person (*you*).
This, and the threefold repetition of the expression *I will betroth
you to me*,[47] emphasizes the personal nature and the intensity of
Yahweh's commitment to restoring Israel. Betrothal indicates a
legally binding commitment to marriage, and between the betrothal
and consummation of the relationship the bride would belong to
her intended husband (Deut. 22:23–24). This does not require that

---

45. See above, p. 26.

46. This may be indicated by the absence of reference to sea creatures,
    which would not be a threat. Where the emphasis is on creation (4:3),
    the fish in the sea are included.

47. The NIV does not include the repeated 'to me'.

Yahweh had previously divorced Israel. Rather, it continues the idea of taking things back to where the relationship began and offering a new start.

Betrothal generally involved the payment of a bride-price by the husband (Gen. 34:12; Exod. 22:16; 1 Sam. 18:25; 2 Sam. 3:14).[48] This would usually be given to the bride's father, but might then be passed to the bride (Kelle 2005: 64–68, 277–279). The gifts mentioned here – *righteousness* (*ṣedeq*), *justice* (*mišpāṭ*), *love* (*ḥesed*), *compassion* (*raḥămîm*) and *faithfulness* (*'ĕmûnâ*) – may be taken as a reference to this bride-price, though in this case they are given directly to Israel (Vogels 1988; Kelle 2005: 277–279; Dearman 2010: 127–128). These are divine attributes, and the primary significance here is that by giving them to Israel for the duration of the marriage, and not just as one-off gifts (Andersen and Freedman 1980: 283), Yahweh provides what was previously lacking and ensures that the future relationship can be sustained.

Righteousness is associated with right action within a relationship. Here, it points to what is expected of both Israel and Yahweh as part of their mutual covenant commitment. It includes legal and ethical integrity and upholding the cause of the weak in society. In accordance with this, Yahweh acts in righteousness to vindicate Israel when they are oppressed by more powerful enemies, and so the term is also associated with salvation (e.g. Isa. 45:8; 51:5). *Justice* is closely linked with righteousness. Yahweh loves righteousness (*ṣĕdāqâ*) and justice (Ps. 33:5);[49] they form the foundation of his throne (Pss 89:14; 97:2) and fill Zion (Isa. 33:5). *Justice* involves punishing the guilty, and where the term appears in Hosea it is frequently in the context of judgment (5:1, 11; 6:5). It also includes ensuring fairness and impartiality (e.g. Deut. 16:18–20) and, like righteousness, is associated with defending those who are too weak to defend themselves (e.g. Exod. 23:6; Deut. 10:18; Ps. 72:2; Isa.

---

48. 2 Sam. 3:14 uses the same expression 'betrothed [*'ēraśtî*] to me [*lî*] for [*b-*]' as in Hos. 2:19–20.

49. The terms *ṣedeq* and *ṣĕdāqâ* seem interchangeable; thus, *ṣĕdāqâ* appears in 2 Sam. 22:21, 25, while *ṣedeq* appears in the parallel passages in Ps. 18:20, 24. See Reimer 1996: 746.

1:17). The significance of *ḥesed* for Hosea has already been discussed.[50] It is associated with righteousness (e.g. Ps. 85:10; Hos. 10:12) and justice (e.g. Ps. 119:149; Jer. 9:24; Hos. 12:6; Mic. 6:8).[51] *Compassion* is also closely linked with *ḥesed* (e.g. Exod. 34:6; Pss 51:1; 103:4; Lam. 3:22) (Clark 1993: 142–149). It is from the same root as the name of Gomer's second child, Lo-Ruhamah ('not shown compassion'; see on 1:6), and indicates deep feelings of tenderness and affection. The final attribute, *faithfulness* (*ĕmûnâ*), is also frequently linked with *ḥesed* (e.g. Pss 88:11; 89:1–2, 24; 92:2; 100:5), and it is, perhaps, no accident that *ḥesed* comes at the centre of this group. Faithfulness has at its heart truthfulness and reliability (e.g. Deut. 32:4; 2 Kgs 12:15; Isa. 59:4). God and his promises are dependable, and he looks for the same faithfulness from his people (cf. 4:1).[52] Faithfulness is also associated with righteousness (e.g. 1 Sam. 26:23; Pss 96:13; 143:1; Isa. 11:5) and justice (e.g. Isa. 1:21; Jer. 5:1).[53]

Before and after the list of bridal gifts are statements of divine intent: *I will betroth you to me for ever* [*lĕ ʿôlām*] . . . *and you will acknowledge* [*yādaʿ*] *the* LORD. Yahweh is committed to his people and offers these gifts to ensure that the renewed relationship will not fail as it did before. It will, too, be marked by a renewed knowledge of God. The term *yādaʿ* ('to know') is significant for the prophecy.[54] Here, it contrasts with Israel's failure to acknowledge Yahweh as the source of blessings (2:8; cf. 11:3) and with the indictment that Israel has forgotten Yahweh (2:13). Elsewhere, *yādaʿ* refers to sexual intimacy (e.g. Gen. 4:1), and while that is not appropriate here, it indicates the depth of the relationship. This is not increased knowledge *about* Yahweh, necessary as that is, but knowledge *of* him.

21–23. This section continues the theme of eschatological restoration *In that day*. It begins with an emphasis on God's control over nature (Macintosh 1997: 87; Dearman 2019: 130; see also

---

50. See above, pp. 31–32.

51. For discussion of the key terms related to *ḥesed*, see Clark 1993: 108.

52. The Hebrew term here is *ʾĕmet*. This is closely related to *ĕmûnâ* and appears in similar contexts. See Moberley 1996.

53. See n. 49 above.

54. See above, p. 15 n. 42.

Boshoff 1992; 2004: 270–273). Israel associated Baal with fertility[55] and with giving the people what they needed to sustain them. Here, Yahweh is given his rightful place as Israel's provider. After being led into the desert, Israel will *respond* (*ʿānâ*) to Yahweh (2:15), and Yahweh's corresponding response will be to supply the needs of his people.[56] Reference to the skies and the earth sets out a sequence whereby Yahweh instructs the heavens to pour rain on the earth, and the earth, in turn, produces *grain, the new wine and the olive oil* (v. 22). These are the very things that the people attributed to Baal (2:8), but here they come at Yahweh's behest (cf. Joel 2:19), indicating that he is the true lord of nature.

The fruit of the earth then responds to *Jezreel*. Here, Jezreel represents Israel,[57] who is the beneficiary of Yahweh's renewed blessing. Jezreel means 'God sows' (cf. 1:4–5), and there is a play on the name at the start of verse 23: *I will plant [sow] her for myself in the land*. This reverses the judgment in 1:4–5 (cf. 1:11) and points to future fertility and prosperity.

The last part of verse 23 continues the theme of the reversal of the judgment associated with the names of Gomer's children. God will show compassion to *Not my loved one*, and *Not my people* will again be called the people of God (cf. 1:10; 2:1). Yahweh's affirmation *You are my people*, together with the reply *You are my God*, reflects the covenant formula 'you will be my people and I will be your God'.[58] This again alludes to the exodus period and points to the full future restoration of the relationship between Yahweh and Israel which began then.

Meaning
These verses emphasize Yahweh's commitment to winning back and restoring his wayward bride. In the previous sections, *Therefore*

---

55. See above, pp. 5–6.
56. The term *ʿānâ* might refer to an answer to prayer (e.g. 1 Sam. 7:9; 8:18; 1 Kgs 18:24–26, 37; Isa. 58:9; Jon. 2:2) or a response to need (e.g. Isa. 41:17). Both are appropriate here.
57. Jezreel (*yizrᵉʿeʾl*) and Israel (*yiśrāʾēl*) look and sound similar (cf. 1:4–5).
58. See above, p. 26 n. 63.

focuses on judgment. However, this passage begins with a different emphasis. Those who are alienated from God because of sin are not able, by themselves, to bring about the changes needed to put things right. However, God is committed to restoring the relationship, and so we see another consequence of sin: God's direct intervention to do what is necessary to make that restoration possible. We see the ultimate demonstration of that in the coming of Christ and in the cross.

Israel has lost sight of God and his provision and so has forfeited the blessings of being in relationship with him. That state, though, is not permanent. God's desire is to give back what has been lost. That includes physical well-being, renewed understanding of God and a reaffirmation of their status as his people, in a renewed covenant bond that will last for ever. To do that, Yahweh will bring them back to where the relationship began and will offer a new start, with all its initial promise. As part of that renewed relationship, he will provide everything necessary to ensure its permanence. That includes bestowing qualities that are crucial to the relationship but which have hitherto been lacking. This amounts to the spiritual renewal of the people (cf. Ezek. 36:26–28).

This new relationship is noted in the New Testament. On the eve of the crucifixion, Jesus announced a 'new covenant in my blood' (Luke 22:20). And, as noted on 1:10 – 2:1, the scope has been widened beyond Israel (cf. Rom. 9:25–26; 1 Pet. 2:10). As a result of divine grace, the hope of future restoration and of a new relationship with God is available to all people.

F. Hosea's love and Yahweh's love (3:1–5)

Context
There is debate about the relationship of this passage to chapter 1. One view is that this is a parallel account of Hosea's marriage to Gomer, maybe following the fall of Samaria, when Hosea recognizes that restoration is possible only after judgment and a period of penance (Green 2003: 87–89; see also Gordis 1954: 30–35; Blenkinsopp 1996: 86; Keefe 2001: 16). However, inclusion of *again* (*ôd*) suggests that this is a subsequent event. There are also differences. Chapter 3 points to discipline and sexual abstinence,

whereas in chapter 1 children are born early in the relationship. Also, while in chapter 1 the children take a prominent role, in chapter 3 they are not mentioned (Routledge 2018: 37–40). Consequently, it seems better to take chapter 3 to refer to a later event in Hosea's life, in response to a further divine command. In this case, the narrative is told in the first person, by Hosea himself.

The identity of the woman in 3:1–3 has been discussed above.[59] The text gives little detail about Hosea and Gomer's relationship after the birth of the children, and there needs to be caution in offering a reconstruction based on limited information. However, arguments that this refers to a different adulterous woman are also built on assumptions.[60] In the light of what we do know, the view taken here is that this refers to Gomer, who by now has left Hosea and needs to be bought back (cf. Routledge 2018: 37–40).

There appears to be a close link between chapter 3 and the message of judgment and restoration in chapter 2 (Wolff 1974: 59; Hubbard 1989: 90). The marriage metaphor is established in chapter 1, with Gomer's actual adultery paralleling the spiritual adultery of Israel. Chapter 2 then applies the metaphor more specifically to Yahweh's dealings with Israel, including the promise to renew and restore the relationship. In chapter 3, in a further sign-act, Hosea is called to demonstrate that same willingness to restore the relationship with his unfaithful wife (Achtemeier 1996: 31).

The reference to David, together with the phrase *in the last days*, is seen by some to reflect Judean eschatology and so to be part of a later redaction (Wolff 1974: 63; Achtemeier 1996: 33; Macintosh 1997: 110–111; Ben Zvi 2005: 31[61]). That conclusion, though, is not necessary.[62] Hosea appears to regard Israel's rejection of the Davidic monarchy negatively, and might well look to a day when the two kingdoms will again be united under a Davidic ruler. This idea of restoration under a future Davidic king underlay Israel's

---

59. See above, pp. 28–29.

60. Moon, for example, speculates that Gomer might have died by this time (2018: 70).

61. Ben Zvi dates the whole book in the Persian period.

62. See above, p. 18.

messianic expectation (Routledge 2008a: 280–289; see also Satter-thwaite, Hess and Wenham 1995; Dearman 2010: 142–144), which began as the hope for an ideal king under whose reign Israel would regain the prominence it had under David. The eschatological aspect of this hope became more prominent in the post-exilic period (e.g. Jer. 23:5–6; 30:8–9; 33:17, 21; Ezek. 34:23–24; 37:24–25) and developed further during the period between the Testaments. However, significant elements were probably already present in the eighth century BC (e.g. Isa. 9:2–7; 11:1–9).

Comment

1. Here, as in 1:2, Hosea hears and responds to a word from Yahweh: 'Go, love a woman' (NRSV).[63] The indefinite '*a* woman' is unusual if the reference is to Gomer. Andersen and Freedman suggest that the language here may be intended to parallel the earlier expression (*Go, marry a . . . woman*), with 'love' replacing 'marry' because they are already married (1980: 295–296). The start of the verse could be read as either 'The LORD said to me *again*' (NRSV; emphasis added) (Mays 1969: 54; Andersen and Freedman 1980: 293; Stuart 1987: 62–63; Hubbard 1989: 90; Dearman 2010: 132) or 'go *again*, love' (cf. NIV) (Wolff 1974: 59; Achtemeier 1996: 33; Macintosh 1997: 93; Moon 2018: 58). Both indicate a further act in the relationship between Hosea and Gomer.

The woman *is loved by another man* [*rēa'*] *and is an adulteress.*[64] This may refer to a single lover, or it may relate more generally to adultery with several partners.[65] Nevertheless, Hosea is called to resume a loving relationship with her. As in 1:2, this mirrors the relationship between Yahweh and Israel: the Israelites have com-mitted adultery by turning to other gods (cf. Deut. 31:18, 20), but

---

63. The term '*iššâ* means, literally, '(a) woman', though it may be translated 'wife'. The NIV *your wife* implies a reference to Gomer.

64. The MT verb is passive. Following the LXX, Wolff (1974: 56) reads it as active, 'who loves'. This better fits the parallel with Israel's love for raisin cakes; cf. Mays 1969: 54. See also Andersen and Freedman 1980: 296.

65. For *rēa'* as 'lover', see Song 5:16; Jer. 3:1.

Yahweh's love for them, and his willingness to restore their broken relationship, continues.

Raisin cakes (*ăšîšê 'ănābîm*) were probably luxury food items.[66] Here, they are linked with the worship of other gods. This may indicate cultic significance,[67] or they may represent the provision that the people saw as gifts from Baal (cf. 2:12). Based on the occurrence of *'ăšîšâ* in Song of Songs 2:5, Andersen and Freedman (1980: 299) suggest that raisin cakes might also have been an aphrodisiac.

The word *love* occurs here four times.[68] It refers to Yahweh's love for his people, which is mirrored in Hosea's love for his wife. This includes commitment, and the willingness to forgive and restore despite infidelity. It is also costly, willing to pay the price of restoration. Hubbard captures the contrast between this and the people's foolish love of sensual pleasure and trivialities: 'while Yahweh is loving the Israelites, what are they loving? Raisin cakes!' (Hubbard 1989: 91; cf. Ben Zvi 2005: 82).

2. In obedience to Yahweh's command, Hosea *bought her for fifteen shekels of silver and about a homer and a lethek of barley*. The word translated *bought* is usually taken to be from the verb *kārâ* ('to buy, acquire'; cf. Deut. 2:6) (Andersen and Freedman 1980: 298; Hubbard 1989: 92; Garrett 1997: 100–101).[69] This may also include the idea of bargaining (Job 6:27; 41:6). The MT includes the term 'for myself', indicating the personal nature of the transaction: Hosea is bringing the woman out from the control of another and accepting her as his own. It is difficult to assign modern equivalents to biblical

---

66. Elsewhere, *'ăšîšâ* on its own is translated 'raisin cakes' (2 Sam. 6:19; Isa. 16:7) or 'raisins' (Song 2:5). Here, the link with grapes (*'ēnāb*) is specific.

67. The NIV reflects this by adding *sacred* (another example of paraphrase rather than translation). 2 Sam. 6:19 may suggest a connection with Yahweh worship. In the context of Baal worship, there may be a comparison with 'cakes' (*kawwānîm*) offered to the 'Queen of Heaven' (Jer. 7:18) (Andersen and Freedman 1980: 298).

68. This translates the noun *'ăhābâ* (once) and the verb *'āhab* (three times).

69. The form is unusual, and Macintosh (1997: 99–100) links it instead with 'to recognize', in the sense of recognizing a transfer of ownership. See also Gruber 2017: 170.

measures. One view is that a homer may be around 100 litres. The term *lethek*, which appears only here in the Old Testament, may be equivalent to half a homer (Powell 1992: 904). The LXX refers instead to a measurement of wine, though the MT seems more likely.

Those who see this as a second marriage take this to be the bride-price (Stuart 1987: 66; Moon 2018: 70). If the woman is Gomer, why and to whom was the payment made? Some estimate that the silver and barley are worth about thirty shekels, which is the price of a slave in Exodus 21:32 (cf. Lev. 27:4). This has led to the suggestion that Gomer needed to be set free from slavery or prostitution (Mays 1969: 57–58; Wolff 1974: 61). Evidence for this valuation, though, is uncertain (Abma 1999: 207; Ben Zvi 2005: 84–85). Alternatively, the payment may have been to cancel a debt (G. V. Smith 2001: 74; Dearman 2010: 135). The text gives no details. The main point, though, is clear: Hosea paid what was necessary to open the way for Gomer to return.

3–5. Gomer's return, though, includes a period of discipline, during which she must abandon her promiscuous lifestyle and refrain from sexual intimacy with any man (literally, 'not be to a man'). This is widely taken to include her husband, and the next part of the verse, which the NIV translates as *and I will behave the same way toward you* (literally, 'and I also to you'), continues that idea: Hosea will also refrain from sexual relations with his wife (NRSV; cf. Mays 1969: 54, 58; Wolff 1974: 56, 62; Stuart 1987: 63; Macintosh 1997: 103; Dearman 2010: 136). Another possibility is that the restrictions relate only to other men, and the emphasis is primarily on faithfulness within the marriage (Moon 2018: 69). The ambiguous 'and I also to you' may then simply mean that Hosea will behave towards Gomer as he expects her to behave towards him. This view, though, seems less likely. First, while we expect some reference to Gomer leaving behind her promiscuous lifestyle, the addition of 'not be to a man' is superfluous. And so is Hosea's reciprocal commitment to faithfulness, which has never been in question. Second, the connective *For* and the use of the same expression *live* [*remain*] . . . *many days* indicate a correlation between verses 3 and 4. Verse 4 points to a period of discipline and privation, and it is reasonable to assume that verse 3 does the same.

Many days suggests, though, that while this may be an extended period, it is temporary. That is clear in the case of Yahweh's relationship with Israel in verse 5, which points to a positive future. We might expect to see a similar positive expression in verse 3, and in the light of this another possibility, while recognizing the temporary suspension of sexual relations between Hosea and Gomer, translates 'and also I to you' along the lines of 'then I will be yours' (Andersen and Freedman 1980: 291, 304–305; see also Hubbard 1989: 93; Garrett 1997: 102). This would then suggest that normal marital relations will eventually be resumed. This interpretation provides a better correlation between the prophet's words to Gomer in verse 3 and their application to the nation in verses 4–5.

Israel's period of discipline and deprivation will include the removal of *king, prince* (*śār*), *sacrifice, sacred stones, ephod* and *household gods*. These represent Israel's political and religious institutions, both of which, in Hosea's view, had become corrupt.[70] Princes include royal officials and maybe military leaders. Sacred stones, or pillars, might have been set up to honour God (e.g. Gen. 28:18; 31:13; 35:14; Exod. 24:4; Isa. 19:19), though they were frequently associated with false worship (e.g. Exod. 34:13; Lev. 26:1; Deut. 7:5; 16:22; 1 Kgs 14:23; 2 Kgs 18:4; 23:14; Mic. 5:13), and that is probably their significance here (cf. Hos. 10:1–2). An ephod is a priestly garment (see Meyers 1992; Jenson 1996). The breastpiece, which contained the Urim and Thummim, was attached to the high priest's ephod (Exod. 28:22–30), linking it with divine revelation (cf. 1 Sam. 23:9–12; 30:7–8). Ornate ephods appear also to have become part of the sanctuary furniture (1 Sam. 21:9) and might also have become objects of improper worship (cf. Judg. 8:27). In Hosea 3:4 the ephod is linked with *household gods* (*těrāpîm*; cf. Judg. 17:5; 18:14, 17–20), small figurines associated with families (Gen. 31:19, 34–35).[71] They are associated with idols and idolatry (1 Sam. 19:16;

---

70. Kings and princes are mentioned together negatively in 7:3–7; 8:4, 10; 13:10–11; kings are further indicted in 5:1; 10:3–4. Israel's sacrifices are condemned in 4:19; 6:6; 8:13; 9:4, and sacred stones in 10:1–2. Ephods and household gods are not mentioned elsewhere in the book.

71. On *těrāpîm*, see Motyer and Selman 1980.

cf. Judg. 18:14, 17–20; 1 Sam. 15:23; 2 Kgs 23:24), and, like the ephod, are also used in divination (Ezek. 21:21; Zech. 10:2). Apart from *tĕrāpîm*, all the things in 3:4 may have a legitimate place, but by Hosea's day they had become associated with false religion. And these, as well as the failed political leadership, must be brought to an end in order for Israel to have hope for the future. Historically, this was brought about by the Assyrian invasion, the fall of Samaria and the exile of the northern kingdom.

This period of discipline will, though, come to an end, and, after it has served its purpose, the people *will return* (*šûb*; v. 5).[72] This may indicate the end of exile (cf. 11:11). Despite the coming judgment, there is hope for the future. The link with *seek* (*bāqaš*) suggests, though, that the primary focus here is the renewal of the relationship with Yahweh (5:15; cf. Deut. 4:29–30).

Seeking Yahweh will be accompanied by seeking *David their king*. The possibility of a single leader has already been mentioned (1:11), though here it is specifically linked with David. As noted above, it is not necessary to assume that this is a later addition. The reference to *in the last days* (*bĕʾaḥărîm hayyāmîm*) has been taken to support a messianic interpretation of the verse (Garrett 1997: 104; Moon 2018: 72). The expression might point to a future age of salvation (e.g. Isa. 2:2; Mic. 4:1), though it does not necessarily have an eschatological significance, and may be taken in the sense of 'in days to come' (e.g. Gen. 49:1; Num. 24:14; Deut. 31:29) (Andersen and Freedman 1980: 308–309; Hubbard 1989: 95; cf. Dearman 2010: 139 n. 22), thus paralleling *Afterwards*, at the start of the verse, and corresponding to *many days* in verses 3–4.

Trembling suggests an element of reverent awe as the people return to God.[73] The term may indicate fear of divine judgment (e.g. Isa. 19:16–17; 44:11; Mic. 7:17), though it is more positive in Isaiah 60:5 where it is linked with a joyful return to Yahweh, and that may be the sense here. A sense of awe is, though, entirely appropriate for people who are returning to Yahweh after a period

---

72. Cf. 2:7. See also above, p. 24.

73. The verb here is *pāḥad*. The NIV also translates *ḥārad* (11:10–11) and *rĕtēt* (13:1) in the same way.

of discipline because of unfaithfulness. The positive nature of the return is further indicated by the reference to Yahweh's *blessings* (*tûb*). This refers to the abundance of Yahweh's provision (e.g. Jer. 2:7). In Jeremiah 31:12 the term is linked with 'the grain, the new wine and the olive oil', the very things forfeited by Israel because of the people's failure to recognize their true source (Hos. 2:8). In the coming days, those blessings will be restored. The term may also refer to God's own character (cf. Exod. 33:19; Pss 25:7; 145:7), and so may point beyond the restoration of material blessings to the renewal of all aspects of the covenant relationship between Yahweh and his people.

Meaning
These verses indicate Yahweh's willingness to restore an unfaithful people. This is motivated by love, and it is significant that Yahweh's love for Israel prompts Hosea to show his love to Gomer. While it is likely that Hosea's unhappy marital situation gave an insight into Yahweh's feelings about unfaithful Israel, the renewal of the relationship is wholly the result of God's initiative. Hosea seems to have been prepared to allow his relationship with Gomer to end. Yahweh, though, will not allow the same with regard to Israel. His is a love that will not let his people go.

Restoration, though, involves a period of discipline. This appears to parallel the privations of chapter 2. Significantly, however, in chapter 3, discipline is directly related to divine love. If their relationship with Yahweh is to be renewed, the people need to turn away from the things that hinder that relationship and turn back to him. Yahweh's restorative love opens the way for that to take place.

Future hope here is linked with a coming Davidic king. This might have appeared subversive for a northern prophet, though prophets were no strangers to political controversy. The people probably expected this hope to be fulfilled within the normal royal succession. In time, though, that gave way to the eschatological hope of a coming Messiah, who was associated with the kingdom of God. Christians see the fulfilment of this expectation in the person of Jesus Christ, through whom hope is extended beyond Israel and Judah to encompass the whole world.

2. ORACLES RELATING TO SINFUL ISRAEL (4:1 – 11:11)

A. Yahweh's case against the people (4:1 – 5:7)

Context

The opening chapters of Hosea's prophecy set the scene of Israel's unfaithfulness through a narrative focused primarily on the prophet's personal life. The remaining chapters include a series of more conventional oracles that build on the same theme and, again, point forward from sin and inevitable judgment to future restoration.[1] There is little in this part of the book to indicate historical context (Andersen and Freedman 1980: 313). The indictments are fairly general, though they fit with what we know of the general situation in the third quarter of the eighth century BC and may include some allusions to political events.

Following on from chapters 1–3, 4:1 – 5:7 refers frequently to Israel's adultery and prostitution. Yahweh has entered into a

---

1. For discussion of the book's structure, see above, pp. 20–21.

relationship with the nation, but the people and their religious leaders have failed to show the faithfulness and the *ḥesed* that their participation in the relationship demanded.

Comment
i. General charge against the people of the land (4:1–3)

1. The verse begins with a common prophetic introduction, *Hear the word of the LORD,*[2] which frequently prefaces oracles of judgment and addresses the Israelites (*bĕnê yiśrā'ēl*) directly. The purpose of the oracle is to bring a charge (*rîb*) against those *who live in the land*. The term *rîb* sometimes points to a legal charge brought by God against the people because of their failure to meet their covenant obligations. That seems to be the case here too, though this oracle does not follow the general pattern of covenant lawsuits.[3]

There are two references to *the land*. Because of the sin of 'the inhabitants of the land' (NRSV, ESV),[4] which here parallels *Israelites*, the land is devoid of the things that are required to maintain the covenant relationship with Yahweh: faithfulness, *ḥesed* and acknowledgment of God. These three ideas occur together in the list of bridal gifts in 2:19–20[5] which ensure that the new covenant relationship will be permanent. Significant here too is the idea that the land is affected by the sin of the people (v. 3).

2. The first part of the verse gives a list of failings, using language that reflects Israel's law. *Murder, stealing and adultery* repeats terms found in the sixth, eighth and seventh commandments respectively (Exod. 20:13–15; see also Jer. 7:9). *Lying* (*kāḥaš*) may allude to the ninth commandment. While not the same term as in Exodus 20:16, *kāḥaš* appears in a similar context in Leviticus 19:11. It is also used to describe the message of false prophets (Jer. 5:12).

---

2. E.g. 1 Kgs 22:19; 2 Kgs 7:1; Isa. 1:10; 28:14; 66:5; Jer. 2:4; 7:2; 19:3; 21:11; 29:20; 42:15; Ezek. 13:2; 36:1.

3. See above, p. 22.

4. The NIV adds *you*, maintaining the direct address to the people.

5. See comments on 2:19–20. *Faithfulness* (*'ĕmet*) and *acknowledgment* (*da'at*) are closely related to the equivalent terms used there. On *ḥesed*, see above, pp. 31–32.

Cursing (*ālâ*) is used in the context of swearing an oath (Deut. 29:12–19), and the NRSV translates it here as 'swearing'. It also refers to the curse that result from reneging on an oath (Deut. 29:20–21) (Scharbert 1974; Gordon 1996a; cf. Routledge 2012: 61–62). Here it may suggest swearing falsely, possibly including taking God's name in vain (cf. Exod. 20:7). The term may have been chosen deliberately to point beyond Israel's sin to its consequences for the land, which is also associated with a curse (cf. Isa. 24:6; Jer. 23:10).

They break all bounds translates the verb *pāraṣ*. This has several meanings in the Old Testament (van Dam 1996), including 'to burst out, break through', implying violence,[6] and 'to spread out, increase'.[7] *Pāraṣ* may be linked with the previous list of sins, indicating their increasing prevalence: 'Swearing, lying, and murder, and stealing and adultery break out' (NRSV; cf. Mays 1969: 60; Garrett 1997: 112; Macintosh 1997: 129). Alternatively, *they* may refer to the people, suggesting excessive violation of Israel's covenant responsibilities: overstepping all accepted boundaries. Or it may be taken with the following expression, *bloodshed follows bloodshed*,[8] an idiom pointing to an inordinate amount of bloodshed. In that case it may indicate violent action which results in the shedding of innocent blood.[9]

---

6. E.g. Exod. 19:24; 2 Sam. 5:20; 6:8; Neh. 2:13; Job 16:14; Ps. 89:40; Eccl. 10:8; Isa. 5:5. The related noun refers to a 'robber' or other violent person (e.g. Ps. 17:4; Jer. 7:11; Ezek. 7:22; 18:10; Dan. 11:14).

7. E.g. Gen. 28:14; 30:30; Exod. 1:12; 1 Chr. 4:38; Job 1:10; Isa. 54:3.

8. Literally, 'bloodshed touches bloodshed', suggesting either that one act of bloodshed leads to another or that one act of bloodshed rapidly follows another.

9. Cf. Ezek. 18:10. Andersen and Freedman (1980: 338) link this with human sacrifice (see also Hubbard 1989: 98). Though primarily connected with Molech (e.g. Lev. 18:21; 2 Kgs 23:10; Jer. 32:35), human sacrifice is also linked with Baal (e.g. Jer. 19:5; 32:35; cf. 7:31), and Molech may have been included in the general category of 'Baals'. On child sacrifice, see J. Day 2000: 210–212; Lange 2007. There is, though, no direct polemic against human sacrifice elsewhere in Hosea (see on 5:2; 8:13; 9:13; 13:2).

3. This verse begins with 'therefore' (NIV: *Because of this*), emphasizing the consequences of Israel's sin for the land and also,
corresponding to the indictment in verse 1, for those who live in
the land. *Dries up* translates *'ābal*. This verb is usually translated 'to
mourn' (NRSV, ESV) and may be understood metaphorically,
indicating the anguish felt by the land because of the sin of its
people. The term occurs in pairings that indicate drought (Isa.
24:4; Jer. 12:4; 23:10; Joel 1:10) and, as here, is often linked with *'āmal*
('to wither, dry up, languish'; Isa. 24:7; 33:9; Jer. 14:2; Lam. 2:8),
leading to the suggestion that *'ābal* may have a second meaning, 'to
dry up' (so NIV) (see Baumann 1974; Hayden 1996; Hayes 2002:
12–18). However, the translation 'the land/earth mourns' (cf. Hayes
2002: 37–64) fits well with the rest of the verse. The removal of
animals, birds and fish echoes Genesis 1:26 (cf. Ps. 8:7–8), though
in reverse order, and may be seen as the undoing of creation
(Deroche 1981; cf. Zeph. 1:2–3). A similar idea, also associated with
'ābal, is seen in Isaiah 24:4–6, and also in Jeremiah 4:23–28, which
suggests a return to a pre-creation world that is 'formless and
empty' (4:23; cf. Gen. 1:2).[10] This reflects the understanding, found
elsewhere in the Old Testament, that human sin affects the stability
of the created order (see Routledge 2010: 85–86; 2014b) and may
allow chaos to return. A similar idea may lie behind the reference
in Romans 8:19–22 to a frustrated and groaning creation.

ii. Israel's spiritual prostitution (4:4 – 5:7)
a. Judgment on priests and people (4:4–19)
4–6. These verses begin the indictment of the nation's religious
leaders. The central issue of false worship makes priests the prime
target, but the failure of prophets is also noted.

The interpretation of verse 4 depends on the disputed translation
of its final section, which, following the MT, the NIV translates:

> *for your people are like those*
> *who bring charges against a priest.*

---

10. The expression *tōhû wabōhû* ('formless and empty') appears only in Jer.
4:23 and Gen. 1:2.

Deroche (1983b: 186–193) suggests that their being like those
who bring charges against a priest indicates that the whole nation
is under sentence of death (Deut. 17:12) and that, rather than trying
to pass the blame on to others (*let no one accuse another*), each must
accept that responsibility. It is not clear, though, why that particular
expression is used to indicate Israel's plight, particularly as it takes
a more reverential view of the priesthood than we find elsewhere
(cf. 4:6, 9; 5:1; 6:9). If we follow the MT, Garrett's suggestion (1997:
116) seems more likely. In his view, 'your people are like those who
bring charges against a priest' refers to the dire spiritual condition
of the nation, which stands as evidence against the priesthood.
And, rather than the people blaming one another, it is the
priesthood that should be held accountable.

The awkwardness of the MT, though, has led other English
versions and commentators to make a small change and read 'with
you' instead of 'your people', giving: 'for with you is my contention,
O priest' (NRSV, ESV; cf. Wolff 1974: 70; Andersen and Freedman
1980: 342, 346–348; Hubbard 1989: 100; Achtemeier 1996: 36;
Macintosh 1997: 134; Dearman 2010: 155; Moon 2018: 78, 79–80).
The first part of the verse may then be an objection by a (chief)
priest to Hosea's message of judgment in 4:1–3 (Andersen and
Freedman 1980: 342, 345–346; Moon 2018: 82), or Hosea's response
to such an objection. This may envisage an actual confrontation,
such as that between Amos and Amaziah (Amos 7:12–17), or it may
be a rhetorical device. It seems better, though, to take *priest* as a
reference to the priesthood as a whole. Priests are responsible for
the nation's lack of spiritual awareness, and, rather than passing the
blame on to others, as in Garrett's view (1997: 116), they must bear
the brunt of the indictment.

Hosea's use of wordplay is evident in verses 5–6, which can be
divided into four pairs of lines, each with repeated terms:

> You *stumble* day and night, and the prophets *stumble* with you.
> So I will *destroy* your mother. My people are *destroyed* from lack
>   of knowledge.
> Because you have *rejected* knowledge, I also *reject* you as my priests;
> Because you have *ignored* the law of your God, I also will *ignore* your
>   children.

The metaphor of stumbling (*kāšal*) indicates failure to walk the right path. Elsewhere in Hosea, the people stumble because of sin (5:5; 14:1, 9). Here, that is traced back to priests and prophets: religious leaders who have collaborated in their support of corrupt cultic institutions, and so have failed to instruct the people in the ways of Yahweh.[11] The NRSV reflects the MT: 'You shall stumble by day; the prophet also shall stumble with you by night', indicating the continual failure of those who should be providing spiritual leadership.

I will destroy your mother may refer to action against the mother of a particular priest (cf. Amos 7:17) (Wolff 1974: 78; Andersen and Freedman 1980: 350), though as a general indictment it may be taken figuratively, to indicate the cutting off of the institutions that spread corruption (Garret 1997: 117; Moon 2018: 84). However, *mother* refers to the nation as a whole in 2:2, 5, and that may be the best interpretation here (Hubbard 1989: 100; Dearman 2010: 158). The action of corrupt leaders will result in the ruin of the nation. This is further linked to a *lack of knowledge*, which is a frequent theme in the book.[12] In this context it refers to the knowledge of God (cf. 4:1; 6:6) and continues the indictment of the priests, whose responsibility it was to instruct the people (cf. Deut. 33:10; Mal. 2:6–7).

The third and fourth pairs of lines, which are linked to the first two by the repetition of *knowledge*, focus particularly on God's judgment as a result of the failure of leadership. *Children*, like *mother*, may refer to the people as a whole who, led by the priests, also *ignore* (NIV) or 'forget' (NRSV) God's law (cf. 2:13). Alternatively, it may refer to the priests' actual offspring (Hubbard 1989: 101), or, more probably, to those who follow the same corrupt path, and so to the

---

11. Hosea's view of prophets seems generally positive (see on 6:5; 9:7–8; 12:10, 13). He would, though, have challenged 'official', state-sponsored prophets who opposed true prophets (1 Kgs 22:5–28; Jer. 14:13–14; 23:16–22) and whom he saw as part of Israel's problem. Priests and prophets appear to have conspired against Jeremiah and are frequently condemned together (Jer. 2:8, 26; 5:31; 6:13; 14:18; 23:11).

12. See above, p. 15 n. 42.

priesthood more generally (Dearman 2010: 159). Part of the responsibility of the priests was to teach the law; ignoring the law would
thereby disqualify them from office. The repetition of *reject* and
ignore/'forget' is another example of the correspondence between
divine judgment and human sin.[13]

7–11. These verses continue the indictment of the priesthood.
'The more *they* increased' (v. 7, NRSV, ESV; emphasis added) better
reflects the MT. The NIV paraphrases to make the reference to the
priesthood clear. During the prosperity under Jeroboam II there
appears to have been growth in the size and prestige of cultic
institutions (cf. 8:11), and therefore of their impact. This should
have helped to deal with the people's sin. Ironically, though,
because of the influence of Baal worship, it only increased the
problem.

In the last part of verse 7, the MT reads 'I will change' (cf. LXX,
ESV). This is frequently emended to 'they (ex)changed' (NRSV, NIV)
(Wolff 1974: 71; Andersen and Freedman 1980: 342; Stuart 1987: 70,
72),[14] and 'glory' is then associated with the worship of Yahweh,
which has been exchanged for the dishonour of serving Baal.
There seems little reason, though, to alter the MT, which continues
the theme of divine judgment. God will remove the priests'
honoured status (Mays 1969: 66; Hubbard 1989: 102; Garrett 1997:
119; Macintosh 1997: 141, 142–143; Dearman 2010: 155; Moon 2018:
78) and will show up the false worship that they revel in for the
shameful practice it is (cf. 10:5). There may be an indication,
too, that the nation's role of revealing God's glory has been compromised (cf. 9:11).

The corruption of the priesthood is further highlighted in
verse 8. The priests *feed on* ('ākal) and *relish* (NIV) or 'are greedy for'
(NRSV, ESV) Israel's sin. Instead of helping them overcome sin, the
priests revel in the people's failure. This may be because it served
to increase the significance and status of the cult. There may also
be a deliberate play on words. The first word for sin, *ḥaṭṭā't*, may

---

13. See above, p. 24.

14. This may follow a later scribal correction, perhaps based on Ps. 106:20;
    Jer. 2:11.

also refer to the 'sin offering' (Andersen and Freedman 1980: 342),[15] which was offered to make atonement for some sins. As part of the ritual, the priests ate some of the sacrifice (e.g. Lev. 6:24–29; 10:17–20). Thus, the more the people sinned, the better the priests ate (cf. 1 Sam. 2:12–17). This further reflects Hosea's view that the priesthood is intentionally self-serving.

Like people, like priests (v. 9) appears to be a proverb. The priesthood cannot evade responsibility by claiming special privileges. Nor can the people escape judgment by blaming the priests. *Ways* and *deeds* together suggest both characteristic misconduct and specific actions. *Repay* translates the Hebrew *šûb* ('return').[16] The sinful actions of priests and people will be brought back on them: both will receive what they deserve (cf. 12:2).

They will eat but not have enough (v. 10) may refer back to the appetite of the priests in verse 8, where the same verb, *ʾākal* ('to eat'), occurs, or may indicate more general dissatisfaction associated with false worship (cf. 2:5–7). Similarly, *prostitution*, which may here be spiritual, actual, or both, will not result in increase.[17] Because the priests have deserted Yahweh, their sinful pursuits will lead only to frustration. *Flourish* (NIV) translates *pāraṣ*, which relates to the spread and severity of Israel's sin in 4:2; its use here may suggest divine action to stem that increase (Stuart 1987: 70, 72; Hubbard 1989: 103).

In the MT, verse 10 ends with the verb *šāmar*. This usually means 'to guard, keep', though it may also suggest devotion. It is usually linked to verse 11: people turn from Yahweh to devote themselves to prostitution (NIV, NRSV; Mays 1969: 66;[18] Wolff 1974: 72; Achtemeier 1996: 39; Dearman 2010: 156), or to prostitution, wine

---

15. The parallel with *ʾāwôn* ('iniquity', NRSV, ESV) suggests the former, though the double meaning allows the wordplay.

16. See above, p. 24.

17. This has been linked to the futility of fertility rites associated with Baal worship, though, as noted above (pp. 7–8), it is unclear how much of that was part of the Baal cult.

18. Mays (1969: 72) suggests that *zĕnût* ('harlotry') both ends v. 10 and begins v. 11, but a copyist has omitted the repeated word.

and new wine (ESV; Garrett 1997: 121; Macintosh 1997: 147; Moon 2018: 78). In Deuteronomy, *šāmar* occurs in connection with observing laws associated with the covenant.[19] Here, it may highlight the sins of the priests who, rather than guarding instruction and keeping the law, are committed to following their own appetites. The repeated reference to wine suggests drunkenness, which here, maybe together with prostitution, inhibits understanding (cf. Lev. 10:9–11; Isa. 28:7).[20]

12–14. These verses begin by focusing on the people. Their failure, though, however willing, is also an indictment of the priests who have led them astray, and so the verses go on to include further judgment on the priests.

The people are accused of seeking guidance from pieces of wood. The first term, *'ēs*, may refer to a wooden idol (as NIV). It is, though, a general term for 'wood', and is used here sarcastically. The second term, *maqqēl*, refers to something that can be carried, such as a 'staff' (ESV). The NIV and NRSV translate this *diviner's rod*, and it may have had some cultic significance, though here again the language is intentionally sarcastic: those who consult idols might as well be talking to any other piece of timber! Isaiah uses similar sarcasm when he describes idols as mere firewood (Isa. 44:14–17). *Consult* (*šā'al*) includes making inquiries of God (e.g. Judg. 18:5; 20:18; 1 Sam. 10:22; 23:2; 2 Sam. 2:1), which is what the people should be doing.

The people are led astray by *a spirit of prostitution* (*rûaḥ zĕnûnîm*). It is unlikely that this indicates something demonic. The range of meanings of *rûaḥ* includes the disposition within human beings that governs their actions (Routledge 2008a: 144–145), and that may be the sense here.[21] *Prostitution* (*zĕnûnîm*) has been discussed already.[22] This, and the parallel expression *they are unfaithful to their*

---

19. E.g. Deut. 4:2; 5:1, 10; 6:2–3; 7:11–12; 8:1–2; 11:1; 12:1; 27:1.

20. *Understanding* here translates *lēb* ('heart'), which in the OT is the seat of will and reason.

21. Mays (1969: 74) refers to 'the intoxication of the mind brought on by desire for the gifts of the Baals'.

22. See above, pp. 27–29.

God, refers to the people's spiritual adultery (cf. 1:2). This is further emphasized in the reference to the location of sacrifices (v. 13a). References to *hill, mountaintops* and the shade of trees parallel closely the location of Canaanite altars, which were to be destroyed when the people entered the land (Deut. 12:2). Altars were frequently located in elevated positions so as to be closer to the deity. Trees provided shade, but also represented fertility, and might be associated with the goddess Asherah (e.g. Deut. 12:2–3; 16:21).[23] These 'high places' (*bāmôt*; cf. 10:8) were not always linked with idolatry (e.g. 1 Sam. 9:11–14). However, they may have included Canaanite altars taken over by Israel and not easily disassociated from their earlier cultic practices. They were also prominent in Baal worship, and became a serious stumbling block for God's people.[24] The significance of the particular trees mentioned seems to be primarily their size and the effectiveness of the shade they offer.[25] This is a practical consideration, though may point further to the superficiality of Israel's worship (Hubbard 1989: 106).

As a direct consequence of what the priests have led the people into, the priests' daughters and daughters-in-law have become caught up in prostitution and adultery. This is unlikely to be only metaphorical (though see Adams 2008: 291–305). It is not clear that illicit sexual practices played a formal part in Baal worship; however, they appear to be closely linked to the cult,[26] and members of the priests' own families have become involved.

---

23. On Asherah, see J. Day 1986b: 385–408; 1992b; 2000: 43–67.
24. Num. 33:52; 1 Kgs 13:33; 14:23; 22:43; 2 Kgs 12:3; 14:4; 17:9–11; cf. 2 Kgs 18:4.
25. *Oak* ('*allôn*) suggests strength (Isa. 6:13; Ezek. 27:6; Amos 2:9; Zech. 11:2). *Terebinth* ('*ēlâ*) is a large tree (Isa. 6:13) with leafy shade (Ezek. 6:13; cf. Judg. 6:11, 19; 2 Sam. 18:9). It is usually translated 'oak', except where it appears with '*allôn* (Isa. 6:13; Hos. 4:13). *Poplar* (*libneh*) occurs only here and in Gen. 30:37.
26. Some relate this to the activities of the people as a whole (Wolff 1974: 86–87; Macintosh 1997: 160–161), maybe as part of fertility rites (see above, pp. 7–8).

Yahweh's response to this promiscuity – *I will not punish your daughters . . . nor your daughters-in-law* (v. 14) – and the rationale, that *the men* are guilty too, seems odd. Dearman (2010: 156, 165–166) addresses this by translating: 'I will not punish (only) your daughters.' Others take the statement as a rhetorical question: 'Will I not punish . . . ?' (Andersen and Freedman 1980: 369; Stuart 1987: 71, 83). Wolff (1974: 87) suggests that the blame for such activities must be levelled at the priests. Moon's explanation seems to fit better with the мт. He argues that *the men* here continues to refer to the priests, and notes that under the law promiscuous daughters of priests were punished primarily because of the shame their actions brought on their fathers (e.g. Lev. 21:9) and thus on the priestly office. Here, though, punishment that was intended to protect the holiness of the priesthood becomes meaningless, because the priests themselves behave in the same shameful way (Moon 2018: 87–88).

Shrine-prostitutes translates qĕdēšôt. The link with sacrifice suggests some cultic association, and, while it is not clear what their precise role was, the parallel with *harlots* (zônâ) indicates sexual activity. Thus, actual promiscuity runs alongside Israel's spiritual unfaithfulness.

The priests' failure results in a widespread lack of *understanding*. The term bîn may apply to discernment generally, though probably refers here to the understanding of who God is and what he requires (cf. 14:9; see also e.g. Isa. 6:9–10; 43:10; 56:11; Jer. 4:22). This is closely related to the failure to acknowledge him (2:8; 4:1, 6). The result of the people's lack of understanding is *ruin* (cf. 4:6). The priests have failed to show true leadership; that, though, is no excuse, and the whole people face divine judgment.

15–16. The prophetic indictment is now directed towards the people as a whole. Verse 15 contrasts Israel and Judah.[27] It is addressed primarily to Israel, and the rhetorical purpose may be to indicate that the nation's adulterous behaviour is not inevitable and, at least for the moment, Judah can avoid falling into the same sin. Further, this might reflect the view that the prophecy links hope

---

27. On references to Judah, see above, pp. 16–19.

for the future with the southern kingdom and the Davidic leader who will come from there (cf. 1:11; 3:5). Israel is likely also to be the main target of the following proscriptions, though they also include a warning to Judah.

Two particular sanctuaries to avoid are singled out: Gilgal and Beth Aven. Gilgal was located close to Jericho. Joshua set up twelve stones there, taken from the Jordan, to represent the twelve tribes of Israel (Josh. 4:19–25). There, too, the Israelites were circumcised, celebrated the first Passover after entering the Promised Land and ate the first produce of Canaan (Josh. 5:8–11). Later, it became a significant centre (e.g. 1 Sam. 7:16; 10:8). Beth Aven (*bêt 'āwen*) appears to be a sarcastic reference to Bethel ('house of God'). Bethel (see Brodsky 1992) has important associations with Jacob (Gen. 28:19; 31:13; cf. Hos. 12:4) and was also one of the sanctuaries set up by Jeroboam after the division of the kingdom (1 Kgs 12:28–29). These sanctuaries appear to have had particular significance in relation to Israel's sin in the eighth century BC. Amos also refers to Bethel and Gilgal (Amos 4:4; 5:5), and the derogatory term *Beth Aven* probably derives from his warning that Bethel would 'be reduced to nothing [*'āwen*]'.[28] Both sanctuaries were close to Judah, and the injunction to stay away may also be directed at potential visitors from the south as well as from the north.

As well as avoiding key sanctuaries, the people are urged not to swear oaths in Yahweh's name. The formula *as the LORD lives* (*ḥay yhwh*)[29] is used legitimately to reinforce oaths and express strong intent (e.g. Judg. 8:19; Ruth 3:13; 1 Sam. 14:39; 26:16; 2 Sam. 15:21; Jer. 38:16). It is, though, an affront when Yahweh's name is invoked as a mechanistic formula, without regard for the covenant relationship that lies behind it.[30]

Verse 16 emphasizes further Israel's intransigence. The contrast here is between God's desire to take care of his people as lambs

---

28. The term *'āwen* may mean 'deceit, nothing'; in 6:8; 12:11 it is better translated 'sin, evil'.

29. The related expression 'living God' appears in 1:10.

30. This may compare with words from the Baal myth: 'For Mighty Ba'lu is alive' (*COS* 1.271); see Mays 1969: 78.

that follow their shepherd and so may enjoy open pasture, and
Israel's stubbornness, like that of a headstrong cow, in resisting the
divine will. The alliteration in this verse, *sōrērâ sārar yiśrā'ēl* ('[like a]
stubborn [heifer], Israel is stubborn'), has already been noted as
part of the wordplay common in the book.[31]

17–19. Israel's intransigence is linked to idolatry (v. 17). *Joined to
idols* indicates alliances with false objects of worship. The people
who were called into covenant relationship with Yahweh have
bound themselves to idols (*'āṣāb*).[32] Andersen and Freedman (1980:
377) note that *ḥābar* ('to join') may also relate to weaving charms or
spells (cf. Deut. 18:11; Ps. 58:5) and suggest, instead: 'Ephraim has
been captivated by idols.'

The imperative *leave him alone!* in the second part of verse 17 may
be aimed at priests, urging them to cease their corrupting behaviour, or it may continue the warning to Judah to stay clear of Israel's
corrupting influence. It may also be directed at Hosea, expressing
frustration that Israel is so in thrall to idols as to be beyond any
correction (cf. 5:4, 6). This is the first time that Israel is addressed
as *Ephraim*, after the largest northern tribe. Hosea uses this designation more than thirty times, often alongside references to Judah
(5:5, 12–14; 6:4; 10:11; 11:12), and its appearance here may indicate
an intended contrast with the south.

The first part of verse 18 links drinking and illicit sexual activity
(cf. 4:10–11): having had their fill of one, people turn, in excessive
measure,[33] to the other. The text of the second part of the verse
is unclear. The NIV reading – *their rulers dearly love shameful ways*
(cf. ESV) – captures its essence,[34] emphasizing the nation's passion
to pursue the shameful practices associated with Baal worship.

---

31. See above, pp. 23–24.

32. The term also appears in 8:4; 10:6; 13:2; 14:8.

33. The infinitive alongside the finite verb, *zānâ* ('to practise prostitution'),
    expresses intensity.

34. [*They*] *dearly love* translates *'āhăbû hēbû*. The first term is from *'āhab*
    (to love), and *hēbû* is probably a dialectical variant or corruption of the
    same verb, with the repetition expressing intensity (as in the first part
    of the verse); see Wolff 1974: 73; Dearman 2010: 156; Moon 2018: 91.

The picture in verse 19 is of Israel caught up in a powerful wind (*rûaḥ*) that confines the people in its (metaphorical) wings (cf. 2 Sam. 22:11; Pss 18:10; 104:3) and sweeps them away. *Rûaḥ* may also relate to the *spirit of prostitution* in 4:12 (Stuart 1987: 86; Hubbard 1989: 111; Dearman 2010: 169; Moon 2018: 95–96). The people are in the grip of false worship and must bear the shameful consequences of their idolatrous sacrifices. Wind may also be an instrument of divine judgment (e.g. 13:15), which, when linked to Israel being swept away, may suggest exile (Ben Zvi 2005: 107–108; cf. Macintosh 1997: 173–174). The people's sin, which now controls them, will carry them ultimately to destruction.

b. Judgment on leaders and people (5:1–7)

1–2. This section widens the scope of 4:1–19 and includes a challenge to the *royal house*. The priests are again indicted. The third group, 'house of Israel' (NRSV, ESV), may refer to the general population (NIV: *Israelites*), though some relate it to a further tier of leadership (Wolff 1974: 97; Garrett 1997: 141; Dearman 2010: 171; however, cf. Hubbard 1989: 112; Moon 2018: 100).

This judgment is against you (NIV) translates more literally as 'the judgment [*mišpāṭ*] is yours'. *Mišpāṭ* (see on 2:19–20) can be translated 'justice' (Wolff 1974: 94; Macintosh 1997: 175) or 'judgment' (Mays 1969: 79; Andersen and Freedman 1980: 380; Hubbard 1989: 112–113) and may have a double meaning (Stuart 1987: 88; Dearman 2010: 171; Moon 2018: 100): leaders should administer *justice*; their failure results in *judgment*.

Failure and judgment are linked with particular sites, though the nature of the sin is unclear. Setting a *snare* or a 'net' is associated with catching birds, though it is also a metaphor for how the wicked prey on the righteous (e.g. Pss 140:5; 141:9; Jer. 18:22) and for divine judgment (e.g. Isa. 8:14; 24:17–18; Jer. 48:43–44). Here, it appears to refer to the seizure, by corrupt leaders, of the people and of the

---

The MT reads 'their shields' (*māgēn*), which may refer metaphorically to protectors and so 'rulers'. Some, with the LXX, read 'pride, insolence': 'they love shame more than their pride' (cf. Stuart 1987: 71; Dearman 2010: 156–157).

nation's religious institutions. Mizpah (see Arnold 1992) is probably the sanctuary in Benjamin which, with Bethel and Gilgal (cf. 4:15), was part of Samuel's judicial circuit (1 Sam. 7:16). Mount Tabor (see Frankel 1992) is in the Plain of Jezreel and was where Deborah and Barak defeated Sisera (Judg. 4:6–15). The reason for the reference to these sites is unclear, though the context suggests that they were associated with Baal worship. Many translations and commentators suggest that the snare was set *at (lě)* Mizpah (NIV, NRSV, ESV; Mays 1969: 79; Macintosh 1997: 175; Dearman 2010: 169) and that people were led astray there. However, *lě* usually relates to what the snare was intended to catch (Pss 69:22; 119:110; 140:5; 142:3; Amos 3:5), and a better translation may be: 'you set a snare *for* Mizpah' (Wolff 1974: 94; Stuart 1987: 88; Garrett 1997: 143; Moon 2018: 101), indicating that the sanctuary, like the people, was the victim of a corrupt regime.

In the first part of verse 2, *the rebels are knee-deep in slaughter* (NIV; cf. ESV) broadly follows the MT (Andersen and Freedman 1980: 380; Hubbard 1989: 113–114; Moon 2018: 98–99). This may pick up on the excessive bloodshed noted in 4:2. Details of the *slaughter* are not given. Andersen and Freedman (1980: 388) relate it to child sacrifice, though if that was happening it is likely that it would have been condemned more specifically (see on 4:2). The main emphasis appears to be that the nation's leaders, who should be guarding and protecting the people, are preying on them. Difficulties with the text have prompted some to emend it to 'and a pit dug deep in Shittim' (NRSV; Mays 1969: 79; Wolff 1974: 94; Stuart 1987: 88; Dearman 2010: 169).[35] This continues the theme of setting a trap, and three place names, corresponding to the three groups addressed in verse 1, better fits the poetic pattern. Shittim is where Moabite women led the Israelites to worship Baal of Peor (Num. 25:1–3; cf. Hos. 9:10) and so fits well with the charge of spiritual, as well as actual, prostitution (cf. 4:12–14; 5:3).

As a result of their corruption, Israel's rulers will face *discipline* (*mûsār*). In Proverbs, *mûsār* frequently refers to right instruction (e.g.

---

35. Reading *šaḥăṭâ* ('slaughter') as *šaḥăt* ('pit') and *śēṭîm* ('rebels') as *šiṭṭîm* ('Shittim').

1:8; 8:10; 13:1; 23:23). It is used, too, in the context of severe punishment (e.g. Isa. 26:16; Jer. 2:30; 30:14), though with the intention of correction, and that may be the sense here. The rulers will be punished severely. Even so, a gracious God wants to bring sinners to repentance.

3–4. These verses are framed by the ironic *inclusio*: *I know* [*yādâ*] ... *Ephraim* (v. 3); *they do not acknowledge* [*yādâ*] *the* LORD (v. 4).[36] Verse 3 takes a poetic form to emphasize both God's knowledge of his people and the nature of their sin. The first part of the verse has a chiastic structure: 'I know ... Ephraim/Israel is not hidden from me.' The second part of the verse notes that Israel has acted as a prostitute (*zānâ*), and parallels that with *ṭāmē'* ('to defile'), which indicates ritual uncleanness. This same pairing also occurs in 6:10. The people's behaviour has defiled them in the eyes of a holy God.

Verse 4 notes the hopelessness of Israel's position. The people's actions have separated them from God and do not allow them to return (*šûb*).[37] This is linked with a *spirit of prostitution* (see on 4:12): the controlling impulse that drives them to worship Baal and prevents them acknowledging God. This suggests that the people's actions have created a barrier that cannot be breached from their side, making divine judgment inevitable. It is significant here that, while earlier the priests were indicted for leading the people astray, the people are, nevertheless, held accountable for their own actions.

5–7. These verses further indict Israel and elaborate on the judgment that has been announced. *Testifies* (v. 5) translates *ānâ* ('to answer, respond'). In 2:15, 21–22 it denotes Israel's proper response to Yahweh, and Yahweh's response in terms of restoration and blessing. Here it appears in a quasi-legal sense, suggesting the testimony of a witness. In this case, it is Israel's *gā'ôn* ('arrogance, pride') that testifies against it (literally, 'in his face'). The term may also

---

36. On *yādâ* see above, p. 15 n. 42.

37. Moon's suggestion that Israel, as a divorced wife who has become attached to another, may not return (2018: 101–102) seems unlikely; see on 2:2, 6–7. On *šûb*, see above, p. 24.

refer to Yahweh's 'majesty' (e.g. Exod. 15:7; Isa. 2:19; 24:14), and it
is possible that 'Israel's pride' here is Yahweh (cf. Amos 8:7), who
testifies against them. It is more likely, though, that Israel's arrogant
self-reliance gives further evidence of the nation's guilt (Glenny
2013: 104; Moon 2018: 102). This hubris may be linked to Israel's
relative prosperity during the reign of Jeroboam II, which appears
to have led to complacency (cf. Amos 5:18–20; 6:1). The consequence of such arrogance is that, like the priests and prophets,
the nation *stumbles* (cf. 4:5) and cannot walk the path that Yahweh
has set out for it.

In the second part of verse 5, the MT presents Israel and Ephraim,
which are synonyms in previous verses, as distinct (ESV; cf. NRSV),
leading to the suggestion that there may have been factions within
the northern kingdom.[38] Sin, though, affects the whole nation,
and the southern kingdom of Judah is also implicated.

Going with *flocks and herds to seek* [*bāqaš*] *the LORD* (v. 6) refers to
people taking animals for sacrifice (cf. Exod. 10:9). Generally,
seeking 'the LORD' is something positive (e.g. Deut. 4:29; Zeph. 2:3;
Zech. 8:20–23) and may indicate repentance (cf. 3:5; 5:15; Isa. 55:6–7;
Jer. 50:4). Here, though, it appears to suggest reliance on ritual
which, without a right attitude, proves fruitless. It may also reflect
arrogance in taking Yahweh for granted and supposing that he will
be available when they choose to seek him (Glenny 2013: 104). But
though they seek him, they will not find him,[39] because Yahweh
has withdrawn himself from them (cf. 5:15).

In verse 7, Israel is accused of having 'dealt faithlessly with the
LORD' (NRSV; cf. 6:7), pointing to the nation's infidelity in
worshipping other gods. The outcome is the birth of *illegitimate*
[literally, 'strange'] *children*. This may refer to children born as a
result of the promiscuity associated with the cult. The primary
reference, though, as with the equivalent expression 'children of
whoredom' (1:2, NRSV), appears to be to a generation which, because
of the failure of its spiritual leaders, is also unfaithful to Yahweh

---

38. See above, p. 3 n. 2.

39. The sequence *seek . . .* [*but*] *not find* also occurs in relation to Israel's
    'lovers' (2:7).

(Glenny 2013: 105). The consequence of this endemic infidelity is the devouring of Israel's fields (cf. 2:9, 12).

While its general meaning is clear, the precise translation of the last part of verse 7 is difficult.[40] The NRSV and ESV (cf. NIV mg.) follow the MT: 'Now the new moon shall devour them [along] with their fields' (Garrett 1997: 146–147; Dearman 2010: 170; Moon 2018: 98; cf. Ben Zvi 2005: 133–134). *Hōdeš* ('new moon') may refer to the New Moon festival (cf. NIV), which was part of Israel's traditional worship but had become corrupted by its association with Baal (cf. 2:11). The sense might then be that Israel's corrupt worship, far from ensuring prosperity, is responsible for the judgment that results in the loss of the land and its produce. Alternatively, the NIV reading takes Yahweh as the subject of *devour* and *hōdeš* as the time when divine judgment will take place.[41] Common to both translations is the idea that the coming devastation is linked with Israel's unfaithfulness and corrupt worship practices.

Meaning

This section begins a direct indictment of the nation. The first part is reminiscent of a covenant lawsuit, reminding the people of their failure to live up to the responsibilities of their relationship with Yahweh. Three key qualities are lacking: faithfulness, *ḥesed* and the knowledge of God. This is apparent in Israel's idolatrous worship, which the prophet describes as spiritual adultery. However, this cannot be separated from behaviour. A failure to understand who God is leads to a compromised understanding of what he requires and this, in turn, results in a lack of moral restraint, including sexual promiscuity, drunkenness, law-breaking, violence and actions that transgress the bounds of common decency. And the further the people go down this path, and the more endemic their infidelity becomes, the more it takes control of their lives and the more difficult it is for them to turn back to Yahweh.

---

40. For suggested emendations see Wolff 1974: 95; Stuart 1987: 88; Macintosh 1997: 189.
41. See also Hubbard 1989: 116. Ben Zvi (2005: 134) suggests the possibility of multiple meanings.

An important factor, again, is the failure of spiritual leadership, and much of the blame for the people's sin is directed towards the priests. Those who should know better, and who should be directing the people in the right way, are themselves corrupt. They have a responsibility to the community of believers, and failure to live up to that responsibility results in divine judgment (cf. Ezek. 34:1–10; Jas 3:1) and the existence of a generation that shares their unfaithfulness. However, though priests bear much of the blame, the people are not thereby exempt from responsibility, and the whole nation faces judgment.

Sin has implications for individuals, particularly for the priests, and for the community, in terms of the loss of land and its produce. Its seriousness is seen in its effect, too, on the created order. A further devastating consequence is Yahweh's withdrawal from the people. They have forsaken him and turned to other gods and so may no longer know the blessings associated with his presence. However, as subsequent passages indicate, because of his continuing love, this is temporary (cf. 5:15), and however difficult it may be for the people to return, judgment is tempered with the hope of eventual restoration.

B. Divine wrath on Israel and Judah (5:8–15)

Context
The trumpet blasts and warnings in the opening verses suggest a military conflict, primarily between north and south. This is widely viewed as the Syro-Ephraimite war and the Assyrian invasion of Israel that followed.[42] That seems a likely backdrop to these verses. However, it is possible, too, that the Syro-Ephraimite war provides only the latest episode in a long-running dispute between Israel and Judah (Macintosh 1997: 195–198; see also on 5:8), and Hosea also has that wider picture in view. Because of the context, references to Judah here are not generally regarded as part of a later redaction.[43]

---

42. See above, p. 3 n. 5.
43. See above, pp. 16–19.

This is the first of a series of oracles that appears to run through to 7:16, maybe focusing on events around 733 BC. Commentators are not agreed on how to divide the sections. Wolff (1974: 110–112) takes this as a single unit, though it may be better, with Dearman (2010: 179), to see it as a collection, linked by key words and themes. Most, however, take 5:8–15 as a single coherent unit which follows on from the theme of judgment in 5:1–7.

Comment

8. The towns mentioned here, Gibeah, Ramah and Beth Aven,[44] are in the territory of Benjamin. All lie close to the Israel–Judah border and so are likely to be caught up in any conflict between them.

The relationship between Benjamin and the kingdoms of Israel and Judah is unclear. When the kingdom divided, Benjamin appears to have supported Judah (1 Kgs 12:21; cf. 2 Chr. 11:5–12). However, some Benjamite towns, such as Bethel, remained, at first, part of the northern kingdom, and it seems likely that the territory of Benjamin became divided, with both north and south vying for possession.[45] Judah appears to have captured territory as far north as Bethel in the early days of the divided monarchy (2 Chr. 13:19). Later, Israel was temporarily in possession of Ramah, with Judah then retaking territory up to Mizpah (1 Kgs 15:16–17, 22). Israel's hold on the region is likely to have been re-established in the eighth century BC, when Jehoash defeated Judah and attacked Jerusalem before returning home (2 Kgs 14:11–14). A less successful advance towards Jerusalem is described during the Syro-Ephraimite war (2 Kgs 16:5). Given the volatility of the Israel–Judah border, it is possible that during Hosea's ministry these three towns were under Israelite control.[46]

The sound of the trumpet (*šôpār*) and horn could be warning of an impending threat, or a call to arms. The third term refers

---

44. Beth Aven may be a derogatory reference to Bethel (see on 4:15) or a town to the east of Bethel (Josh. 7:2; 18:12).

45. On Benjamin, see Schunk 1992.

46. For further discussion, see above, p. 3 n. 5.

to a shout, and this, too, may be an alarm (NRSV, ESV) or a *battle cry* (NIV).[47] The last part of the verse reads simply 'behind you Benjamin', and this, too, could be a warning: 'look behind you' (NRSV), or a rallying call: 'we are behind you' (cf. NIV, ESV).[48] If this is a warning it might indicate Judah's incursion into Benjamite territory, possibly after the intervention of Assyria in the Syro-Ephraimite war, to recover land previously lost to Israel (Mays 1969: 86–88; Stuart 1987: 101; Hubbard 1989: 118–121; Achtemeier 1996: 48; Macintosh 1997: 194–198). There is no explicit biblical reference to such a counter-attack, but it is not unlikely, given the history of border disputes. The order in which the towns are listed might also suggest an advance from south to north, and this is consistent, too, with the reference to Judah removing boundary stones (v. 10). If this is a call to arms, it might be an encouragement to Benjamin to resist Judah's incursion. The limited historical evidence makes a firm conclusion impossible, and while a counter-attack by Judah seems the most likely setting, the primary concern is the internecine conflict between Israel and Judah, which Hosea regards as sinful (cf. 1:11), and which will result in judgment on both nations.

9. The result of divine judgment is that Ephraim, which appears here to refer to the whole of the northern kingdom, will be *laid waste (šammâ)*. This will take place on *the day of reckoning*. This expression occurs only here and may refer to coming judgment at the hands of Assyria. Or it may be similar to the 'Day of the LORD', when Yahweh would intervene decisively in world history (Stuart 1987: 103; Dearman 2010: 184). Israel expected this event to bring vindication, the defeat of their enemies and restoration (cf. 2:16–23). However, it would also bring judgment on God's unfaithful people (cf. Amos 5:18–20). The 'Day of the LORD' is associated with the 'desolation [*šammâ*] of the earth' in Isaiah 13:9 (cf. Hos. 4:3), and

---

47. Good's suggestion that this has cultic rather than military associations (1966a: 282–283) seems less likely.

48. The same expression (*'aḥăreykā binyāmîn*) occurs in the song of Deborah and Barak (Judg. 5:14) and may have become familiar as a battle cry.

that future devastation may be foreshadowed by Israel's defeat by Assyria.

The second part of the verse emphasizes the certainty of coming judgment, and notes that its proclamation is *among the tribes of Israel*. In the Old Testament, *tribes of Israel* generally relates to the nation before the division of the kingdom, though it is also associated with God's choice of Jerusalem (e.g. 1 Kgs 8:16; 11:32; 14:21; 2 Kgs 21:7) and with Ezekiel's vision of a restored and reunited nation (Ezek. 47:21; 48:19, 29, 31). Here, Hosea refers to the northern kingdom as *Ephraim*, and *tribes of Israel* appears to indicate the whole nation, including Judah. This suggests the ideal of a united people of God, which is undermined by hostility between the northern and southern kingdoms (cf. Emmerson 1984: 68–69, 99).

10. Focus on the whole nation continues with an indictment of Judah. If the primary context here is the Syro-Ephraimite war, the northern kingdom is the main aggressor. However, the leaders of Judah – probably a reference to military commanders, officials and the royal house – have also undermined the unity of God's people by acting *like those who move boundary stones*. The term *gĕbûl* refers to the border of national and local territories. It may also refer to the marker that separates neighbouring plots of land; moving that marker in an attempt to appropriate property was condemned as a breach of covenant responsibility (Deut. 19:14; 27:17; cf. Job 24:2; Prov. 15:25; 22:28; 23:10). In the Old Testament, this use of the term relates to local, rather than national, boundaries. That may explain the inclusion of *like*. Annexing northern towns might not involve the actual movement of boundary markers, but it represents the same kind of covenant violation as when a local landowner attempts to steal a neighbour's land.[49] The MT refers to Yahweh pouring out his wrath 'like water' (NRSV, ESV). As this is referring to judgment the NIV is probably right in interpreting it as *like a flood of water*. Isaiah 8:7 uses similar language when referring to Assyria as an instrument of divine judgment on Judah. This may also allude to the reversal of creation (cf. 4:3) and the return of chaotic waters as a

---

49. If this related to Judah's internal injustices (Ben Zvi 2005: 140), *like* would be unnecessary.

symbol of judgment (cf. Amos 5:8; 9:6) (cf. Routledge 2008a: 133–136; 2010: 85–86).

11. The focus of judgment now moves back again to Ephraim. The nation will be *oppressed* (*ʿāšaq*) and *trampled* (*rāṣaṣ*). The same terms describe injustices within Israelite society (Amos 4:1) and so represent appropriate retribution. They also occur together in the list of covenant curses (Deut. 28:33). This will come about through the coming Assyrian invasion.[50]

The particular sin mentioned here is Israel's intent to go after *ṣāw*. The meaning of this term is unclear (cf. Macintosh 1997: 204–205). Its only other occurrences are in Isaiah 28:10, 13, where it is repeated with other short sounds, maybe to reproduce the meaningless ramblings of drunkards (Andersen and Freedman 1980: 409; Stuart 1987: 97, 99). The LXX (cf. NRSV) relates it to an Arabic term meaning 'empty, worthless' (Wolff 1974: 104; Achtemeier 1996: 48; Macintosh 1997: 204; Dearman 2010: 180). Another suggestion is that it is a shortened form of a word meaning 'filth' (cf. ESV; Andersen and Freedman 1980: 399; Moon 2018: 105, 110–111), maybe referring to idols (NIV). The sense seems to be of something disgusting or of no account. In a political context, it may refer to Israel's alliance with Syria, or its overtures to Assyria (Hubbard 1989: 123; cf. Macintosh 1997: 205).

12–14. With the northern and southern kingdoms having been indicted separately, they are now placed together and face parallel judgment for their mutual hostility. *Moth* (*ʿāš*) and *rot* (*rāqāb*) in verse 12 indicate decay. In the Old Testament, *ʿāš* is associated with the destruction of clothes (e.g. Isa. 50:9; 51:8), though it may also refer to maggots (cf. NRSV) that infest open wounds (Andersen and Freedman 1980: 412; Garrett 1997: 153), or to the pus associated with sores (Wolff 1974: 104; Stuart 1987: 97, 105).[51] *Rot* relates to wood (Isa. 40:20) and to bones (e.g. Prov. 12:4; 14:30; Hab. 3:16), and so may also indicate bodily decay. The terms occur in parallel in Job 13:28, referring to wasting away. The sense may be that

---

50. It is unlikely that this refers to the relatively limited encroachment by Judah.

51. Macintosh (1997: 207) prefers 'emaciating disease'.

Yahweh will cause Ephraim and Judah to waste away, or, when taken alongside verse 13, it may point to the putrefaction associated with wounds that are left unattended, or even aggravated by Yahweh.

Ephraim's and Judah's response to their wounds was to turn to Assyria (v. 13). The verse does not specifically note Judah's dependence on Assyria, though in the light of the parallelism in the verse some take Judah as the subject of *sent to the great king* (Hubbard 1989: 123; Macintosh 1997: 209). The northern kingdom elicited Assyrian support under Menahem, and, following the death of Pekah, Hoshea relied on Assyria to secure his appointment.[52] In the south, Ahaz asked Assyria for help against the Syro-Ephraimite coalition, and consequently Judah, too, became an Assyrian vassal. It is also possible that Hosea deliberately breaks the parallelism at this point to focus on Ephraim (cf. Wolff 1974: 115; Emmerson 1984: 70). In either case, dependence on Assyria is condemned. The wound, here represented as a weeping sore (*māzôr*), has been inflicted by God, and neither Assyria nor anything else apart from God can offer healing.

Great king translates *melek yārēb*. This means, literally, 'a king who contends' (Ben Zvi 2005: 143) or it may refer to an otherwise unknown 'King Jareb'. Dividing the Hebrew words differently (*malkî rāb*) gives the more likely reading *great king*,[53] referring to the Assyrian ruler (Andersen and Freedman 1980: 413–414; Stuart 1987: 99; Garrett 1997: 154; Moon 2018: 105–106).[54] Its use here is probably ironic: even the so-called 'great king' is no match for Yahweh.

The parallelism between Judah and Ephraim resumes in verse 14. Yahweh will come against both as a lion[55] which tears and devours its prey. This emphasizes the ferocity of Yahweh's judgment and

---

52. See above, pp. 2, 4.

53. This requires, too, that the *-î* is read as part of the particular Hebrew construction and not translated.

54. The term 'great king' is also attested in an Akkadian inscription from Sefire (*COS* 2.214).

55. *Lion* (*šaḥal*) and *great lion* (or 'young lion', NRSV, ESV; *kĕpîr*) are synonymous terms.

so, also, the extent and seriousness of the people's sin. The futility of seeking help elsewhere is also highlighted: there is *no one to rescue them*.

15. The purpose of judgment is that the people will, in their distress, turn, not to Assyria, but to Yahweh. In the meantime God withdraws. Continuing the imagery of God as a lion, the NIV interprets *māqôm* ('place', cf. NRSV, ESV) as *lair*. While this may refer to Yahweh the lion taking his prey to his lair (Moon 2018: 111–112), it seems better to see it, again, as Yahweh's withdrawal from the people (cf. 5:6), leaving them to face their distress. However, in stark contrast to 5:6, there is the implication that, when the people are in earnest about turning to him, he may be found, and is able to offer the healing that is available nowhere else. The people cannot escape the suffering associated with their guilt, but its aim, emphasized by parallel references, is that they will *seek* (*bāqaš*) his face and earnestly search him out (*šāḥar*).

Meaning

A key theme in these verses is the judgment on both nations because of their hostility to one another. The conflict between Israel and Judah, in both the Syro-Ephraimite war and numerous border incidents over a long period, threatens the unity of the people. Yahweh's desire is for one people that can stand as a witness to the nations, but that is undermined by continuing rivalry and infighting. This remains a serious problem for the church today, where division can undermine its effectiveness for service.

Another feature is the horrific imagery associated with divine judgment. This indicates the seriousness with which God takes sin, and the desperate state of those who have turned from him. But that very desperation is intended to drive them to recognize their guilt, to seek God and to find healing. For the world today, the horrific image of Christ dying on the cross proclaims that same message of judgment and hope for those who put their trust in him.

The desperation of Israel and Judah led them to turn instead to Assyria. These verses emphasize the futility of asking for help from anyone but Yahweh. In earlier chapters, he removed blessings that the people associated with Baal in order to demonstrate their true source. Here, he withdraws from the people until they recognize their need of him. The people of God in every generation face the temptation to put confidence in other things. But for all its military might, the extent of its empire and the 'greatness' of its king, Assyria's power is no match for God's. Nothing is. God alone is the source of his people's help and strength, and believers then and now need to depend on him.

C. Failure to repent (6:1 – 7:2)

Context

The emphasis here is on the lack of true repentance by Ephraim and Judah. The first section (6:1–3) uses language similar to that in the previous verses and appears to be a response to the judgment announced there. The nature of the response, though, is debated.[56] It may be spoken by the people (Wolff 1974: 116–117; Hubbard 1989: 124–125; Achtemeier 1996: 50), led by the priests, possibly as a formal expression of penitence in the light of the disastrous consequences of the Syro-Ephraimite war. If so, the following verses, which point to the people's insincerity (6:4–6) and covenant unfaithfulness (6:7–11a), and which include a further catalogue of sins which prevent a true turning back to Yahweh (6:11b – 7:2), indicate that their repentance does not go far enough. However, there is nothing in 6:1–3 to suggest that it is not genuine, and it may be better to see it instead as a call by Hosea, setting out what the people need to do (Stuart 1987: 107; Garrett 1997: 156–157; Macintosh 1997: 216–219; Moon 2018: 114). The rest of the section makes it clear, though, that this is not forthcoming. In either case, the people's response to God falls short of what it needs to be (Dearman 2010: 191–193).

Comment

i. Call to repentance (6:1–3)

1–3. Verse 1 reflects the judgment in the previous section. It repeats the reference to 'tearing' (*ṭārap*) (cf. 5:14), and the idea of

---

56. Macintosh (1997: 216–219) notes the main options.

binding wounds may reflect the imagery of putrefying sores in
5:12–13, which only Yahweh can cure (*rāpā'*).

Despite the absence of an admission of guilt (Hubbard 1989: 125),
the call to return (*šûb*), which echoes Yahweh's returning to his place
(5:15), seems an appropriate response to the challenge to *earnestly seek*
him (5:15), and is accompanied by the further exhortation to *acknowledge* (*yāda'*) Yahweh (6:3). The repetition *acknowledge . . . press on to
acknowledge* may also reflect the earnestness called for in 5:15.[57] *Rādap*,
translated here 'to press on', occurs in 2:7 in relation to Israel
'chasing after' her lovers. That futile endeavour is now better
directed. As noted already, both *šûb* and *yāda'* are key terms for
Hosea,[58] and together they indicate repentance and a right understanding of who God is and what he requires of his people. These
verses, so understood, offer the hope of national healing and
restoration.

In verse 3, Yahweh's coming is likened to the sun and rain that
ensure the land's prosperity. In 2:8–13, Yahweh threatens to with-
draw his blessings because the people do not acknowledge (*yāda'*)
that they come from him, and attribute them instead to Baal. Here,
there is a proper recognition of Yahweh as their source, and that,
along with the repentance in verse 1, opens the way for assurance
that divine blessing will return. 'Dawn' (NRSV) suggests hope and
a new beginning (cf. Isa. 58:8), though the main emphasis here is
on its certainty: however dark the night, dawn will come.[59] And
with the right response of the people, Yahweh's coming is also sure.
Rain watering the earth is a common image of renewal and
restoration (e.g. Isa. 44:3; Joel 2:23). *Winter rains* here translates a
general term for rain (*gešem*), while *spring rains* (*malqôš*), also referred
to as 'latter rain', refers, more specifically, to the second of the two
major periods of rainfall in Israel's agricultural year (Deut. 11:14;
Jer. 5:24). The autumn or early rain softens the ground for sowing;

---

57. Some take the first *acknowledge* with v. 2 (e.g. Stuart 1987: 98; Dearman
    2010: 191).
58. On *šûb*, see above, p. 24; on *yāda'*, see above, p. 15 n. 42.
59. Similarity between 'dawn' (*šaḥar*) and 'earnestly seek' (*šāḥar*, 5:15)
    suggests another link with the previous section.

the spring rain provides the crops with the water necessary to continue their growth and ensure a harvest.

Verse 2 begins with two parallel lines:

After two days he will revive us [*ḥāyâ*];
   on the third day he will restore us [*qûm*].[60]

Following the theme of verse 1, this could refer to healing (Mays 1969: 95; Wolff 1974: 117; Eidevall 1996: 95; Macintosh 1997: 220–221; cf. Johnston 2002: 221–222). However, in the Old Testament, *ḥāyâ* and *qûm* appear as a word pair only in reference to resurrection (Isa. 26:14, 19; cf. 2 Kgs 13:21; Job 14:12, 14) (J. Day 2000: 118–119). The distinction between healing a nation at the point of death and restoring it to life may not be too great (Johnston 2002: 222). Nevertheless, the language of death and resurrection is used elsewhere to refer to national restoration (e.g. Isa. 26:19; Ezek. 37), and it seems reasonable to take it that way here (Andersen and Freedman 1980: 420; Stuart 1987: 108; Hubbard 1989: 125; Garret 1997: 158–159; Dearman 2010: 193–194; Moon 2018: 115).[61] Thus understood it points to a radical new beginning for the nation: death (cf. 6:5) in the form of defeat and exile and, when all pretensions and false hopes are removed, resurrection to new life.

The significance of three days is also debated. If verse 2 refers to healing, this may indicate a short period.[62] With reference to resurrection, one suggestion is that three days may be the time

---

60. Examples of x/x+1 parallelism include Ps. 62:11; Prov. 30:15b; Amos 1 – 2. Barré (1978: 129–135) argues that *ḥāyâ* and *qûm* are also a recognized parallel pairing and interpretation should focus on the whole expression.

61. J. Day (2000: 118–220) suggests that this reapplies imagery relating to Baal's dying and rising; cf. Levenson 2006: 206–207. Here, though, the people die and rise, emphasizing that Yahweh, not Baal, is the source of his people's life.

62. Barré (1978: 139) notes that a prognosis of recovery within three days, probably indicating a short time, is common in Akkadian medical, and other ANE, texts.

between death and the soul leaving the body (Andersen and Freedman 1980: 420), or when decomposition begins (Hubbard 1989: 125; Pickup 2013). Three days appears frequently in the Old Testament as a significant period of time, and it may be better to take it that way here.[63] Resurrection on the third day has a particular resonance with a Christian audience, and when Paul talks about Christ's resurrection 'on the third day according to the Scriptures' (1 Cor. 15:4), he probably has this passage in mind.[64] However, links with the New Testament are primarily typological, presenting correspondences between the narratives of God's people in the Old Testament and Christ, the ideal Israel (Garrett 1997: 159).[65] Such correspondences are generally noted in retrospect. The Old Testament sets out patterns of divine activity which are recognized and reapplied by later writers, and that appears to be the significance of 'according to the Scriptures'. However, in their original context, they are not predictive.[66]

The resurrection/healing of the nation will result in life in the presence of God, literally 'before his face'. This echoes the language of 5:15, where Yahweh withdraws until the people 'seek his face'. The people's repentance brings not only new life to the nation, but restoration, too, of a broken relationship with Yahweh.

ii. A fickle and unfaithful people (6:4 – 7:2)
These verses indicate that the call to repentance in verses 1–3, with the hope of recovery and restoration that it might have brought, goes unheeded.

---

63. The removal of threats or a reversal from death to life is indicated in Gen. 22:4; 40:12–13; 42:18; Josh. 2:16; 1 Sam. 30:12; 2 Kgs 20:5; Jon. 1:17; see Russell 2008; see also Dempster 2014. Moon (2018: 115) suggests a link with Yahweh's appearing on the third day on Mount Sinai (Exod. 19:11, 16).

64. See further, Dempster 2014. Moon (2018: 118–122) notes that several Jewish writings take 6:2 to suggest general resurrection.

65. For an overview of typology see Routledge 2008a: 43–47; see further, Baker 2010: 169–189.

66. Some suggest that elements of the typological understanding were known to the original writers; cf. Beale 2012. See also on 11:1.

4–6. Verse 4 begins with two rhetorical questions indicating Yahweh's frustration with Ephraim and Judah, given all he has done for them. *Love* here translates *ḥesed*, which is the proper response of the people to Yahweh, and to one another, on the basis of their covenant relationship.[67] This, though, is as transient as morning mist or as dew that evaporates quickly in the heat of the day. This suggests that the people may have made some effort, but it was fleeting and has come to nothing.

Verse 5 begins with two parallel lines describing divine judgment. Like the images in 5:11–14, this is portrayed in stark terms. 'To cut in pieces' (*ḥāṣēb*) usually relates to cutting stones, but in Isaiah 51:9 it describes God's action in defeating Rahab, who is usually viewed as a monster representing chaos[68] and so is opposed to the order established in creation. The fate of Israel and Judah, whose sin also challenges the divine order (cf. 4:3), is similar. Less dramatic, but no less severe, is the parallel expression *I killed [them]*. This judgment is closely associated with the *prophets*, which parallels *the words of my mouth* and emphasizes the divine origin and authority of their message. The prophetic role was to call the people back to God and warn them of the dire consequences of continued apostasy. However, when those warnings were not heeded, the prophets had the responsibility, too, to proclaim divine judgment, which, as noted already, was viewed as the death of the nation. The reference is probably to the full sweep of prophets, including Hosea's own ministry. He refers to Moses in 12:13, and 5:6 may echo Samuel's conflict with Saul (1 Sam. 15:21–22).

The MT of the last part of verse 5 reads, 'your judgments the light goes forth', perhaps pointing to the idea that prophetic announcements shine a light on to the people's sin (Garrett 1997: 161). By dividing the consonants differently, it may be read as 'my judgment goes forth like light [*'ôr*]' (so LXX, NRSV, ESV and most commentaries). The NIV translates *'ôr* as *sun*, possibly echoing the reference

---

67. See the discussion of *ḥesed* above, pp. 31–32.
68. Like Leviathan (see above, p. 9), Rahab appears in the context of God's victory over the primaeval sea (Job 26:12; Ps. 89:9–10). See J. Day 1985: 6, 38–40; 1992d.

to 'dawn' (*sun rises*, 6:3): Yahweh's deliverance is as sure as the dawn, but where there is no repentance, his judgments are just as sure.

Verse 6 refers again to *ḥesed* (NIV: *mercy*), which is paralleled with *acknowledgment* [*da'at*] *of God*. These are important ideas for Hosea, and their absence (along with *faithfulness*) has already been noted (see on 4:1). They are contrasted with sacrifices and burnt offerings. This does not denigrate sacrifice, and the wider prophetic vision of the future includes animal sacrifices (e.g. Jer. 33:18; Ezek. 40:38–43; 46; Zech. 14:21; Mal. 1:11). However, Yahweh does not desire cultic observance which seeks to manipulate rather than respond properly to him, and *ḥesed* and the knowledge of God emphasize the importance of relationship with him. Sacrifices offered with the right inner attitude remain important, and will do so until Christ's death makes them unnecessary (Routledge 2009).

7–9. The MT of the first part of verse 7 reads, 'they, like Adam, have transgressed [*'ābar*] the covenant [*bĕrît*]'. Some take Adam as a reference to the first human being (Achtemeier 1996: 53; McComiskey 1998: 95; Moon 2018: 127–130).[69] Allusions to creation (4:3) and to the covenant with Noah (2:18) indicate that Hosea was familiar with Israel's prehistory. And, while no covenant is specifically associated with Adam, there may have been a more general relationship implicit within the act of creation and confirmed in the covenant with Noah (Routledge 2008a: 164–165, 321). Adam's disobedience, then, exemplifies Israel's current violation of its covenant obligations. There are, though, no other references to Adam in the prophetic books, suggesting that the comparison was not widely recognized. A further problem is that Adam is the antecedent of 'there', which usually indicates a place. Moon (2018: 127–129) suggests it may refer instead to a rhetorical scenario, though the examples he notes (6:10; 13:8) could still indicate locations. The majority of translations and commentators take it as a place and read 'at/in Adam' (NRSV, NIV; cf. Andersen and Freedman 1980: 437–439; Hubbard 1989: 128; Macintosh 1997: 67; Dearman 2010: 189, 197), referring to the town mentioned in Joshua 3:16. This is not directly associated with covenant unfaithfulness,

---

69. Another possibility, 'like a man' (cf. LXX), seems unlikely.

however. Joshua 3:16–17 uses the same verb *ʿābar* ('to cross, transgress') to refer to Israel crossing the Jordan and also refers to *běrît* ('covenant'). This suggests a possible allusion to that earlier, better time (cf. 2:15). If, as seems likely, the place is the focus, there may have been a contemporary incident at Adam that we are unaware of. One suggestion is that Adam was linked with the rebellion of Pekah, which had the support of men from Gilead (v. 7; cf. 2 Kgs 15:25). On this view, insurrection spread from Adam to Shechem (v. 9), and eventually to Samaria, where it resulted in the assassination of Pekahiah (Macintosh 1997: 238; Dearman 2010: 197–198; see also J. Day 1986a: 6). Andersen and Freedman suggest that at Adam, which is in the region of Gilead (v. 8),[70] travellers on the road to Shechem were murdered by bands of priests (v. 9), who may have been on their way to join Pekah's rebellion (Andersen and Freedman 1980: 432, 436; cf. Hubbard 1989: 128–129). Achtemeier suggests that it refers to hostility by the priests to the levitical reformers whose movement may have centred on Shechem (1996: 54). While no explanation is entirely satisfactory, a key emphasis appears to be on political upheaval, possibly in the context of Pekah's uprising, which in turn precipitated the Syro-Ephraimite war, in which the priests played a significant part. But it is possible that the text has multiple meanings: the current covenant violations at Adam recall the sin of the first human (Garrett 1997: 162–163; cf. Curtis 2009), and Israel's unfaithfulness contrasts with God's faithfulness in opening the way into the Promised Land.

Mention of Shechem (v. 9) may also recall previous internecine conflict. Abimelek was made king there after killing his brothers (Judg. 9:1–6), and the city was the centre of Jeroboam's rebellion that led to the division of the kingdom (cf. 1 Kgs 12:1, 25).

Sin is described in various ways. Breaking the covenant (v. 7) is paralleled with being *unfaithful* (*bāgad*). The term means 'to act treacherously'. It is also associated with marital unfaithfulness (5:7;

---

70. V. 8 is generally translated *Gilead is a city of evildoers*, though Andersen and Freedman read, instead, 'in Gilead is the city [i.e. Adam] of evildoers'.

cf. Jer. 3:20; 9:2), and so links to the reference to prostitution in verse 10 and may reflect the corruption within the priesthood. Hostility between north and south may also be viewed as a covenant violation. The city's *evildoers* (v. 8) are *stained with footprints of blood*,[71] indicating the violent nature of their crimes. That is followed by the more specific reference to murder (v. 9), by gangs of priests who are likened to *marauders* (*gĕdûd*) who lie in wait to ambush travellers. *Wicked schemes* refers to general acts of villainy, though includes sexual depravity (e.g. Lev. 19:29; 20:14; Judg. 20:6; Jer. 13:27; Ezek. 23:48–49), a charge that has already been levelled at the priesthood (cf. 4:14).

10–11a. This summarizes the nation's guilt. Yahweh himself is witness to what is described as 'something horrible'. In keeping with the wider theme of the book, this is specifically linked with *prostitution* (*zĕnût*). This may include turning to other nations, including Syria and Assyria, but may also refer to actual immorality. This is evident throughout the nation (literally, 'in the house of Israel'). This brings defilement (cf. 5:3), ritual uncleanness that would normally exclude them from God's presence. The reference to Ephraim alongside Israel may again indicate the factions in Israel noted in 5:5. Most translations and commentators read the reference to Judah in 6:11a with 6:10 (though see Stuart 1987: 98, 112), and this may indicate that same threefold division.

Harvest (v. 11a) appears in the context of judgment in Jeremiah 51:33 and Joel 3:13. Most link this with judgment on Judah, though if, following the LXX, the first words of 6:11 are included with 6:10 ('Israel is defiled, also Judah'), it might relate to the whole nation (Moon 2018: 122). It is not necessary to view the reference to Judah as a later addition. The Syro-Ephraimite war brought condemnation of both kingdoms.

11b – 7:2. Like 6:1–3, the first part of this section indicates that Yahweh does not seek to destroy his people, but instead offers the possibility of restoration and healing. *Restore* (6:11b) translates *šûb* and echoes the call in 6:1. If the people return to Yahweh, he will *restore* [*their*] *fortunes*. This expression appears more than twenty

---

71. *Evil* translates *'āwen* (see on 4:15).

times in the Old Testament, usually in the context of deliverance from exile,[72] and this fits with Hosea's view of coming judgment (cf. 8:13; 9:3; 10:5–6; 11:5–6). Restoration is paralleled with healing (*rāpā'*), which again reflects the language of 6:1. The reference to iniquity suggests that healing may be linked with forgiveness (see O'Kennedy 2001).

However, as in 6:1–3, repentance is not forthcoming. The parallel expressions *the sins [āwôn] of Ephraim are exposed and the crimes [rā'â] of Samaria [revealed]*[73] emphasize the failure of the nation. The reference to Samaria also indicates that 6:11b – 7:2 is aimed primarily at the northern kingdom. The people practise *deceit*. Thieves break into homes; *bandits* (*gĕdûd*; cf. 6:9) rob in the streets. The link with 6:9 suggests that the main target here may be Israel's priests. And the perpetrators *do not realise* ('do not say to their heart') that Yahweh is aware of all their evil (*rā'â*). Their deeds *engulf* (literally, 'surround') them, hemming them in and preventing their escape. At the same time, their sins are before Yahweh's face, and stand between him and the restoration that he wants to bring.

Meaning

A key idea in this section is God's willingness to restore his people. Here it occurs twice: in the call to repentance in 6:1–3, and in the expression of frustration in 6:11:a – 7:1a. This is an important theme in the opening chapters but has faded from view with the catalogue of Israel's sin in chapters 4 and 5. In the divine purpose, though, it is never far away. Sin brings judgment, which is described here in sometimes graphic terms. The people need to be aware of the seriousness of their situation. Yet, despite their failure, if they are prepared to turn back to God, he will reverse the judgment and give healing and new life. Looking at the promise of national resurrection 'on the third day', a Christian audience will be reminded of the true basis for restoration: the death and resurrection of Jesus.

However, the response needed by the people is not forthcoming. That is, perhaps, not surprising when those who should be giving

---

72. E.g. Deut. 30:3; Jer. 29:14; 31:23; 32:44; Ezek. 39:25; Joel 3:1; Amos 9:14.

73. The verb appears in the first expression; in the second, it is assumed.

a spiritual lead, the priests, are themselves involved in political conspiracy and murder. The priesthood has already been the subject of damning indictment (4:4 – 5:7). Here that criticism continues, and highlights again the particular responsibility of those called to positions of spiritual leadership.

Another problem is the people's failure to demonstrate *ḥesed* (6:4, 6; cf. 4:1). The importance of this term for the prophecy has already been noted. Its repetition here emphasizes God's desire for a meaningful relationship with his people. Here it is contrasted with religious ritual, which has its place but must never be allowed to take the place of devotion and love.

D. Internal and international politics (7:3–16)

Context
The focus on Ephraim in 7:1–2 provides a bridge from the wider indictment of all the people to what appears to be a more specific indictment of the northern kingdom.

The reference to a baker's *oven* (7:4, 7) marks verses 3–7 as a separate subsection, dealing primarily with internal political intrigue (cf. 6:9). The setting may be the Syro-Ephraimite war and its aftermath, though it may have wider significance. Reference to kings falling (v. 7b) will include the assassination of Pekahiah by Pekah, though may indicate, too, the death of Pekah at the hands of Hoshea (2 Kgs 15:30) and, possibly, earlier murders leading to Menahem's accession (2 Kgs 15:8–14). Calling on Assyria (v. 11) may reflect Hoshea's request for support after the Syro-Ephraimite conflict (2 Kgs 17:3), though may also relate to Menahem (2 Kgs 15:19).

Verses 8–16 focus on Israel's relationship with the nations. The reference to Egypt (v. 11) may allude to Hoshea enlisting Egyptian support for his eventual rebellion against Assyria (2 Kgs 17:4), so may be later than the previous verses. The two subsections are linked by the baking imagery (7:8) and may be best viewed as a single unit (Ben Zvi 2005: 149–150; Lim and Castelo 2015: 136). Even if taken separately, they may be seen to represent complementary aspects of Israel's unfaithfulness (Dearman 2010: 207). Andersen and Freedman (1980: 447, 462) take the two sections to reflect aspects of 'the state of the nation'.

Comment

i. Israel and its kings (7:3–7)

3. *They* here appears to refer to an unidentified group of conspirators, possibly the priests, noted in 6:9 (Andersen and Freedman 1980: 447; Hubbard 1989: 132), though Garrett (1997: 168) sees a more general reference to those in power. *Wickedness* (*rā'â*) is mentioned for the third time in three verses, highlighting its all-pervasiveness; the parallel with *lies* (*kāḥaš*; cf. 10:13; 11:12) suggests that while the term has wider implications, the main issue here is conspiracy.

The parallel references to *king* and *princes* probably indicate the whole royal court (cf. 7:5; 8:10). Their *delight* in the lies of the conspirators may indicate that wickedness reaches the highest levels of society (cf. 5:1) (Moon 2018: 135), and perhaps more specifically points to the joy of the new king and officials as the beneficiaries of conspiracy (Mays 1969: 104; Wolff 1974: 124; Hubbard 1989: 132). Another possibility is that pleasing the royal court is part of the conspirators' treachery (Andersen and Freedman 1980: 448; Garrett 1997: 163; Dearman 2010: 202): they curry favour with a view to assassination. The latter is perhaps more likely (cf. v. 5), though in the light of frequent changes in monarchy, it may have elements of both: the new regime celebrates its position, while others await their opportunity.

4. *They* and *all* refer to the same group as in verse 3. *Adulterers* is a common theme in the prophecy (cf. 3:1; 4:2, 13, 14) and in this context probably indicates disloyalty to Yahweh (Hubbard 1989: 132; Macintosh 1997: 257; Dearman 2010: 203): the spiritual counterpart to political treachery.

The *oven* (*tannûr*) would usually be used to bake bread. It is likely to have been an upright clay cylinder with a fire in the bottom that would be allowed to burn very hot (Ross 1996: 434; Curtis 2001). When it was hot enough, dough would be pressed on to the inside of its upper walls to bake. The heat of the oven might indicate the burning ambition that drives treachery (cf. vv. 6, 7).

The significance of the baker is unclear. Andersen and Freedman (1980: 456; cf. Hubbard 1989: 132–133) see this as an official who should protect the king but whose inattentiveness allows his downfall (cf. v. 6). Garrett (1997: 169) sees a reference to the king himself, whose inactivity allows treachery to flourish. More likely, the baker is part of the oven simile. Despite needing little attention from the baker while the dough is rising, the oven remains hot, suggesting the unseen growth of conspiracy (Wolff 1974: 124–125; Macintosh 1997: 258–259; cf. Dearman 2010: 203). Paul (1968: 116) takes this to indicate periods when the baker left the fire smouldering, before stirring it up again. This corresponds to the fire being left overnight, before being brought to life in the morning (v. 6). Alternatively, the baker's neglect could allow the fire to burn too hot, and thus indicates desire that is out of control (Moon 2018: 135; cf. Hubbard 1989: 132–133).

5. *The day of the festival of our king* (NIV; literally, 'the day of our king'; cf. NRSV, ESV) is likely to refer to a feast held to honour the king, though specific details are not given.

Inflamed with wine (NIV) translates more literally as 'sick with the heat of wine' (NRSV, ESV). The verb *ḥalâ* could be translated 'to be ill', suggesting general drunkenness, in which the inebriated king reached out to *mockers*, possibly those plotting against him. In the Hiphil, *ḥalâ* more usually means 'to make ill'. Garrett (1997: 167) suggests that the princes make the king ill, though kings and princes are better taken together. A more likely translation is 'they make the princes ill', where 'they' relates to the 'mockers', who use the intoxication of the king and those around him to further their conspiracy. On this interpretation, verse 3 points to deceiving the king and princes in order to overthrow them, rather than being part of the conspiracy that brought them to power.

Macintosh (1997: 261) suggests that the relatively sympathetic reference to *our king* indicates that this refers to the assassination of Pekahiah, the only king in Israel's recent history who had not seized the throne by violence. However, while particular situations may be in view, the details are unclear, and it is better to focus on the more general picture of a royal court seething with intrigue.

6–7. These verses continue the imagery of the oven. Again, the text is difficult, though the overall theme of burning ambition, deception and conspiracy leading to the overthrow of kings seems clear.

The MT of verse 6 reads: 'For they approach, their hearts like an oven, in their ambush. All night their baker (is) sleeping. In the morning it burns like a raging fire.' The first part is relatively straightforward. Lust for power burns like an oven in the hearts of the conspirators as they set their ambush (for the king). The idea of ambush reflects the image in 6:9 of robbers lying in wait, and reinforces the view that the plotters may be priests. 'Their baker' seems obscure. Some retain it (Andersen and Freedman 1980: 447; Hubbard 1989: 132–133; Garrett 1997: 168; Moon 2018: 133), and the reference to him sleeping may correspond to his lack of attention in verse 4. Most translations, though, emend the pointing to read 'their passion/anger' (cf. NIV, NRSV). Both suggest that, just as a baker's fire smoulders through the night (while the baker sleeps) before being brought to life in the morning, so treachery bides its time, waiting for the time when it will become a raging fire.

The heat of the oven is noted again in verse 7, where it is specifically linked with devouring the nation's *rulers* (*šōpĕṭîm*). This term may also be translated 'judges', referring to those responsible for administering justice. This includes the king and probably the princes already mentioned. The oven of lust and ambition has become so hot that it consumes the institutions of state that maintain government and ensure fairness and decency in society.

The reference to kings falling probably refers to the assassinations of four kings between the deaths of Jeroboam and Hoshea, though might be more pertinent at the time of Menahem, who acceded to the throne after two kings were killed in the space of a month. Significantly here, Yahweh was excluded, and this is particularly pertinent if priests were involved in the conspiracy. Each new regime may have claimed religious legitimacy. Yahweh, though, distances himself from them. There may also be an ironic allusion to the charge already levelled, that the conspirators did not turn to Yahweh but were all too ready to seek help from foreign powers (cf. 5:13).

ii. Israel and the nations (7:8–16)

8–10. The emphasis now changes from internal to international politics. The possible allusion to turning to Assyria (rather than Yahweh) at the end of verse 7 and the continuation of the baking metaphor provide a link with the previous section.

In verse 8, the verb 'to mix' (*bālal*) usually relates to mixing flour and oil to make bread for the grain offering (e.g. Lev. 2:5; 23:13; Num. 6:15), though it also refers to the confusion of languages at Babel (Gen. 11:7, 9). In such a mixture, individual elements become indistinguishable, suggesting that Israel's involvement with surrounding nations – Syria, Egypt and Assyria – has led to its loss of distinctiveness as God's people. The second description, *Ephraim is a flat loaf not turned over*, also relates to bread-making: dough needed to be turned during baking, otherwise one side would be uncooked and the other burnt. Ephraim here is half overdone and half underdone. This may further indicate Ephraim's loss of identity. It may hint, too, at the inattentiveness of the baker (7:4, 6), here referring to the nation's leaders.

A significant feature of verse 9 is the repeated reference to 'he does not know it' (NRSV, ESV).[74] The nation, caught up in political intrigue and foreign alliances, remains unaware of how desperate its condition is. *Foreigners sap* [literally, 'eat, devour'] *his strength* probably refers to the economic and agricultural consequences of paying tribute to foreign powers. *His hair is sprinkled with grey* (NIV) is better translated 'grey hairs are sprinkled upon him' (NRSV, ESV). This is usually understood to refer to the loss of physical vitality associated with old age: Ephraim has become weak but does not know it! It may be better, though, to relate *śêbah* ('grey hairs, old age') to an Akkadian word referring to the white-haired mould that grows on bread (Paul 1968: 118–120; Andersen and Freedman 1980: 467; Hubbard 1989: 137–138; Garrett 1997: 170), thus pointing to the decay that pervades the nation. This might then suggest a pairing of ideas in verses 8–9: Ephraim mixes with the nations/foreigners devour his strength; Ephraim is an unturned loaf/mould is spread on him (cf. Andersen and Freedman 1980: 467).

In verse 10, *Israel's arrogance testifies against him* repeats the beginning of 5:5. It points to the self-reliance that contrasts with trust in Yahweh, and, ironically, confidence in the ability to negotiate foreign alliances (cf. 7:11). Again, that arrogance is linked with their failure to return (*śûb*) to God (cf. 5:4). The language ('return', 'seek',

---

74. See above, p. 15 n. 42.

'Yahweh their God') echoes 3:5, where it points to future restoration. For the moment, though, the nation is oblivious to the seriousness of its plight and, despite everything (*despite all this*), it looks elsewhere for help, rather than to the one who alone can secure its future.

11–12. Ephraim is further likened to a senseless dove (v. 11), flying first one way, then another. Two expressions sum up the nation's folly. *Easily deceived* (*pātaḥ*) suggests simple-mindedness, naïvety and gullibility. *Senseless* translates, literally, 'without heart', and, because the heart (*lēb*) was the seat of the will, indicates an inability to make sound judgments.[75] That has led to vacillation between Assyria and Egypt, depending on which seemed better able to provide the help needed. *Calling* (*qārā'*) to Egypt contrasts with the nation's unwillingness to 'call' on Yahweh (v. 7), and the futility of *turning* (literally, 'going' [*hālak*]) to Assyria has already been noted (5:13).

The verb 'to go' (*hālak*) is repeated at the start of verse 12. *When they go*, Yahweh will intervene directly to frustrate their plans. A fowler laid bait, and when a bird, tempted by the bait, came to the ground, the fowler caught it in his net. Here Ephraim is lured by the apparent security of Egypt or Assyria, but that security is illusory and will bring disaster.

The last part of verse 12 is difficult. The MT reads literally, 'I will discipline them according to the report to their assembly' (cf. NRSV, ESV).[76] This probably refers to the report to an Israelite assembly of negotiations with a foreign power,[77] though Moon's suggestion that it refers to Yahweh's words delivered to the assembly by the prophet (2018: 139–140) is also possible. The details of any such assembly are unknown, but condemnation of agreements with other nations is clear (cf. 12:1).

---

75. *Pātaḥ* also occurs with *lēb* in 2:14, though in a more positive context.

76. The NIV translation, *When I hear them flocking together, I will catch them*, maintains the imagery of the fowler but is unlikely.

77. 'To their assembly' is emended by Andersen and Freedman (1980: 469) to 'of their treaty', and by Wolff (1974: 107) to 'of their wickedness', but these have little textual support.

13. The first part of verse 13 comprises parallel lines announcing divine judgment. *Woe to them* implies a threat, specified as *destruction.* *Strayed* (*nādad*) often occurs in the context of fleeing (e.g. Isa. 21:15; 22:3), and this is paralleled with the charge of rebellion. Ephraim has rejected Yahweh's authority and runs from him, and so must face the consequences.

Again, though, alongside the threat of judgment we see Yahweh's willingness to restore his people. *Redeem* (*pādâ*) implies rescue, usually with the payment of a price (cf. Exod. 13:15; Num. 18:15) (cf. Hubbard 1996b), and echoes Hosea's own experience of buying back his wayward wife. It also recalls the exodus (cf. Deut. 7:8; 9:26; 15:15), and that is seen, further, in similarities in structure between verses 13 and 15 (Andersen and Freedman 1980: 473; cf. Garrett 1997: 172). However, the people have refused. *Speak . . . falsely* suggests misrepresentation of Yahweh. This was, no doubt, rife within a syncretistic worship system promoted by a corrupt priesthood, and it prevented the kind of response that would open the way for redemption.

14–15. Israel's failure to offer a sincere response to Yahweh is further highlighted in verse 14. The people have cried out (*zā'q*) to God in the past (e.g. Exod. 2:23; Judg. 3:9; 1 Sam. 7:8–9). Their prayer here, though, is insincere. It is not *from their hearts*, indicating a lack of will and commitment. Instead, they *wail on their beds.* This may refer to anguish that prevents sleep or, more likely, to fertility rituals, linked to lamenting the death of Baal (Garrett 1997: 174). Self-laceration is also associated with Baal worship (1 Kgs 18:28; cf. Jer. 49:3).[78] These actions are to ensure the provision of *grain and new wine.* In chapter 2, this is attributed to Baal rather than Yahweh (cf. 2:8–9), and by engaging in these fertility rituals the people are still making the same mistake.[79] They may think they are crying out to Yahweh (cf. 8:2), but their prayer is syncretistic, worshipping him as just another 'baal' (cf. 2:16). As the last part of verse 14 indicates, this is no different from turning away from him.

---

78. Following the LXX, and reading *gādad* ('to cut, slash') for *gārar* ('to gather').

79. The NIV has added *appealing to their gods.*

Ignorance of Yahweh's provision is seen, too, in verse 15, whose structure is similar to that of verse 13b:

I long to redeem them	*but they speak about me falsely* (v. 13).
I trained them . . .	*but they plot evil against me* (v. 15).

Verse 15 recalls the exodus. *I trained them* (*yāsar*) reflects Deuteronomy 8:5, where Yahweh disciplines (*yāsar*) Israel as a father disciplines a child (cf. Prov. 29:17). *Strengthened* suggests sustained support and encouragement (e.g. Deut. 1:38; 3:28; Josh. 1:9) and is also linked with the occupation of Canaan (Deut. 11:8). Taken with 7:13b, this suggests that Yahweh's faithfulness to his people in the past, and particularly in the events of the exodus, is reflected in his readiness to redeem them now as before.

In contrast, the people *plot evil* (*rāʿ*) against him. Israel's wickedness (*rāʿâ*) has already been noted (e.g. 7:1–3).[80] Here the emphasis may be on Israel's attitude: the evil intent and ingratitude which contrast with Yahweh's help through their history. The link with verse 13b suggests that it includes false representation of Yahweh and what he requires (cf. 7:14).

16. This verse begins with a further play on the term *šûb*.[81] Despite the call to return to Yahweh (cf. 6:1), Israel continues to look elsewhere. According to the MT, they turn to *lōʾ ʿal* ('not high/height, not above').[82] The NIV relates *ʿal* ('height') to Yahweh: *They do not turn to the Most High* (cf. 11:7) (see also Moon 2018: 139–140). Andersen and Freedman (1980: 477–478; cf. Hubbard 1989: 142) prefer 'no god' (cf. Deut. 32:21). Others, in line with the image of a *faulty bow*, and with possible support from the LXX, emend to *lōʾ yôʿilû* ('no profit'; cf. Jer. 2:8) (NRSV; Mays 1969: 110; Dearman 2010: 207). The sense, though, seems clear: the people do not turn to their only source of help, and, as a result, they have become useless

---

80. Here the noun *rāʿâ* and the adjective *rāʿ* mean the same.

81. See above, p. 24.

82. Further suggestions include 'not to me' (Wolff 1974: 108); 'Not on High', as a parody of 'God on High' (Garrett 1997: 173); 'not what is above' (Macintosh 1997: 284–285; cf. ESV).

(cf. Jer. 2:5). A *faulty bow* (cf. Ps. 78:57) is unreliable and dangerous: it may misfire when needed in battle, and possibly injure its user. This may refer to the disastrous consequences of Israel's unfaithfulness in pursuing foreign alliances.

Continuing the military imagery, Israel's leaders will *fall by the sword*. This is because of *their insolent words* (literally, 'the anger/indignation [*za'am*] of their tongue'). *Za'am* (cf. Gordon 1996b) often refers to divine wrath associated with judgment (e.g. Isa. 10:5; 30:27; Jer. 10:10; Ezek. 21:31; Hab. 3:12). The verb *zā'am* also means 'to curse' (e.g. Num. 23:7–8; Mic. 6:10). This suggests that the leaders' words are tantamount to cursing Yahweh and so are *insolent* (NIV, ESV; cf. Mays 1969: 110; Wolff 1974: 108; Moon 2018: 139), or that they bring Yahweh's wrath (Andersen and Freedman 1980: 479). These, though, amount to the same thing. The *words* may be the spoken commitments that accompany treaty-making with foreign powers (cf. 7:12) and which are in defiance of the people's covenant relationship with Yahweh, or the lies spoken about Yahweh (7:13).

A further consequence is that Israel will be ridiculed in Egypt. This may be because of their failed alliance with Assyria, or it may point to the coming exile, which is portrayed as a return to Egypt (8:13; 9:3, 6; cf. Ezek. 36:3). There may, too, be an ironic reference to the exodus (cf. 7:13, 15): those who were brought out of Egypt will become an object of scorn there (Garrett 1997: 175; Dearman 2010: 215).

Meaning

These verses describe corruption at the highest levels of society. Hardly surprising, therefore, that the nation at large has gone astray. Priests should give instruction, and princes should maintain justice. Instead, those called to lead are consumed by their own ambitious schemes, with dire consequences for themselves and for those they should be serving.

Central to that corruption is the people's failure to trust God, relying instead on their own devices. Internally, this results in the political conspiracy and intrigue that brings about the rise and fall of kings (7:7; cf. 8:4). On the international scene it includes alliances with stronger nations (cf. 7:11). Putting confidence in other things is a constant temptation for God's people. He, though, is the only source of true security. Turning elsewhere is arrogant self-deception which may give the impression of strength, but which masks underlying weakness and decay (7:9). It is folly (7:11) and represents rebellion against Yahweh (7:13–14). The result is mockery by enemies, and divine judgment (7:12–13, 16).

However, despite the people's sin, Yahweh wants to redeem them (7:13). Here we see a further expression of the divine husband's willingness to restore his unfaithful wife. There is a way back (cf. 7:10, 14), but then, as now, many who are caught up in persistent wrongdoing refuse to admit their need and turn to Yahweh with the kind of meaningful repentance that can open the way for forgiveness and restoration.

E. False confidence and impending judgment (8:1 – 9:9)

Context

This section recalls earlier parts of the prophecy. The reference to the *trumpet* (*šôpār*) in 8:1 may deliberately echo 5:8, and the passage continues other themes from 5:8 – 7:16, including internal political corruption (8:4; cf. 7:3–7) and dependence on other nations, especially Assyria (8:8–10; cf. 5:13; 7:11). The notion of Israel going after *lovers* (8:9) recalls chapter 2, though here it relates to foreign nations rather than other gods. The issues of idolatry and false worship also recur (cf. 4:1 – 5:7). A key emphasis is on the people's misplaced confidence in their corrupted religion and in other nations, and the judgment that must surely follow.

While there is general agreement that 8:1 marks the beginning of a new section, some view 8:1–14 and 9:1–9 as separate units (Wolff 1974; Macintosh 1997; Ben Zvi 2005: 185; Moon 2018).[83] There are, though, common elements (Hubbard 1989: 143; cf. Ben Zvi 2005: 164). As well as having similar themes, both include Hosea's only references to *the house of the LORD* (8:1; 9:4; cf. 9:8);

---

83. Andersen and Freedman (1980) further divide 8:1–14 into two sections (8:1–8, 9–14).

using near-identical language, both deliver the same verdict: *he will remember their wickedness and punish their sins* (8:13; 9:9); and both view punishment as a *return to Egypt* (8:13; 9:3). It seems reasonable, therefore, to take them as two parts of a single section.

While it is difficult to assign a particular historical context to these verses, the harvest language in 9:1–9 suggests that they were delivered at the feast of Tabernacles, Israel's autumn harvest celebration (Wolff 1974: 153; Stuart 1987: 141; Hubbard 1989: 155; Dearman 2010: 237; however, cf. Macintosh 1997: 335–336). They appear to emphasize that coming judgment will bring religious celebrations to an end, including offering sacrifices. References to Ephraim and Samaria indicate that this, like the previous section, is directed primarily at the northern kingdom, and the anticipation of imminent judgment (cf. 2 Kgs 17:6) may point to a time late in Hoshea's reign. Judah is also mentioned briefly (8:14).

Comment
i. A broken covenant (8:1–3)
1–3. The first part of verse 1 reads literally, 'to your palate a trumpet, like an eagle/vulture [*nešer*] over the house of the LORD'. The terseness of the text makes it difficult to be clear about its meaning. Sounding a trumpet might be a warning of impending attack (cf. 5:8), suggesting that the eagle represents an enemy (cf. Deut. 28:49; Jer. 4:13; Hab. 1:8) (NRSV, ESV; Achtemeier 1996: 63–64; Eidevall 1996: 127–128; Macintosh 1997: 291; Dearman 2010: 216; Moon 2018: 144).[84] Verse 3 also talks about being pursued by an enemy, and there is also a twofold reference to Israel's sin (vv. 1b, 3a). This suggests a concentric structure, emphasizing judgment as the consequence of sin:

---

84. Garrett (1997: 181) likens the vulture, as something unclean, to the priesthood. Emmerson (1975: 704) emends *nešer* to *naššār*, which, based on an Arabic term, she translates 'herald': 'set the trumpet to your lips like a herald'. She then gives a cultic interpretation, linking pursuit by an enemy to covenant curses rather than a specific military threat.

a   [*one like*] *an eagle is over the house of the* LORD
   b   *because the people have broken my covenant and rebelled against
        my law.*
      c   *Israel cries out to me, 'Our God, we acknowledge you!'*
   b'   *But Israel has rejected what is good;*
a'   *an enemy will pursue him.*

In this case, 8:1a is addressed to the prophet, who is acting as the nation's watchman (cf. Ezek. 3:17; 33:7; cf. Hos. 9:8), warning of coming judgment.

The house of the LORD usually refers to the temple (Emmerson 1975; Garrett 1997: 181), but that seems unlikely in a message addressed primarily to the northern kingdom. Here it appears to refer, maybe ironically, to the land (cf. 9:4, 8, 15). Israel were set apart as God's people through the covenant established at Sinai, but they have broken that covenant relationship and rebelled (cf. 7:13–14) against God's law (*tôrâ*).

Verse 2 describes Israel's empty cry to Yahweh: *Our God, we acknowledge* [*yāda'*] *you!*[85] This may reflect language used in worship, and many worshippers may believe it to be true. However, the prophet is clear that the people do not know or acknowledge Yahweh (2:8; 5:4; 11:3; cf. 4:1).[86] Their worship of Yahweh as just another baal indicates how inadequate their knowledge is. There may also be an implicit rebuke of the priesthood, who were responsible for making Yahweh known.

Verse 3 continues the theme of sin and judgment. Israel has rejected what is *good* (*tôb*). This may refer to Yahweh himself, to Israel's behaviour in failing to act in the way they should as God's people (cf. Deut. 12:28; Isa. 65:2; Jer. 6:16), or to the prosperity and

---

85. *Israel* in the verse is awkward. It may be the subject of 'to cry out' (NIV; cf. NRSV), or taken in apposition to 'we': 'we, Israel, know you' (NRSV, ESV; cf. Emmerson 1975: 702; Macintosh 1997: 294; Moon 2018: 144). Andersen and Freedman (1980: 481, 490) suggest 'God of Israel'. It is not in the LXX and may be a dittograph from v. 3, or a gloss (Dearman 2010: 216).

86. See also above, p. 15 n. 42.

blessing associated with their relationship with Yahweh (e.g. Deut. 26:11; 28:12; 30:15). All have been spurned by the people, and the consequence is pursuit by an enemy. This is a further example of the punishment corresponding to the crime. *Rādap* ('to pursue') refers to Israel's vain pursuit of what is wrong (2:7; 12:1) and the failure to *press on* to know Yahweh (6:3). Here, appropriately, it also refers to Israel's punishment. The unnamed enemy is probably Assyria.

ii. Kings and idols (8:4–6)

In these verses, political and religious corruption are closely linked. Political appointments and worship of idols both represent human attempts to ensure security and blessing. But neither takes account of God, and so both will fail.

4. The reference to setting up northern kings and princes (8:4a) echoes 7:3–7 and probably reflects the political intrigues noted there. The appointment of kings is motivated by ruthless ambition, not divine call. *Without my consent* (NIV) translates more literally as 'not from me'. The parallel expression 'I did not know [*yāda'*]' indicates that this was without Yahweh's acknowledgment and approval (cf. NIV), rather than suggesting a lack of awareness (Macintosh 1997: 297; Dearman 2010: 216; Moon 2018: 144). Hosea may not have been against the northern monarchy per se (though see Cook 2004: 107–114). However, in its closing days it had little to commend it, and, as we have seen, Hosea linked hope for the future with a Davidic king (3:5).

Silver and gold are mentioned in the context of Baal worship in 2:8. Here they are explicitly linked with making idols (cf. 13:2). This obsession with idols has already been noted (4:17; cf. 14:8), but it is to no avail. *To their own destruction* (NIV) may be translated 'with the result that (they) will be cut off'. The subject in the MT is singular, but most English versions and commentators follow the LXX, where it is plural ('they are destroyed'). This could then refer to the idols, to the silver and gold, or to the people. Some retain the singular, without changing the sense, and relate it to the calf-idol noted in the following verses (Andersen and Freedman 1980: 492), Israel's wealth (Garrett 1997: 183) or Israel itself (Dearman 2010: 222). The effects are similar: Israel looks to other gods for prosperity and security, but they can offer neither, and everything that the people rely on, and even the nation itself, will be removed.

5–6. These verses focus on 'the calf [*ʿēgel*] of Samaria' (v. 5). An *ʿēgel* was a young bull, and, in the Ancient Near East, was a symbol of strength and fertility. Here it probably refers to the golden calf set up by Jeroboam I at Bethel (1 Kgs 12:28–29; cf. Hos. 10:5). Bethel had national prominence (cf. Amos 7:13), and *Samaria* here appears to stand for the whole of Israel.[87] Jeroboam's sanctuaries at Dan and Bethel were to provide people in the north with alternatives to Jerusalem, and the calf may originally have been associated with Yahweh, possibly as a pedestal, corresponding to the ark in the Jerusalem temple (Walton, Matthews and Chavalas 2000: 368; Hill and Walton 2009: 298–299). It appears, though, to have become linked with Baal, who is represented as a bull. Whatever the intention, this, like the calf constructed by Aaron in the desert (Exod. 32:4; cf. 1 Kgs 12:28), was considered the height of idolatry, and Jeroboam became known as the one who caused Israel to sin (e.g. 1 Kgs 14:16; 15:30; 16:26; 2 Kgs 3:3; 10:29). The calf seems to have become a symbol of the religion of the northern kingdom, and Israel's continued reverence for it caused Yahweh's anger (*ʾap*).

The first clause of verse 5 is unclear. In the MT, 'your calf' is the subject of *zānaḥ* ('to reject'), but there is no object. As an intransitive verb *zānaḥ* may also mean 'to be foul-smelling', and Dearman (2010: 216) suggests: 'your calf is wretched' (cf. Macintosh 1997: 301–302). The NRSV repoints it as a passive: 'Your calf is rejected' (cf. Mays 1969: 113; Garrett 1997: 183). Some take Samaria as the object: 'your calf has rejected you, Samaria' (Moon 2018: 144). The NIV, following the LXX, repoints the verb as an imperative: *Throw out your calf-idol* (cf. Wolff 1974: 132). A further suggestion is to take *my anger* as the subject of both clauses: 'my anger has rejected . . . my anger burns' (Lundbom 1975; Hubbard 1989: 147; Ben Zvi 2005: 165; though see Gruber 2017: 349–350). Most variations indicate the calf's rejection

---

87. It is less likely that there was such a calf in Samaria (see Dearman 2010: 224–226) or that the calf was moved there (Gruber 2017: 348). Cook (2004: 111) suggests that the reference to *Samaria* links the calf-cult to the Israelite king.

by Yahweh (cf. ESV: 'I have spurned your calf'), and that seems the most likely sense. This rejection of the symbol of Israel's fertility and prosperity corresponds to Israel's rejection of what is good (v. 3). There is also a likely play on words: Yahweh rejects (*zānaḥ*) the calf-cult to which the nation has prostituted itself (*zānâ*).

The final part of verse 5 expresses Yahweh's dismay over Israel's lack of purity. This is linked with the cleanness necessary to come before God (Pss 26:6; 73:13; cf. Gen. 20:5). Despite calls to turn back to Yahweh, the people persist in idolatrous disobedience.

Verse 6 begins with 'because from Israel'. Following the LXX, some take this with the last part of verse 5 and relate it to the people: *They are from Israel!* (NIV; Wolff 1974: 132; Hubbard 1989: 147–148), maybe expressing hope that the people's disobedience will not continue for ever because they are from Israel and have a higher call (Wolff 1974: 143). A more likely reading, though, is 'because it [i.e. the calf] is from Israel' (cf. NRSV, ESV; Garrett 1997: 183; Macintosh 1997: 307; Dearman 2010: 216; Moon 2018: 144), emphasizing, with the rest of verse 6, the calf's non-divine origins. It was made at Israel's behest, not Yahweh's. It was manufactured by a craftsman (cf. Isa. 40:19–20; Jer. 10:3, 9) and, contrary to what may have been said about it in the past (cf. Exod. 32:4; 1 Kgs 12:28) and to its present role at the centre of a corrupt worship system, it has no claim to be revered as a god (cf. 14:3). And as a mere human creation, it will be destroyed. The term describing the fate of the calf occurs only here in the Old Testament.[88] It is commonly translated *broken in pieces* (NIV, NRSV, ESV; Wolff 1974: 132; Garrett 1997: 183; Dearman 2010: 216), though it may mean 'given to the flames' (cf. NRSV mg.; Moon 2018: 144, 146). By whatever means it comes about, the calf's demise further emphasizes its lack of divinity and the futility of placing confidence in it.

iii. Trust in foreign alliances (8:7–10)

7. The verse begins with a familiar proverbial idea: 'you reap what you sow'. For Israel, though, the consequences are disproportionate. Sowing wind may suggest the emptiness and futility of

---

88. For discussion of possible translations, see Macintosh 1997: 308–310.

looking elsewhere for help rather than to Yahweh. The result, corresponding to reaping the whirlwind (*sûpâ*), is that not only will the people not receive the help they seek, but they will face catastrophe. *Sûpâ* denotes a destructive wind associated with a storm and symbolizes disaster (e.g. Prov. 1:27; Isa. 21:1). It may also herald Yahweh's coming in judgment (e.g. Isa. 29:6; 66:15; Jer. 4:13), and that may be the implication here.

The second part of the verse continues the agricultural imagery. Seed that is sown may grow, but the corn stalks will not produce grain. And if they do, the grain will be swallowed up (*bāla*ʿ) by enemies. This logical inconsistency is a rhetorical device known as *pseudosorites*, which says that something will not happen, but even if it does, it will be negated by something else, and if that happens, something else will negate it, and so on (see Andersen and Freedman 1980: 393–394, 496–498; O'Connor 1987; Patterson 2010: 30–36) (cf. 9:11b–12). Again, the emphasis is on the futility of Israel's actions. While this may point literally to the failure of the harvest, it also applies metaphorically to Israel's attempts to ensure its own security by appointing kings, worshipping other gods and seeking help from surrounding nations, rather than looking to Yahweh. Because the idea of sowing wind seems strange, some understand prepositions – 'they sow *in* the wind and will reap *in* a storm' – and so take all of the elements in verse 7 to emphasize the futility of Israel's efforts (Andersen and Freedman 1980: 496–497; Stuart 1987: 127; Garrett 1997: 184). The rhetorical impact is increased by using words that have similar sounds; for example, *qāmâ* ('stalk'), *qemaḥ* ('flour'), *ṣemaḥ* ('stalk').

8. Wordplay continues into verse 8, with a repetition of *bāla*ʿ ('to swallow up'). The nation will share the same fate as the grain, and will disappear among foreign peoples, notably Assyria. And, as a result of divine judgment, and maybe partly, too, due to its vacillating, pleading for help with one nation then another (cf. 7:11) and forming and breaking alliances, Israel has become worthless (literally, 'a vessel without value') on the international stage. The NIV's *something no one wants* is a paraphrase but it expresses the general idea (cf. Wolff 1974: 132; Stuart 1987: 127). Jeremiah uses the same expression to refer to Moab (Jer. 48:38), and to Jehoiachin, who was taken into a foreign land following the first Babylonian attacks on Judah (Jer. 22:28).

9–10. Verse 9 refers again to Israel seeking help from Assyria. In 7:11, the general term *ḥālak* ('to go') is used. Here, 'to go up' (*ʿālâ*) is more geographically specific, suggesting that this may refer to a particular embassy, northwards to Assyria, maybe by Menahem or Hoshea.[89] The wordplay linking *ʾeprayim* (*Ephraim*) and *pereʾ* (*wild donkey*) has already been noted,[90] and it is likely that they should be taken together here: 'Ephraim is a wild donkey, wandering alone' (Andersen and Freedman 1980: 501; Stuart 1987: 127; Garrett 1997: 185; Dearman 2010: 226). This may suggest stubbornness: Israel insists on following its own path (Eidevall 1996: 133–135). Or it may indicate that, for all its efforts to secure the support of other nations, Israel remains friendless (cf. v. 8).

In most translations, turning to Assyria is related to seeking after lovers (e.g. NIV, NRSV, ESV), echoing the imagery of earlier parts of the book.[91] The translation, though, is not straightforward. The verb *tānâ* is usually translated 'to hire' (ESV), implying that, rather than selling herself (cf. NIV, NRSV) and receiving a prostitute's pay (cf. 2:12), Israel must now pay for the attention of her lovers (Hubbard 1989: 149; Garrett 1997: 186; Dearman 2010: 229). This emphasizes again how worthless the nation has become. Another possibility is to understand *tānâ* as 'to recount' (cf. Judg. 5:11; 11:40). This might suggest celebrating relationships with other nations (Macintosh 1997: 316; Moon 2018: 146), thus highlighting further Israel's false confidence in Assyrian help.

Tānâ is repeated in verse 10. The *lovers* whom Israel seeks to hire, or whose help it celebrates, are the nations to whom it looks for security. Those efforts, though, will come to nothing. Yahweh will *gather* (*qābaṣ*) the people. And, while *qābaṣ* is often associated

---

89. See above, pp. 2, 4. Irvine (1995) sets 8:8–10 at the end of Hoshea's reign.

90. See above, p. 23.

91. The term translated *lovers* is *ʾahab* ('love gift'); Macintosh (1997: 316) translates it 'love affair'. It is probably better to repoint as *ʾāhab* ('lovers'); cf. 2:5, 7, 10, 12.

with deliverance from exile (e.g. Isa. 43:5; 60:4; Jer. 23:3; 29:14; Ezek. 11:17), here the context suggests rather that it refers to assembling them for judgment (cf. Isa. 44:11; Joel 3:2; Mic. 4:12; Zeph. 3:8).

The MT in the second part of verse 10 is unclear, and commentators note a range of emendations. The expression *melek śārîm* may be translated 'king of princes' (cf. NIV: *mighty king*), referring to the Assyrian ruler (Mays 1969: 114, 112; Hubbard 1989: 150; Macintosh 1997: 319, 321; Moon 2018: 145, 146–147). Others read it as 'kings (and) princes' (NRSV, ESV; Andersen and Freedman 1980: 501; Garrett 1997: 186; Dearman 2010: 226) and relate it to Israel's leadership (cf. 8:4). In the former case, the 'burden' is probably the tribute exacted by Assyria (Macintosh 1997: 319), though may include oppression more generally. In the latter, it may again be the tribute under which Israel's kings and princes suffer (ESV; Andersen and Freedman 1980: 501; cf. Dearman 2010: 226), or the burden imposed on the people by its kings and princes – though that, too, may be exacerbated by the need to raise revenue to pay Assyria (cf. 2 Kgs 15:19–20) (Garrett 1997: 185).[92] The nature of the suffering is also debated. Some take *mě'aṭ* as a verbal form, 'to become few', indicating Israel's decline: *They will begin [wayyāḥēllû] to waste away* (NIV; Garrett 1997: 185). Others translate *mě'aṭ* as 'soon' and repoint *wayyāḥēllû* to *wayyāḥîlû* ('they will writhe') (NRSV, ESV; cf. Wolff 1974: 133; Dearman 2010: 226; though see Moon 2018: 146). Whatever the precise translation, though, the emphasis is on the impact of the judgment that will overtake Israel through the failed policies of its leaders and, ultimately, through Assyria.

iv. Empty sacrifices (8:11–14)

11. As in 8:4, Hosea moves from condemning Israel's politics to attacking its religious practices. A literal translation of verse 11 is: 'because Ephraim has increased [*rābah*] altars for sinning, they have become altars for sinning' (cf. ESV). It seems best to take this as

---

92. The LXX, 'they will cease to anoint kings and princes' (cf. 3:4), reading *māśah* ('to anoint') for *maśśā'* ('burden') (see Stuart 1987: 127), seems less likely.

ironic: the altars set up to deal with sin have simply provided more opportunities for sinning (NIV, NRSV):[93] each new altar was a means of extending Ephraim's corrupt worship practices (cf. 4:7). The verb *rābah* also occurs in verse 14, in relation to Judah increasing fortifications. But the multiplied effort of both kingdoms is futile and counterproductive.

12. This points to the people's disregard for Yahweh's written instruction, and includes an indictment of the priests, who have failed to teach the people as they should (cf. 4:4–10; Mal. 2:6–9). Indeed, it appears that Israel's religion has become so corrupted by false worship that what is set out in the law and should be intrinsic to Israel's covenant faith is now considered 'strange' (*zār*). This term also occurs in relation to the priests' illegitimate children (5:7) and to foreigners (7:9; 8:7). The implication is that Israel has turned so far away from Yahweh that his instruction is now alien to them. The reference to *many* may be a foil to the reference to the increased number of altars: Israel already has enough of what it needs to meet Yahweh's requirements.

13. The second word of this verse, *habhābay*, occurs only here, and its translation is uncertain (see Nicholson 1966). The NIV links it with 'to give' and takes it with 'they sacrifice': *they offer sacrifices as gifts to me* (cf. ESV; Stuart 1987: 127; Moon 2018: 147). It is probably better, though, to relate *habhābay* to *'āhab* ('to love'). This may underlie the NRSV translation 'choice sacrifices', suggesting sacrifices that the people mistakenly think are acceptable (Garrett 1997: 187). Or it could be translated: 'they love sacrifice' (Dearman 2010: 232).[94] This is accompanied by eating the meat of the offerings, and some extend 'love' into this next clause, suggesting that they also love meat (cf. Mays 1969: 114; Wolff 1974: 133; Hubbard 1989: 152–153). This appears to have become the primary reason for sacrifice; they appear to be concerned to please God but are more motivated by their greed.

---

93. For alternatives, see Andersen and Freedman 1980: 508–509; Macintosh 1997: 823–825.

94. Andersen and Freedman's suggestion, they sacrifice 'my loved ones', indicating child sacrifice (1980: 501), is less likely (see on 4:2).

The verb *rāṣâ* ('to be pleased with') is often associated with the acceptability of sacrifices (e.g. Lev. 1:4; 7:18; 22:23; Ps. 51:16; Mic. 6:7). Here, though, it probably relates to the acceptance of the people (cf. Jer. 14:10, 12; Ezek. 20:40–41). Sacrifice was intended to bring divine favour by dealing with sin. However, despite Israel's efforts, Yahweh is not pleased and, instead, will remember and punish the nation's sin. That punishment will involve a *return [šûb] to Egypt*,[95] which points to coming exile in a foreign land.

14. The apparent change of focus in verse 14, and the reference to Judah, has prompted suggestions that it is part of a Judean redaction, though that is not necessary (Andersen and Freedman 1980: 511–512; Dearman 2010: 233–234).[96] It continues the theme of sin and judgment, with the indictment that the people have forgotten (*šākaḥ*) Yahweh (cf. 2:13; 4:6; 13:6) and engage instead in building projects, which are probably aimed at flaunting their wealth and providing security.[97] There may be an intentional contrast between Israel forgetting Yahweh, and Yahweh remembering Israel's sin in the previous verse.

Yahweh here is referred to as Israel's *Maker*. This title relates primarily to the establishment of the nation[98] and, with the reference to returning to Egypt in the previous verse, recalls the exodus. Yahweh has made this people for himself and entered into a covenant with them. But they have forgotten him! The result will be judgment, in the form of divine fire (cf. Ezek. 39:6; Amos 1 – 2) which will destroy the fortifications in which the people have put their confidence.

---

95. On *šûb*, see above, p. 24.
96. Some suggest that this is original to Hosea but placed here by a redactor (Wolff 1974: 146; Emmerson 1984: 74–77; Macintosh 1997: 332–333).
97. Garrett (1997: 188) notes that palaces were often heavily fortified.
98. Other passages which accuse the people of forgetting their Maker (e.g. Ps. 95:6–7; Isa. 17:7–10; 51:13) use the term primarily to assure them of his ability to redeem them.

v. The end of festivals (9:1–9)

1–2. As noted, the context for this oracle may be the feast of Tabernacles, which included gathering the produce from *threshing-floors and winepresses* (v. 2; cf. Deut. 16:13). Threshing-floors were the place where grain was separated from the crops by crushing the stalks. This might be done by hand, or more usually by a cow or ox walking over the stalks (cf. Deut. 25:4). Winepresses were used to crush the newly harvested grapes, ready to make wine. Hosea begins by challenging the exuberant celebrations that usually accompanied the feast, as the people rejoiced in God's provision.[99] Rejoicing at the harvest was common across the Ancient Near East, though the reference to *other nations* here may be a specific indictment of Israel's syncretistic worship and attribution of Yahweh's blessing to other nations' gods. A successful harvest would give the impression that Yahweh was blessing the people, and the prophet wants to dispel such false confidence.[100] The nation has been *unfaithful* (*zānâ*; cf. 1:2; 2:5; 3:3; 4:10–15; 5:3), and what they have received, rather than being a sign of divine blessing, is no more than the pay given to a prostitute (cf. 2:7, 12).[101] Consequently, Israel's celebrations will be short-lived. Yahweh's judgment will remove material signs of prosperity (cf. 2:7), and the produce of threshing-floors and winepresses will not meet the people's needs. The term translated *fail* can also mean 'deceive', probably referring to the self-deception that material blessings are a sign of divine favour.

3–5. In verse 3, judgment is further linked with exile. *Remain* translates *yāšab* ('to live, dwell'), which occurs in Deuteronomy in connection with occupying the land (e.g. Deut. 12:29; 17:14; 19:1).

---

99. The opening expression in the MT is, literally, 'do not rejoice to rejoicing'. Following the LXX, 'to' is often emended to repeat 'do not' (cf. NIV, NRSV, ESV). Alternatively, the repetition may indicate exuberant rejoicing (Macintosh 1997: 337).

100. Garrett's suggestion (1997: 189–190) that this refers to a failed harvest prefiguring judgment seems less likely.

101. This may suggest having sex on threshing-floors (Andersen and Freedman 1980: 523; Hubbard 1989: 156), which may have become significant within the fertility cult.

This is, though, God's land, and the people may live in it only for as long as they are obedient to him (e.g. Deut. 11:31–32; 30:20); the consequence of sin is, therefore, expulsion from it. Exile in Assyria is again viewed metaphorically as a return (*šûb*) to Egypt (cf. 8:13). There is also wordplay using similar-sounding terms: instead of continuing to dwell (*yāšab*) in the land, they will return (*šûb*) to a place of foreign oppression.

Eating *unclean food* may be ironic: the people have defiled the land and its produce and so will be exiled to Assyria, where all food is unclean (Garrett 1997: 191). Or it may link with verse 4 and relate to the people's inability to bring acceptable offerings (cf. 8:13) (Dearman 2010: 238–239; Moon 2018: 157). They have failed to do so in the land God has given and so they will be removed to a place where such sacrifices cannot be offered. In both cases, the punishment corresponds to the crime. Verse 4 notes two kinds of offering – drink offerings of wine (cf. Num. 28:7; 2 Sam. 23:16) and animal sacrifices – though these probably represent the whole sacrificial system, which will not be effective in exile.

The bread of mourners suggests food associated with death, and so considered unclean.[102] It may also include an oblique reference to the exile as a form of national death (cf. 6:2) (Dearman 2010: 239). In exile, food will only be to sustain life:[103] it will not be acceptable for offerings and will not enter Yahweh's house (*bêt yhwh*). *Bêt yhwh* is the same expression as in 8:1. It may refer to the temple (cf. NIV), though in a passage applied to Ephraim it seems better to take it, as in 8:1, as a reference to the land of Israel (Dearman 2010: 240; Moon 2018: 157).[104] The people in exile will be cut off from the land, and so from opportunities to offer appropriate sacrifices. This is

---

102. Andersen and Freedman (1980: 526) suggest that the term translated *mourners* may indicate a pagan deity and that this is bread offered to idols.

103. The term used here, *nepeš*, may be translated 'throat, neck', hence 'hunger' (NRSV, ESV); more usually it refers to a 'living being' (cf. Gen. 2:7), and 'their *nepeš*' could mean 'their lives', i.e. 'to keep them alive', or simply *themselves* (NIV).

104. Macintosh (1997: 343) sees this as part of a later redaction.

further highlighted in verse 5, where the reference may be to the impossibility of the general observance of festivals (cf. NIV). The term, though, is singular, so may relate more specifically to the feast of Tabernacles (cf. 12:9).

6. Instead of celebrations, the people will face disaster. When the Babylonians invaded Judah, people fled to Egypt, including to Memphis (Jer. 44:1). And, given the false confidence placed in Egypt, it is likely that Israelites might flee there to escape the destruction of an Assyrian invasion. However, they will be gathered up and will die there, among its graveyards, which include the significant burial ground at Saqqara. Joseph did not want his bones left in Egypt (Gen. 50:25), but that will be Israel's fate. And what remains in Israel, including their tents and the silver they treasure, perhaps a reference to idols (cf. 2:8; 8:4), will become overgrown. The pairing of *briers* (*qimmôš*) and *thorns* (*ḥôaḥ*) also occurs in Isaiah 34:13 to describe once-occupied land that has become desolate and uninhabitable.

7–9. Verse 7 begins straightforwardly, with a further announcement of divine judgment. The repeated verb is in the perfect tense, indicating that these days 'have come' (NRSV, ESV). This is an example of the 'prophetic perfect', where imminent events (cf. NIV) are referred to as though they have already occurred. The repetition of *days* here may correspond to the repetition of *day* in verse 5, suggesting that celebration will give way to judgment (Andersen and Freedman 1980: 532). The parallel of 'recompense' and 'punishment' (NRSV, ESV) indicates that that judgment is wholly deserved. The next phrase, *Let Israel know*, is sometimes emended to 'Israel cries' (NRSV; cf. Wolff 1974: 150; Stuart 1987: 139–140), though that seems unnecessary. *Let Israel know* probably relates to the previous announcement: Israel will understand that the days of judgment are upon them (Mays 1969: 128; Hubbard 1989: 158; Moon 2018: 155). Andersen and Freedman (1980: 515) link it with what follows in verse 9, and place the reference to prophets in parentheses, though that seems less likely.

The NIV reverses the order of the remaining two parts of verse 7. The next part in the MT translates literally as 'the prophet (is) foolish; the man of the spirit (is) mad'. In 4:5, Hosea condemns prophets alongside priests, and this might continue that condemnation of prophets who remain oblivious to coming judgment (Dearman 2010: 243–244; Ben Zvi 2005: 199). Odell (1996) regards all references to prophets in Hosea as negative; however, her arguments are not convincing, and several texts appear to regard the prophetic role positively (6:5; 9:8; 12:10, 13). It seems more likely, therefore, that 9:7 reflects the words of the people or religious leaders who are attacking Hosea (Mays 1969: 129; Wolff 1974: 156–157; Andersen and Freedman 1980: 532; Seow 1982: 221; Hubbard 1989: 158–159; Achtemeier 1996: 77–78). The parallel expressions 'prophet' and 'man of the spirit' emphasize the close link between the Spirit and prophetic inspiration.[105] The characterization of prophets as mad is evident elsewhere (cf. 2 Kgs 9:11; Jer. 29:26) and may be related both to the strange behaviour that sometimes accompanied their message[106] and to its frequently unacceptable content. The sign-act of Hosea's relationship with Gomer and his announcement of impending doom both fit this category. The rest of verse 7 may continue the people's criticism of Hosea (Moon 2018: 155), though, more likely, it gives the reason for their reaction. It is their great sin (*ʿāwōn*),[107] and their great hostility towards Yahweh, that results also in hostility towards the one who reminds them of their true condition (Wolff 1974: 157; Stuart 1987: 146; Hubbard 1989: 159).

The MT of verse 8 reads: 'Ephraim watches/stands guard with my God, the prophet (is) a fowler's snare over all his ways, hostility (is) in the house of his God.' Moon (2018: 155, 158) takes this as a continuation of the words of Hosea's opponents, who exalt Ephraim's position and accuse Hosea of causing trouble. Macintosh (1997: 354–355) regards 'prophet' as a gloss and takes 'to stand guard' in the sense of 'confront': 'Ephraim stands in confrontation with my God.' It seems better, though, to link 'prophet' with watchman (cf. Ezek. 3:17; 33:7): *The prophet, along with my God, is the watchman over Ephraim* (NIV; cf. NRSV, ESV; Hubbard 1989: 159–160;

---

105. Num. 11:25–29; 24:2–3; 1 Sam. 10:6; 19:20; 2 Sam. 23:2; Neh. 9:30; Ezek. 2:2; 11:5; Zech. 7:12.

106. Isa. 20:1–6; Jer. 13:1–11; 19:10–13; 27:1–7; Ezek. 4; 5:1–4; 12:1–16.

107. The same term (*ʿāwōn*) occurs in 4:8; 5:5; 7:1; 8:13; 9:9; 10:10; 12:8; 13:12; 14:1–2.

Dearman 2010: 236). This sets out a positive view of what a true prophet, like Hosea, should be: standing with God and watching over the people. The second part of the verse may refer to Ephraim (cf. Macintosh 1997: 354–355). 'A fowler's snare' (NRSV, ESV) may indicate coming judgment (cf. 7:12), and *hostility*, repeated from 9:7, may indicate Yahweh's hostility towards Israel or Israel's hostility towards God. More likely, though, both refer to the continuing opposition to the prophet as he seeks to fulfil his God-given calling. *The house of his God* should be understood as a reference to the land of Israel (cf. 8:1; 9:4). The prophet is rejected in the very place where God's word should be welcomed, giving a further indication that Israel is unfit to remain in the land.

Verse 9 re-emphasizes the depths of Israel's corruption. The *days of Gibeah* probably refers to the incident of the Levite's concubine in Judges 19. The conclusion there is that 'Such a thing has never been seen or done, not since the day the Israelites came up out of Egypt' (Judg. 19:30), and, because the tribe of Benjamin stood by the perpetrators of the crime, it resulted in its near annihilation (Judg. 20).[108] Israel's sin will have similar consequences. The reference to Gibeah may also be linked to 5:8, which is probably set in the context of the Syro-Ephraimite war and so also relates to internecine conflict. And if there is a link between Hosea and the Levites,[109] the mistreatment of the Levite might have resonated with Hosea's own experience. The final lines of verse 9 repeat the statement in 8:13 and point again to the inevitability of divine punishment.

Meaning
This section continues the theme of judgment on an unfaithful people. Israel claims to know God (8:2) and goes through the

---

108. The statement in Judg. 19:30 comes after the events at Gibeah, but
    before the reprisals against Benjamin (Judg. 20), and it is unlikely that
    those reprisals are its primary focus (contra Arnold 1989: 452–454).
    However, the allusion to the whole incident raises the issue of
    internecine conflict (Andersen and Freedman 1980: 534).
109. See above, p. 14.

motions of religious observance. The people may believe they are doing what God requires, but it is empty ritual. Israel has been called into a covenant relationship with Yahweh (8:1) which should be expressed in faithful obedience. Yet they do not acknowledge him in their political decisions, they look to other things for security and their worship is tainted with idolatry. In all this they have lost sight of the God who made them, they disregard his requirements and they reject his messages of correction. As a result, they are unfit to live in the land, here referred to as Yahweh's *house*, and will be removed to a place of exile, where festivals will no longer be celebrated and sacrifices no longer offered. These privations correspond to the discipline referred to earlier (cf. 2:11; 3:4). The aim there, however, is eventual restoration, and although 8:1 – 9:9 focuses primarily on judgment, further passages will refer again to the hope of return and renewal.

Going through the motions of worship, losing sight of God as the source of blessing, putting trust in other things, excluding God from decisions and disregarding his requirements in everyday life are not limited to Israel. Within the Christian community there is the same danger of moving God to the sidelines, of forgetting who he is, what he has done and what the proper response to him should be. And sometimes, being given up to the choices they make and having a glimpse of life without God's provision may be necessary to bring wanderers to their senses. However, such is the love of God in Christ that he always provides a way back.

F. Unfulfilled promise (9:10 – 10:15)

Context

This section contains a series of examples with a common theme: Israel's early but unfulfilled promise (cf. 2:15). The view of Israel's past, though, is not all positive, and further episodes from Israel's history are invoked to demonstrate that the current apostasy is not new.

The analysis adopted here divides these verses into three sections (9:10–17; 10:1–10; 10:11–15). Many include 10:9–10 in the third section (Wolff 1974: 182; Andersen and Freedman 1980: 560; Eidevall 1996: 155; Garrett 1997: 212; Macintosh 1997: 383; Ben Zvi

2005: 205). While there are no compelling arguments either way, including the verses in the second section preserves the pattern of each beginning with a simile or metaphor (Hubbard 1989: 169; Dearman 2010: 258; Moon 2018: 169–170).

These sections include agricultural imagery, giving continuity with the harvest theme in 8:1 – 9:9, and they follow a similar rhetorical pattern: what Israel was and has become (though see the comment on 10:1), and the judgment that will follow. Other points of continuity with the previous section include further *pseudosorites* (9:11–12, 16; cf. comment on 8:7), and references to Israel's 'princes' (9:15, ESV; cf. 8:4), God's *house* (9:15; cf. 9:4, 8), multiplying altars (10:1; cf. 8:11), the doomed calf-idol (10:5; cf. 8:5) and sowing and reaping (10:12; cf. 8:7). There are links, too, to earlier parts of the book, with mention of Gilgal (9:15; cf. 4:15), Gibeah (10:9; cf. 9:9; 5:8) and the use of the derogatory term Beth Aven for Bethel (10:5; cf. 4:15).

Comment
i. Fruit becoming unfruitful (9:10–17)
This section has repeated elements. Verse 10 notes Israel's early promise followed by failure at Baal Peor. Judgment is then presented using a *pseudosorites* (vv. 11–12).[110] There is another reference to what Israel was (v. 13), followed by the prophet's interjection (v. 14). Verse 15 notes Israel's further failure at Gilgal, which is followed by judgment, again using a *pseudosorites* (v. 16). The passage ends with a second prophetic interjection (v. 17).

10. Yahweh *found* (*māṣāʾ*) Israel *like . . . grapes in the desert*, and the people's ancestors who came out of Egypt were like 'early figs' (*bikkûrâ*). The desert is an unlikely place to come across choice fruit but it would be a pleasant surprise for a traveller who found it. For Hosea (as for Jeremiah) the desert is where Israel's relationship with Yahweh began, and this suggests that in those days Israel was a source of delight to Yahweh (cf. 2:15).[111] *Bikkûrâ* is related to *běkōr* ('firstborn'), which is also applied to Israel (Exod. 4:22) (Ben Zvi

---

110. See above, p. 123.

111. See above, pp. 27–28; cf. Eidevall 1996: 149–150.

2005: 200; Dearman 2010: 251). This may be a further allusion to Israel's early status, and it provides a link to 11:1–11. That delight, though, soon turned to anger.

The reference to Baal Peor recalls the incident in Numbers 25:1–9, when Israelite men became involved in sexual immorality (*zānâ*) with Moabite women and were seduced into worshipping the 'Baal of Peor'. This had immediate consequences, resulting in the deaths of thousands of Israelites, and had also a lasting impact (Josh. 22:17). There 'they dedicated [*nāzar*] themselves to shame [*bōšet*]' (MT). 'Shame' is sometimes associated with Baal (cf. Jer. 11:13), and Baal worship is clearly in view here (cf. NIV: *they consecrated themselves to that shameful idol*). *Nāzar* is also used in connection with those set apart as Nazirites by making a vow (Num. 6:1–21), and Israel's dedication to Baal may have involved a specific cultic act by which the people 'yoked themselves to the Baal of Peor' (Num. 25:3). Consequently, Israel became 'like the one they loved' (so NIV, NRSV, ESV; Macintosh 1997: 360; Dearman 2010: 250; Moon 2018: 161). The MT text could also be repointed to read 'like their lover' (Mays 1969: 131; Stuart 1987: 148), or, possibly, 'like the one who loved them' (Andersen and Freedman 1980: 536; Hubbard 1989: 165), without substantially changing the meaning. All emphasize the same problem: Israel's continuing involvement with Baal results in the people sharing his detestable qualities. The references to Baal and *zānâ* in Numbers 25 have clear resonance in Hosea's day, indicating that Israel's current spiritual condition is nothing new and that drastic action (cf. Num. 25:7–8) is necessary to avert an even greater catastrophe.

11–12. *Glory* (v. 11) contrasts with shame (v. 10). It may refer to Ephraim's honoured status, or to its strength, which may be related to its population (cf. vv. 11b–12a) (Wolff 1974: 166; Hubbard 1989: 165; Macintosh 1997: 365–367). This will quickly disappear. More likely, taken with 12b and in contrast to the shame associated with Baal, *glory* should be taken to refer to Yahweh and his presence among the people (Andersen and Freedman 1980: 542; Garrett 1997: 200; Dearman 2010: 252). Because of Israel's sin, Yahweh will fly away from them (cf. 5:6, 15; Ezek. 10:18–19).

The people attributed fertility to Baal. Yahweh's withdrawal will leave them in no doubt where fertility really lies. This has already been emphasized in relation to crops (e.g. 8:7; 9:2; cf. 2:9). Here it is seen in the inability to have children. This is highlighted in a *pseudosorites* in verses 11b–12a. There will be no birth, pregnancy or conception; and even if children should be born and brought up, parents will be bereaved of them (cf. v. 16b). Yahweh's withdrawal in 12b echoes 11a and with the *pseudosorites* forms a chiasm. The people experience woe because of the departure of the one who is the true source of their life.

13–14. The second part of verse 13 points to Ephraim's impending fate: the nation's children will be brought to *the slayer*. This may continue the idea of the deaths of children and the corresponding infertility of the nation. Andersen and Freedman (1980: 538; cf. Hubbard 1989: 168) see a further reference to child sacrifice (though see on 4:2). More likely, it is a wider reference to the deaths of Ephraim's people at the hands of Assyria, which will result in the loss of hope for future generations.

The first part of the verse is less clear. It points again to Ephraim's early potential: planted in a meadow. A difficulty is the translation of *ṣôr*. This usually refers to Tyre (as NIV) and suggests a comparison (Garrett 1997: 201; Moon 2018: 161): Ephraim's beginnings had all the promise exhibited by Tyre (cf. Isa. 23:8; Zech. 9:3), but now, like Tyre, they face destruction. It may be better, though, to link *ṣôr* with an Arabic term for 'palm tree' (as NRSV, ESV; cf. Hubbard 1989: 166; Macintosh 1997: 370; Ben Zvi 2005: 200; Dearman 2010: 250). Ephraim was planted in a fertile place, but, despite Yahweh's care, the nation has become unfruitful (cf. Isa. 5:1–4).[112] The picture of fertile beginnings contrasts starkly with the nation's infertility and its imminent demise.

In verse 14, the prophet speaks. Reference to wombs that miscarry and dry breasts echoes the theme of infertility and contrasts with the promise of fruitfulness made to Joseph, Ephraim's father (Gen. 49:25). The prophet's interjection may subvert a common prayer for fertility. Its significance, though, is not clear. Some see it

---

112. Following the LXX, some suggest a parallel with the second part of the verse: 'Ephraim . . . has made his sons a hunter's prey' (Mays 1969: 131; cf. Wolff 1974: 160), though this is unnecessary.

as intercession: better for children not to be born than that they
face the horrors to come (Mays 1969: 134–135; Wolff 1974: 166;
Macintosh 1997: 372; Moon 2018: 164). Others see it as a prayer
against Israel (Andersen and Freedman 1980: 544; Stuart 1987: 153),
agreeing with the divine pronouncement.

15. The verse begins with a verbless sentence: 'all their evil, in
Gilgal'. This continues the theme of unfulfilled promise. At Gilgal,
Israel first ate the fruit of the land, and celebrated the Passover as
an indication of what was a new beginning (Josh. 5:10–12). However, in Hosea's day Gilgal was linked with Bethel as a centre of
corrupt worship (4:15; cf. 12:11), and there may have been other
recent events associated with Gilgal that are unknown to us. It was
also the place where Israel's first king, Saul, was anointed and
rejected (1 Sam. 11:14–15; 15:10–23), and the reference to rebellious
leaders may be linked with that (cf. 13:11). Hosea may have seen
Saul as representative of the failed northern monarchy (Ben Zvi
2005: 202). Whether or not that was the case, for Hosea, disobedient
rulers continue to play a significant part in the nation's troubles.
And it may be that Gilgal, like Adam (6:7), was linked with political
intrigue and rebellion.

Whatever the precise crimes associated with Gilgal, their effect
is tragic: *I hated them* and *I will no longer love* [*āhab*] *them*. The relationship that began well has now broken down. As a result, the people
will be expelled from Yahweh's *house*, which, as in 9:8 (cf. 8:1; 9:4),
refers to the land of Israel. As well as this being a stark statement
of judgment, there may be allusions here to the marriage metaphor
in the first part of the book. The term *śānā'* ('to hate') is used in the
context of marriage breakdown (Deut. 21:15–17; 22:13; 24:3) and
may include the wife being sent out of the husband's house (Deut.
24:3). *Gāraš* ('to drive out') may also mean 'to divorce' (Lev. 21:7,
14; 22:13) (Dearman 2010: 256–257). Also, although the Hebrew
term is different, *I will no longer love them* echoes the name Lo-
Ruhamah (1:6). This emphasis on judgment should not be watered
down. Nevertheless, there is hope that that name will be reversed,
that the relationship will be restored, and that Yahweh will again
show love to his people (2:23; 3:1; 14:4).

16–17. Verse 16 repeats the judgment of infertility and includes
ironic wordplay on the similarity of the name Ephraim to *fruit*

(*pĕrî*).[113] The idea of a withered root suggests a return to an agricultural metaphor. The *pseudosorites* emphasizes that the nation will be barren, but even if children are born, Yahweh will kill them. The reference to *cherished* [*maḥmād*] *offspring* may correspond to their *treasures* [*maḥmād*] *of silver* (9:6). By setting their affections on the wrong things, the people will lose what is truly precious to them.

Verse 17 is a further prophetic interjection, reiterating earlier themes. Despite calls for them to listen (e.g. 4:1; 5:1), the people and its leaders have not obeyed Yahweh; so, because they have rejected him and his word, he will reject them (cf. 4:6). The result, as noted already several times, will be expulsion from God's land. They have strayed (*nādad*) from Yahweh (7:13), so now they will be taken into exile and will 'wander' (*nādad*) among the nations.

ii. A vine overrun by thorns and thistles (10:1–10)

1–2. Here Israel is referred to as a *spreading* [*bôqēq*] *vine*. The meaning of *bôqēq* is debated. It may mean 'laid waste' (e.g. Nah. 2:2), and several commentators describe Israel here as a 'damaged vine' (Garrett 1997: 204; Macintosh 1997: 383–384; Moon 2018: 166). However, taken with the second part of the verse, which suggests increase, the sense seems to indicate past fruitfulness, and some link it instead with an Arabic term indicating fertility (cf. LXX; see also NIV, NRSV, ESV; Wolff 1974: 170; Andersen and Freedman 1980: 547; Hubbard 1989: 170–171; Dearman 2010: 258). It is possible, though, that there is an intentional double meaning (Stuart 1987: 157; Ben Zvi 2005: 207; Lim and Castelo 2015: 162): Israel was fruitful but, because of its misuse of divine blessing, it is also profoundly damaged. In the next phrase, the verb, *šāwā*, means 'to be like, suitable', suggesting the translation 'fruit suitable for him [*lô*]' (Stuart 1987: 157; Ben Zvi 2005: 207; Moon 2018: 166). This could be interpreted negatively or positively: a damaged vine producing damaged fruit or a luxuriant vine producing abundant fruit. Some take it instead to mean 'to yield', and *lô* is translated as 'his/its' (NRSV, ESV) or *for himself* (NIV). This suggests that Israel used the

---

113. See above, p. 23.

fruit for its own purposes, which may include furtherance of the Baal cult.

Whatever the precise translation of the first part of the verse, the second part gives the overall sense of the indictment: increased fruit led to a corresponding increase in altars (cf. 8:11), and the more prosperous the land, the more ornate the sacred stones. Altars and sacred stones or pillars could feature in the legitimate worship of Yahweh (see on 3:4). In this context, however, they are associated with Baal (cf. v. 2): the more Yahweh prospered them, the more they lavished on false worship.

Verse 2 notes that the people's sin is deep-seated; it stems from their hearts (cf. Deut. 6:5; 29:18). Most translations take *ḥālaq* from a root meaning 'to be smooth or slippery' and refer to hearts that are false or deceitful (NIV, NRSV, ESV). Ben Zvi (2005: 209) suggests a pun relating to Jacob, who was both 'smooth' (Gen. 27:11) and duplicitous. Consequently, the people must bear their guilt and the punishment it brings. This includes breaking down the altars and sacred stones that have become the object of Israel's affection.[114]

3–4. In verse 3, the prophet repeats the words of the people. *King* (*melek*) here may refer to Yahweh, with the statement reflecting their unwillingness to recognize Yahweh and their turning instead to Baal (Andersen and Freedman 1980: 553; Achtemeier 1996: 85–86). However, in Hosea, *melek* generally appears in the context of political leadership, and so more likely refers to the human monarch. *Then* (NIV) is better translated 'now' (NRSV, ESV), and the reference to having no king could suggest that this was written after the fall of Samaria. It may be better, though, to take it as anticipating coming judgment, which would include living without a king (3:4; cf. 10:7, 15; 13:10–11). As they experience divine judgment the people will become painfully aware of their failure to 'fear' (*yārē'*) Yahweh, a term which includes awe and reverence and which is closely associated with obedience to Israel's covenant obligations (e.g. Deut. 6:2; 10:12–13; 17:19; 31:12; cf. Hos. 4:6; 8:12). They will be equally aware of the failure of their kings to protect

---

114. The term here usually refers to breaking the neck of an animal (Exod. 13:13; Deut. 21:4; Isa. 66:3).

them from their enemies, both militarily and by giving the spiritual leadership that would have ensured God's continued blessing.

In verse 4, the prophet resumes his indictment. The catalogue of sins may be an ironic answer to the question *what could [the king] do for us?* (Mays 1969: 140; Stuart 1987: 161; Macintosh 1997: 395). However, the switch in person from 'he' to 'they' suggests that this is now aimed at the people and gives examples of the duplicity noted in verse 2. The opening phrase reads literally, 'they speak words' (cf. NIV, *They make many promises*; see Dearman 2010: 258), suggesting that what the people say is empty. This is elaborated in what follows: 'swearing falsely, making covenants'. This may relate to the people's covenant relationship with Yahweh, which they show no intention of honouring. It may also have a wider application – to relationships within society, perhaps between king and people, to international treaties, and possibly to their unworthy commitment to other gods. The result is dysfunction within society. The NIV's *lawsuits* (cf. NRSV) translates *mišpāṭ* ('justice, judgment'). 'Justice' fits the context better. What should be a hallmark of the nation has become corrupted. The imagery is of fields that have been ploughed in preparation for sowing, but what emerges is poisonous weeds.

5–6. References to the king (v. 3) lead to further mention of the calf-idol. The plural (MT) may be a plural of 'majesty', indicating the reverence given to the calf, or it may refer more generally to the calf-cult. The calf appears to have a close association with Israel's monarchy[115] and, as the references to Samaria here and in 8:5 indicate, with the nation as a whole. It was situated at Bethel, which is again referred to derogatively as Beth Aven. Here we see the calf-idol being taken as spoil to Assyria, and the general understanding is that the inhabitants of Samaria fear for its fate (cf. NIV; Stuart 1987: 161–162; Hubbard 1989: 174–175; Macintosh 1997: 400–401; Dearman 2010: 265; Moon 2018: 171).[116] *Fear (gûr)*, though, may also

---

115. See above, p. 121 n. 87.

116. 'Inhabitant' is singular but is better understood collectively (NIV: *The people who live in Samaria*). Some see 'Resident/Inhabitant of Samaria' as a title for the calf (Andersen and Freedman 1980: 556; Hubbard 1989: 174).

suggest the people's reverence for the calf (Pss 22:23; 33:8) (Wolff 1974: 175; Garrett 1997: 209) which now proves futile. The reference to 'mourning' probably further illustrates the concern of the people. Some, though, take it with *rejoiced* (*gîl*, NIV) to suggest cultic activities associated with Baal worship which will no longer be possible (Moon 2018: 171). Others read 'to be distressed' instead of 'to rejoice' (cf. NRSV; Mays 1969: 138; Andersen and Freedman 1980: 556; Hubbard 1989: 174; Macintosh 1997: 399) and take mourning and distress as the response to the loss of the calf. *Priests* (NIV) translates *kōmer*, which in the Old Testament refers to those who lead idolatrous worship (cf. 2 Kgs 23:5; Zeph. 1:4). If there is a close connection between Hosea and Levites,[117] it may allude to non-levitical priests (Dearman 2010: 265).

Though the precise translation here is elusive, the emphasis on reverence for the calf-idol, which has been at the centre of Israel's idolatrous worship (cf. 8:5), is clear. That reverence is further highlighted in what may be an ironic reference to the calf's 'glory' (NIV: *splendour*). In 9:11, it was noted that Israel's glory, probably referring to Yahweh's presence among the people, would be removed. Now, the calf-idol, to which the people looked instead of acknowledging Yahweh, will also depart (*gālâ*). The language here is reminiscent of 1 Samuel 4:21–22 where, following the capture of the ark by the Philistines, Phineas's wife names her child 'Ichabod', declaring, 'The Glory has departed from Israel.'[118] The term *gālâ* may also be translated 'to go into exile' (NIV; see e.g. Isa. 5:13; Amos 5:5; 6:7; 7:11). Like the idol they worship, the people will also soon be taken into exile in Assyria. There may also be wordplay here between the similar-sounding words *gālâ* and *gîl*.

The calf, unable to save itself, will be taken to Assyria as tribute for *the great king* (v. 6; cf. 5:13), a reference to either Shalmaneser V or Sargon II.[119] Ironically, the thing in which the nation gloried will bring only national disgrace and humiliation. *Foreign alliances* (NIV) translates *'ēṣâ* ('plan, advice'), but this is too restrictive. Israel's

---

117. See above, p. 14.

118. *Kābôd* ('glory') and *gālâ* ('to depart') occur in both passages.

119. See above, p. 4.

plans included seeking foreign alliances, and these have brought international humiliation (cf. 8:8), but its internal political intrigues and the hostility between north and south have also brought disgrace. Another possibility is to take *'ēṣâ* to mean 'tree' (cf. Jer. 6:6) and to see it as a further reference to the calf: however ornate, the calf is nothing more than a piece of wood (Andersen and Freedman 1980: 558; Hubbard 1989: 175). Some make the link with the calf clearer and emend the MT to read 'his idol' (NRSV, ESV; Mays 1969: 138). Whatever the precise translation, this emphasizes that Israel's confidence in things other than Yahweh will come to nothing and result only in shame.

7–8. Some interpret *Samaria's king* (v. 7) as the calf-idol (cf. v. 3) (Mays 1969: 142; Andersen and Freedman 1980: 558; Hubbard 1989: 175). It seems more likely, though, that it is a reference to the human king (Stuart 1987: 162–163; Macintosh 1997: 407–408; Ben Zvi 2005: 217; Dearman 2010: 266–267) who, like the idol with which he was closely associated, will perish. *Twig* (NIV) translates *qeṣep*. This usually refers to divine anger, though here it is widely viewed either as a small piece of wood, carried helplessly by the current, or as the foam on the water that quickly disappears.[120]

Verse 8 returns to the Baal cult and signals the destruction of Bethel, here mockingly referred to as Aven (NIV mg.; cf. 4:15; 10:5).[121] Judgment is directed particularly at the *high places* (*bāmôt*), referring to the altars in and around Bethel where false worship, including possible fertility rites, took place (see on 4:13). These are described as *the sin of Israel*, emphasizing their central place in the nation's corrupt practices, and they will be destroyed. Their being overrun by *thorns and thistles* indicates neglect and dereliction (cf. 9:6). That specific pairing, though, occurs only here and as part of the cursing of the ground following Adam's sin (Gen. 3:18). There

---

120. A similar term in Joel 1:7 refers to a strip of wood; see also LXX; Mays 1969: 138; Hubbard 1989: 175; Garrett 1997: 211–212. 'Wrath' may be linked to 'boiling' or 'bubbling', hence the translation 'foam'; see also Macintosh 1997: 406–407; Ben Zvi 2005: 213; Dearman 2010: 259; Moon 2018: 167.

121. The same term (*'āwen*) refers to 'evil, sin' in 6:8; 12:11.

is a close relationship between that curse and the return to chaos resulting from the undoing of creation (cf. 4:3) (cf. Routledge 2014b), and because of its sin, the nation will feel the impact of both.

The final part of the verse indicates despair. In the face of impending judgment, the people cry out for the mountains and hills to fall and cover them (cf. Luke 23:30; Rev. 6:16), either to hide the shame of their actions or to avoid the horrors of coming judgment.

9–10. In verse 9, Hosea returns to the theme of the sin of Gibeah (cf. 9:9). The name 'Gibeah' (*gibʿâ*) means 'hill', and this may provide an intentional link with verse 8 (Hubbard 1989: 176). *There you have remained* translates 'they stood there', which may allude to the Benjamites who stood alongside the perpetrators of the crime against the Levite's concubine (Judg. 20:13–16). More probably it indicates the adoption of the same sinful mindset that characterized the people of Gibeah and Benjamin and persists to the present day (cf. NIV, NRSV). The final part of the verse in the MT reads: 'war will not overtake the evildoers [*běnê ʿalwâ*;[122] literally, 'children of wickedness'] in Gibeah'. As a simple statement (Sweeney 2000: 107–108; Lim and Castelo 2015: 165) this does not fit the context of judgment in Hosea, or Judges 20. Consequently, it is usually taken as a question: *Will not war . . . overtake [them]?* (NIV, NRSV; Mays 1969: 143; Dearman 2010: 259; Moon 2018: 167); though it may be understood rhetorically, 'surely war will overtake them' (Wolff 1974: 179; Macintosh 1997: 411), or ironically: '(they think that) war will not overtake them' (Garrett 1997: 213). In the MT, 'evildoers' is included in verse 9 (NIV, ESV; Wolff 1974: 178; Macintosh 1997: 411; Lim and Castelo 2015: 165; Moon 2018: 167). The possible reference to war against evildoers may, further, recall the battle against the perpetrators of evil (*běnê bělîyaʿal*) in Judges 19:22; 20:13 (Sweeney 2000: 108; Lim and Castelo 2015: 165). This possible allusion is less clear if 'evildoers' is read with verse 10 (NRSV; Mays 1969: 143; Garrett 1997: 313; Dearman 2010: 259), though the sense of the passage remains: evildoers will be punished.

---

122. Most see *ʿalwâ* (MT) as a copyist's error and read instead *ʿawlâ* ('injustice, wickedness') (cf. 10:13).

The NIV translation *When I please* (v. 10) reflects the MT *bě'awwātî* (cf. ESV; Macintosh 1997: 414; Moon 2018: 167). The LXX reads instead, 'I have come', suggesting the emended term *bā'tî* (cf. NRSV; Andersen and Freedman 1980: 560; Stuart 1987: 165; Hubbard 1989: 178; Garrett 1997: 213; Dearman 2010: 259). The main emphasis, though, is clear. Just as Benjamin was punished by the tribes of Israel, so now Yahweh will gather the nations against Israel. The plural appropriately describes the Assyrian army, which included people from different nations.

The use of the term *yāsar* ('to discipline, teach'; cf. 7:12) indicates that the purpose of Yahweh's action is corrective. The second verb, *'āsar* ('to bind'), sounds similar. It emphasizes that the people are bound by their iniquity and face inevitable judgment. The *double sin* may be the crime historically associated with Gibeah and the present iniquity, which includes engaging in internecine conflict against Judah.

iii. A trained heifer ploughing wickedness (10:11–15)

11–12. The contrast between past obedience and present sin continues in a further metaphor. The first part of verse 11 translates as 'Ephraim, a trained heifer, loving to thresh'. The first finite verb in the MT (*'ābar*) is past tense, suggesting, again, a contrast between an idealized past, in which Israel is portrayed as an animal prepared and willing to thresh grain (cf. NRSV, ESV), and the nation's present condition as a *stubborn heifer* (4:16). *Heifer* translates *'eglâ*, the same term used in 10:5 for the calf-idol. This may reflect the close connection between the calf-idol and the nation, and this, too, contrasts with Israel's earlier faithfulness to Yahweh. The verb *'ābar* means 'to pass by'. The NIV emends the MT to read: 'put a yoke on' (Mays 1969: 144; Stuart 1987: 165; Garrett 1997: 214). Some interpret 'pass by' in the sense of 'to spare' (NRSV, ESV), suggesting that in the early days Israel's compliance made a yoke unnecessary. However, in the context of the reference to the heifer's *'fair* neck', it may be better understood as taking note of Israel's early potential (Wolff 1974: 179; Eidevall 1996: 160; Macintosh 1997: 417–418; Lim and Castelo 2015: 165; Moon 2018: 175).

The second part of verse 11 refers to Yahweh harnessing (*rākab*) Ephraim for a more arduous role. Threshing was a relatively easy task, and the animal was allowed to eat grain as it worked (Deut. 25:4). Going forward, Israel and Judah will be called upon to plough and harrow, to break up and flatten the hard ground, in preparation for planting seeds. This change may reflect Israel's current sinful condition, which requires increased discipline and correction (cf. 4:16; Jer. 31:18) (Hubbard 1989: 180–181; Achtemeier 1996: 90). More likely, this still refers to Israel's past, and to the increased responsibility of life in the Promised Land (Wolff 1974: 185; Emmerson 1984: 84; Eidevall 1996: 160–161; Macintosh 1997: 421–422; Moon 2018: 175). The contrast with those early expectations appears in verse 13. Some take *Judah* as part of the later redaction (Mays 1969: 144; Emmerson 1984: 83–86; Macintosh 1997: 418–419).[123] In relation to the nation's early history, though, a reference to both kingdoms is appropriate (Wolff 1974: 185; Dearman 2010: 271; Moon 2018: 176).

Verse 12 continues the theme of breaking up ground ready for sowing and reaping, though with the order reversed. The Hebrew expression suggests preparing ground that has not yet been cultivated, reinforcing the view that this reflects Israel's new life in the Promised Land. The key qualities expected of Israel are *righteousness* (*ṣĕdāqâ*) and *unfailing love* (*ḥesed*). This pairing also occurs in the list of bridal gifts in 2:19 and reflects the essence of Israel's covenant relationship with Yahweh. These go hand in hand with 'seeking Yahweh', which indicates dependence on him rather than on Baal. And, just as ploughing, sowing and reaping is futile without the divine provision of rain, as the people play their part Yahweh will respond by a corresponding blessing of *righteousness* (*ṣedeq*),[124] which includes justice and right behaviour within society and also salvation in the face of oppressive nations (cf. Isa. 45:8–9).

13–15. The first part of verse 13 continues the agricultural metaphor, emphasizing again how Israel, throughout its history, has failed to live up to early expectations (cf. 8:7). Instead of sowing

---

124. The terms *ṣedeq* and *ṣĕdāqâ* appear interchangeable; see above, p. 63 n. 49.

righteousness, they have ploughed *wickedness* (*reša'*);[125] instead of *ḥesed*, they have reaped *evil* ('*awlâ*); and instead of enjoying the land's good fruit, the people feed on *deception* (*kāḥaš*). This is a frequent theme for Hosea[126] and indicates an endemic problem of Israelite society. It includes the self-delusion of placing trust elsewhere than in Yahweh, and that is picked up in the next part of the verse.

The rest of the passage (vv. 13b–15) focuses on warfare. The nation is charged with putting trust in military might and in its own plans (v. 13b). This begins: 'because you have trusted in your way [*derek*]'. This may refer to Israel pursuing its own policies (Macintosh 1997: 425; cf. Dearman 2010: 270; Moon 2018: 174). Some, following the LXX, amend 'way' to 'chariots' (Wolff 1974: 181; Stuart 1987: 165–166), to correspond with *warriors*. Andersen and Freedman understand it in the sense of 'power, dominion' (1980: 569; cf. NIV, NRSV; Hubbard 1989: 183; Ben Zvi 2005: 222). This may relate to the rebellions against Assyria by Pekah and Hoshea,[127] both of which led to the severe reprisals noted in verse 14. Or it may be a more general indictment of what was a common problem for God's people: trust in their military capabilities and alliances rather than in Yahweh (cf. 1:5; 8:14; cf. Isa. 22:8–11; 31:1; Jer. 5:17).

As a result of the nation's preparations, war will come, and the fortresses in which the nation trusted will be destroyed (v. 14a). The horror of coming warfare is emphasized by likening it to the destruction of Beth Arbel by Shalman, which included the slaughter of mothers and children (v. 14b). This atrocity must have been well known in Hosea's day, but it is unknown to us. Beth Arbel may be a town in Gilead, east of the Jordan. Suggestions for the identity of Shalman include Shalmaneser III, who defeated Israel in the ninth century BC and is depicted receiving tribute from Jehu on the Black

---

125. *Planted* (NIV) translates *ḥāraš*, 'to plough' (NRSV); cf. v. 11. *Reša'* is contrasted with righteousness in Job 35:8; Pss 45:7; 125:3; Ezek. 33:12.

126. *Kāḥaš* refers to political treachery (7:3) and *lies* (11:12). The verbal form is included in the general indictment of the nation (4:2) and refers to the failure of the crops that the people depend on (9:2). A related term, *kāzāb*, appears in 7:13; 12:1.

127. See above, pp. 3, 4.

Obelisk (841 BC; *COS* 2.269); and Salamanu, a Moabite ruler mentioned in Tiglath-Pileser III's Annals (*COS* 2.289). It is also possible that this refers to Shalmaneser V's reprisals against Hoshea (Moon 2018: 176–177; cf. Ben Zvi 2005: 219), though if it was part of the invasion culminating in the fall of Samaria, it must have taken place early in the campaign.

   While the precise details surrounding Beth Arbel are unclear, the horrors described are clear enough. So, too, is the warning that Bethel will face the same fate (v. 15a). In the MT the verbs are past tense and are generally viewed as prophetic perfects (cf. LXX; Hubbard 1989: 184; Macintosh 1997: 431). Judgment on Bethel is because of its 'great wickedness' (NRSV; *rā'â*). Israel's *wickedness* is a familiar theme (cf. 7:1–3; 9:15). Here, the reference to the cultic site of Bethel suggests that the primary focus is Baal worship (cf. 4:15; 10:5–6, 8) which, though centred on Bethel, infects the whole nation (cf. 10:8).[128] The loss of Israel's king (v. 15b) has been anticipated (10:3, 7) and here completes the picture of devastation. 'Dawn' (NRSV, ESV) was, traditionally, when battles began, and suggests the speed of the demise of king and nation.

Meaning

The simile and metaphors in 9:10 – 10:15 highlight Israel's early promise. They look back to the exodus, to where Yahweh's covenant relationship with Israel began, and note Israel's failure to live up to early expectations. Despite all Yahweh has done for them, instead of trusting him they put confidence in other things, including military power, political institutions and foreign alliances. And they persist in their devotion to other gods. The severity of divine judgment emphasizes the seriousness of sin. Judgment will result in the loss of the things that are dear to the people and which they depend on, including the fertility of the land, military strongholds and the calf-idol dedicated to Baal. The imminent Assyrian invasion will also bring about the deaths of precious offspring and put the future of the nation in jeopardy.

---

128. The LXX reads 'house of Israel' instead of Bethel, though there is no need to emend the MT.

The struggles of everyday life, when other things press in and become priorities, can lead to the loss of the early excitement of relationship with God. So, for example, Jesus similarly challenges the church at Ephesus: they have forsaken the love they had at first and need to return to the way things were (Rev. 2:4–5).

G. Divine commitment to a beloved but ungrateful child (11:1–11)

Context

Hosea 11:1–11 fits with the general pattern in the previous verses of Israel's unfulfilled calling. However, the imagery becomes more intense, and the portrayal of Israel as God's child reintroduces the tender familial relationship between God and his people. Consequently, it may be viewed as a separate section (Wolff 1974: 193; Stuart 1987: 176; Dearman 2010: 274). It complements the picture of God as husband and, as with that metaphor, also contains the hope of restoration beyond judgment. This passage also concludes the second major part of the book.

Comment

1–4. These verses point to Yahweh's love for Israel, whom he describes as *my son* (v. 1). Like the marriage metaphor, this emphasizes Yahweh's deep familial ties to his people,[129] and the further reference to Egypt again links this with the exodus (cf. Exod. 4:22; see also Jer. 31:9, 20). The description of Israel as a *child* (*na'ar*) suggests youth (cf. 2:15; Jer. 2:2) and points to Israel's vulnerability and dependence in those early days. The MT, 'from Egypt I called [*qāra'*] my son', is generally taken to indicate a divine summons to come *out of Egypt* (NIV, NRSV, ESV; cf. Stuart 1987: 174; Hubbard 1989: 187; Macintosh 1997: 436; Dearman 2010: 275; Moon 2018: 179). Alternatively, giving 'from Egypt' a temporal sense (cf. 12:9; 13:4) and taking *qāra'* with 'my son', this could mean 'from (the time he was in) Egypt I called (him) my son' (Andersen and Freedman 1980: 574). The former is

---

129. For a comparison between Israel's adoption and adoption in the ANE, see Melnyk 1993.

more likely, though a double meaning, linking deliverance from Egypt with election as Yahweh's son, may be intentional (Yee 1987: 217; Eidevall 1996: 168–169; Ben Zvi 2005: 233).

Matthew 2:15 quotes the end of verse 1 (*out of Egypt I called my son*) in relation to Jesus' flight to Egypt. Some link this with what was in the past regarded as a somewhat flexible use of Scripture by Matthew (McCasland 1961), though that view is no longer widely held. Others suggest that the text has intentional messianic significance (Sailhamer 2001; cf. Lim and Castelo 2015: 171–172). It is true that the call to sonship is linked with the Davidic king (cf. Ps. 2:7), and already by the eighth century BC David was associated with messianic hope (cf. Routledge 2008a: 281–282). However, it is unlikely that the description of Israel as Yahweh's son has direct messianic connotations. It is better to see this as typological: Matthew notes a correspondence between the narrative of Israel and the life and ministry of Jesus, and points to him as the ideal Israel (see on 6:2; see also McCartney and Enns 2001; Hamilton 2008; Kirk 2008; Kwakkel 2011). As indicated earlier, this correspondence is observed retrospectively and is not implicit within the original text.[130]

The beginning of verse 2 in the MT reads: 'the more *they* called to them, the more they went from *them* [literally, 'from their faces']'. The NRSV, following the LXX, emends this to: 'The more *I* called them, the more they went from *me*' (emphasis added; Mays 1969: 150; Wolff 1974: 190; Stuart 1987: 174; Dearman 2010: 275; Moon 2018: 179). If the MT is retained, it may refer to the call of prophets (cf. 9:8; 12:10) to the people (McComiskey 1998: 184). The NIV translates as a passive: *the more they were called, the more they went away from me*, without specifying from whom the call came. Others emend only the second part: 'the more they went from *me*'. Andersen and Freedman (1980: 577; cf. Hubbard 1989: 187) link this to the Baal Peor incident

---

130. LaSor (1978) takes 11:1 as *sensus plenior*, by which the fuller significance of the text is implicit in the prophecy; Garrett (1997: 220–222) takes a typological approach but suggests that Hosea recognized that his words had further significance; see also Beale 2012. A fully typological approach, though, makes finding a link with Matt. 2:15 from Hosea's side unnecessary.

(cf. 9:10), when Moabite women called to Israel and so drew them away from Yahweh. It is probably better to follow the LXX in both cases. The key role of the prophets in delivering Yahweh's message means that there is, perhaps, not much difference between the MT and the LXX in its practical outworking. However, the LXX preserves the intimacy of the relationship between father and child (which generally does not require an intermediary), and highlights Israel's perversity: the more Yahweh, as loving father, sought to draw the people to him, the more they turned away. This is evident particularly in their sacrificing to the *Baals* and burning incense to *images* (*pāsîl*), a term applied to false gods in Deuteronomy 7:5, 25; 12:3. The verbs suggest continuing activity: what happened at Baal Peor (cf. 9:10) has continued to the present day. Lim and Castelo (2015: 169–170) note a possible link between references to coming out of Egypt and worshipping images, and the opening of the Decalogue ('I am the LORD your God, who brought you out of Egypt, out of the land of slavery. You shall have no other gods before me . . . You shall not bow down to them or worship them' [Exod. 20:2–3, 5]). The language is not precise but, as in 4:2, the allusion may be intentional (cf. 4:2).[131]

Verse 3 begins emphatically: *It was I*, Yahweh not Baal, who cared for Ephraim, which here appears to represent the nation as a whole. *I . . . taught . . . to walk* (NIV) translates the unusual term *tirgaltî*, which is probably linked with *regel* ('foot'). It may suggest the idea of going ahead, and so of giving guidance (Andersen and Freedman 1980: 574; Eidevall 1996: 170–171; Dearman 2010: 275; cf. Hubbard 1989: 188). Several, though, support the picture of a father teaching his child to take his first steps (NRSV, ESV; Mays 1969: 150; Stuart 1987: 174; Garrett 1997: 223). The next phrase, *taking them by the arms* (cf. ESV; Stuart 1987: 174; Hubbard 1989: 188; Garrett 1997: 223), or, possibly, 'taking them up in my arms' (cf. NRSV; Mays 1969: 150; Wolff 1974: 191; Macintosh 1997: 441; Kakkanattu 2006: 52; Dearman 2010: 275; Moon 2018: 179), continues that theme. Reference to God's arm(s) indicates divine

---

131. Suggestions that Hosea may have had access to a different version of the Decalogue seem speculative.

protection (cf. Exod. 6:6; 15:16; Kakkanattu 2006: 53–54) and may suggest picking the child up when he stumbles. The reference to healing (*rāpā'*) might, further, suggest tending to cuts and bruises.[132] Healing may also point to the deliverance at the exodus and the experience of divine grace and protection in the desert (cf. Exod. 15:26), or, possibly, to forgiveness following the sin noted in verse 2 (cf. O'Kennedy 2001: 463–464). This also repeats the significant theme that, for all Yahweh's blessings, Israel does not *realise* (*yāda'*) what he has done (see on 2:8).

There is debate about whether verse 4 continues the parent–child metaphor or changes to the training of a farm animal (cf. 10:11). The latter is based on the MT, which includes *'ōl* ('yoke'): 'I became to them as one who eases the yoke on their jaws' (ESV; Eidevall 1996: 172–174; Garrett 1997: 224; Dearman 2010: 275; Moon 2018: 275). However, a yoke is not placed on the jaws,[133] and this, with the parent–child imagery in the previous verses, has led some to emend *'ōl* to *'ul* ('infant'): *I was like one who lifts a little child to the cheek* (NIV; cf. NRSV; Mays 1969: 150; Wolff 1974: 191; Hubbard 1989: 188–189; Kakkanattu 2006: 57–63).[134] *I led them* [*māšak*] *with cords of human kindness, with ties of love* [*'ahăbâ*] could relate to training an animal, but could also refer to the gentle application of restraint to a child. And the same terms, *māšak* and *'ahăbâ*, appear together in a similar context in Jeremiah 31:3. While both interpretations are possible, the emendation is minor, and it is reasonable to see this as a continuation of the parent–child metaphor.

---

132. There may be wordplay between Ephraim (*'eprayim*) and *rāpā'* (Dearman 2010: 282).

133. Comparison with Isa. 30:28, which refers to putting a bridle 'on the jaws' (Dearman 2010: 283), is not convincing: a bridle is put on the jaws, whereas a yoke is not. Moon's suggestion that lifting the yoke enables the animal to feed (2018: 184) still does not explain the yoke being 'on the jaws'.

134. Schüngel-Straumann (1995) amends *lĕḥî* ('jaw', 'cheek') to read 'breast' and argues that the imagery is of God as mother. That, though, seems unlikely, as does the suggestion that 'I am God and not man' (v. 9) indicates non-masculine behaviour. See also Wacker (2012).

The term translated *human kindness* (NIV, NRSV) is *'ādām* ('man, human'). This may suggest that any restraint imposed by the *cords* is humane, and some refer to 'cords of friendship' (Macintosh 1997: 445; Moon 2018: 179). Or it may indicate that the restraint is administered by human beings (Dearman 2010: 284) – for example, the prophets.

The final section continues the theme of Yahweh's loving care. *Bent down* translates *nāṭâ*, which frequently has the sense of inclining towards (e.g. Josh. 24:23; Judg. 9:3; 1 Kgs 11:2; Pss 17:6; 40:1; Jer. 7:24). Following the parent–child imagery, it may suggest the idea of the divine father reaching out to attend to the needs of his child, though it could also refer to feeding a farm animal. *Nāṭâ* is also used of Yahweh's 'outstretched' arm (e.g. Exod. 6:6; 7:5; Deut. 5:15), again recalling the exodus. The reference to feeding may relate specifically to the miraculous supply of food and water during Israel's time in the desert period, though also, more generally, to his continued provision in the Promised Land (cf. 2:8).

5–7. It is possible to read the beginning of verse 5 as a negative: 'They shall not return [*šûb*] to the land of Egypt' (ESV). Macintosh (1997: 450) sets this in the context of Hoshea's ineffective appeal to Egypt, which resulted in control by Assyria. The exodus theme of the passage, though, suggests that the reference is to captivity in Egypt. Others take it to imply that, instead of going back to Egypt, Israel faces a new exile in Assyria (Garrett 1997: 225; Macintosh 1997: 450; Dearman 2010: 276). However, other verses state the opposite (8:13; 9:3; cf. 11:11). Another suggestion is to replace *lō'* ('not') with *lô* ('to him') and link it with verse 4 ('bent down *to him*') (cf. NRSV; Mays 1969: 150; Wolff 1974: 191). It seems better, though, to read the text rhetorically: *Will they not return . . . ?* (NIV) or 'surely they will return' (Andersen and Freedman 1980: 574; Hubbard 1989: 190; Moon 2018: 179). Because Israel refuses to repent (*šûb*), the deliverance of the exodus will be reversed, and the people will again face oppression in a foreign land, though now it will be Assyria that rules over them. The correspondence is again evident: Israel will not *return* to Yahweh, and so must *return* to captivity.[135]

---

135. See above, p. 24.

Verse 6 notes the havoc associated with the coming judgment. The military threat from Assyria is indicated by the reference to a *sword*, which appears to be the subject of the following three verbs, all indicating coming destruction. *Flash* translates a form generally thought to be from the verb 'to whirl', and that whirling blade will bring devastation to Israel's cities. The second verb is best translated 'destroy'. The object (*bad*) is unclear, though the parallel with 'diviners' in Isaiah 44:25 (cf. Jer. 50:36) suggests that it could be corrupt religious leaders (cf. NIV, NRSV; Mays 1969: 150; Stuart 1987: 174; Hubbard 1989: 191; Eidevall 1996: 176). *Bad* may also be translated 'pole' (Exod. 25:14), hence 'bars of their gates' (ESV; Dearman 2010: 276); 'branch' (Ezek. 19:14), referring to trees (Moon 2018: 182) or 'villages', as branches of cities (Macintosh 1997: 452–453); or 'boasting' (Isa. 16:6; Wolff 1974: 192; Garrett 1997: 226). Andersen and Freedman (1980: 585) suggest a reference to military personnel. The third verb means 'to devour' (cf. 2:12; 5:7; 7:7, 9; 8:14). Its object may be Israel's plans (NIV; Hubbard 1989: 192; Garrett 1997: 226), which include seeking help from Egypt and so failing to trust Yahweh. Alternatively, judgment is because of those plans (cf. NRSV, ESV; Wolff 1974: 192; Stuart 1987: 174; Macintosh 1997: 452; Moon 2018: 180) and will fall on those religious leaders at the heart of the political system who influence the foolish schemes of the nation's rulers. Again, though the precise translation is not certain, the message of judgment, and the underlying concern that the people and their leaders are placing their confidence in other things, is clear.

The key indictment in verse 7 is that the people *are determined to turn from me* (cf. NRSV, ESV). A more literal translation is 'they are hung up [*tālā'*] in their turning [*mĕšûbâ*] from me'. *Tālā'* here points to being firmly attached to something (Wolff 1974: 192; Andersen and Freedman 1980: 574; Stuart 1987: 174; Yee 1987: 221; Hubbard 1989: 192; Eidevall 1996: 177). It may, though, indicate something unstable (Macintosh 1997: 455), and as part of Deuteronomy's covenant curses it refers to a precarious future (Deut. 28:66), one that 'hangs by a thread' (Craigie 1976: 352) or 'hangs in the balance' (McConville 2002: 399; Moon 2018: 180). It may be that both ideas are present here. Because the people are firmly attached to ways that lead them away from Yahweh, their future has become uncertain. *Mĕšûbâ* is derived from *šûb*, continuing the prophet's play on the term: the people refuse to repent (*šûb*) and instead embrace apostasy (*mĕšûbâ*).

The rest of verse 7 is difficult. There is a recurrence of *qārā'* ('to call'; cf. 7:11; 11:1–2) and the subject is probably the people, or, possibly, prophets (Dearman 2010: 286–287). The object, *'al* ('height'; cf. 7:16), may refer to Yahweh, 'the Most High' (NIV, NRSV, ESV; Moon 2018: 180). This suggests that the people call to Yahweh, or the prophets call the people back to Yahweh, but because of their insincerity (cf. 8:2) he will not respond and raise them up. Some emend *'al* to *ba'al* (Mays 1969: 150; Wolff 1974: 192; Stuart 1987: 174), or *'al* as it stands may be an ironic reference to Baal, whom the people view as the high god (Hubbard 1989: 192) but who cannot help them. Several commentators read *'ōl* ('yoke') instead of *'al*, with the idea that the people are summoned to the yoke (cf. 11:4) which no-one will lift (Eidevall 1996: 177, following Yee 1987: 223). The precise translation may be uncertain, but the emphasis is on the impossibility of respite from impending judgment while Israel's apostasy continues.

8–9. Following the message of judgment, we again see Yahweh's compassion (*niḥûmîm*), which here relates to offering comfort or consolation (cf. Isa. 57:18; Zech. 1:13) (Moon 2018: 210–211). As in chapter 2, the familial ties between Yahweh and his people outweigh their apostasy and open the way for restoration.

Verse 8 comprises three parallel pairs. The first expresses Yahweh's unwillingness to 'give up' Ephraim or 'hand over' Israel. The second contrasts this with the judgment that fell on Admah and Zeboyim, cities of the plain which were destroyed alongside Sodom and Gomorrah (Deut. 29:23). According to Deuteronomy, Israel's apostasy will result in exile, and the impact on the land is likened to what happened to those cities. But this will not be annihilation, and Israel may be restored (cf. Deut. 30:1–6). This is explained in the third pair, which notes Yahweh's change (*hāpak*) of heart (cf. 1 Sam. 10:9; Ps. 105:25; Lam. 1:20). This is not, though, vacillation. The term *hāpak* means 'to overturn', and the strong language reveals tension between divine judgment and compassion, and the upheaval in Yahweh's heart as he contemplates the destruction of his people.[136]

---

136. *Aroused* (NIV) translates *kāmar* ('to agitate, grow hot'; cf. NRSV, ESV).

There may also be an inner conflict between divine compassion and
what the law requires for a rebellious son (Deut. 21:18–21) (cf. Lim
and Castelo 2015: 171). *Hāpak* also refers to the overthrow of the
cities of the plain (Deut. 29:23) and may be used intentionally:
Yahweh's heart, not Israel, is overthrown.

This unwillingness to make a full end of Israel is further
emphasized in verse 9. Though Israel's sin deserves it, Yahweh will
not execute his *fierce anger* ('*ap*; cf. 8:5). This idea may be repeated
at the end of the verse, where '*îr* may be translated 'city' (NIV;
Hubbard 1989: 195–196; Garrett 1997: 227; Macintosh 1997: 463),
though more likely it refers to 'agitation' and hence 'anger' (cf.
NRSV, ESV; Wolff 1974: 193; Stuart 1987: 174; Eidevall 1996: 179;
Dearman 2010: 276). *Šûb* is usually translated as an auxiliary verb,
meaning 'again': 'I will not *again* destroy' (NRSV, ESV; cf. NIV),
suggesting no further judgment beyond the one already announced.
An alternative is 'I will not *return* to destroy' (Wolff 1974: 193;
Emmerson 1984: 40; Eidevall 1996: 179; Macintosh 1997: 463; Moon
2018: 180), continuing Hosea's wordplay on *šûb*.[137]

Yahweh's reason for not effecting his wrath is, *I am God, and not
a [human] – the Holy One among you* (for a detailed discussion, see
Dearman 2010: 291–292). The emphasis on the distinction between
God and humanity (cf. Num. 23:19; Isa. 31:3) may suggest that
Yahweh's passion, unlike that of human beings, does not result in
arbitrary outbursts of rage. It also indicates that Yahweh cannot be
defined by metaphor (Mays 1969: 157–158; Eidevall 1996: 179–180).
The portrayal of Yahweh as a father or husband, and even of one
struggling with his emotions, may give us insights into his character, but he is not bound by those analogies and remains beyond
any anthropomorphic representation of him. Here that freedom
includes Yahweh's capacity to show mercy as well as to judge (cf.
Exod. 34:6–7). This may be evident, too, in the title *Holy One*,
which is particularly prominent in the book of Isaiah. 'Holy' in the
Old Testament describes the essential character of Yahweh (cf.
Routledge 2008a: 105–106) and points to what sets him apart from
humanity. It may be linked with judgment, but, as the 'Holy One',

---

137. See above, p. 24.

Yahweh also offers salvation and redemption (e.g. Isa. 10:20; 12:1; 43:3, 14; 48:17; 54:5). Here, too, Yahweh is *among* his people, in their midst. This emphasizes his commitment to them and his unwillingness to allow them to come to ultimate harm.[138] Sin makes judgment inevitable. However, consistent with the character of a holy God, judgment is intended to discipline, not destroy, and beyond it lies the promise of restoration.

10–11. Some suggest that one or both of these verses are editorial (Macintosh 1997: 467–468). Nevertheless, they fit into the overall discourse of 11:1–11 (Moon 2018: 183). In particular, they form an *inclusio* with verses 1–2, tying the passage together. Those who *went* [*hālak*] *away* from Yahweh (v. 2) will now *follow* (literally, 'go [*hālak*] after') him (v. 10); those who were called 'from Egypt' (v. 1) but whose sin has led to their return there (v. 5) will again come *from Egypt* (v. 10) (Yee 1987: 214–217; Eidevall 1996: 166–167, 180).

Yahweh's summons to the exiles will be like the roar of a lion (cf. Amos 1:2; 3:8), causing them to 'tremble' (*hārad*), as they did when Yahweh appeared on Mount Sinai (Exod. 19:16). Despite the tenderness of Yahweh's relationship with his children, he remains God, and his call should strike fear, particularly among those who face exile because of their sin (cf. 3:4). In response to Yahweh's call, people will come from the west (v. 10),[139] as well as from Egypt and Assyria (v. 11). The reference to Egypt suggests the exodus and may be figurative, though Egypt was also a likely place of flight from the Assyrians, as it was later from the Babylonians (cf. 2 Kgs 25:26; Jer. 42:14; cf. Hos. 9:6). The reference to *doves* recalls the senseless fluttering between Egypt and Assyria (7:11). Here, though, that is reversed, as the people turn instead to Yahweh. *I will settle them* (NIV) translates the Hiphil of *yāšab* ('to dwell'), though, following the LXX, some prefer a slight emendation and read instead, 'I will return [*šûb*] them' (cf. NRSV; Stuart 1987: 174). This promise of restoration, followed by the statement *declares the LORD*, brings the

---

138. The same expression, 'Holy One . . . among you', occurs in the context of salvation in Isa. 12:6.

139. Literally, 'the sea' (i.e. the Mediterranean) and so *the west*.

section of the book that began at chapter 4 to a hopeful conclusion.

Meaning

Here, as in the preceding sections, Israel fails to live up to early expectations. And, as before, the consequence is divine judgment. However, that judgment is tempered by grace, and there is also the hope of restoration. Like the prodigal in Jesus' parable, the son, despite the father's care, wanders away. But the hardship that accompanies judgment is educative; its purpose is to bring the people to their senses. The loving commitment of the divine parent will not finally let them go. This imagery gives a profound insight into the tension within Yahweh's heart: between the judgment that Israel's sin and rebellion demand, and the divine compassion that, for all their apostasy, will not give his people up. That tension is resolved ultimately in the cross, where judgment on sin falls, but where the way is open for sinners to be forgiven.

3. PAST INGRATITUDE AND FUTURE HOPE (11:12 – 14:9)

A. Yahweh's case against the people (11:12 – 12:14) [MT 12:1–15]

Context

Following the hopeful conclusion to the second section of the book, the prophecy returns to the repeated cycle of sin, judgment and promise. As in 4:1, it includes Yahweh's charge (*rîb*) against the people (12:2). The opening verses (11:12 – 12:1) may be seen to introduce the whole of the final section of the book, though the reference to *deceit* (11:12; 12:7) links them more specifically with the historical references to Jacob in 12:2–12 and the verses may, therefore, serve as an introduction to both (Ben Zvi 2005: 246). As with the metaphors in the preceding chapters, references to the patriarch set the current problems of the nation in the context of past promise and failure. The references to Jacob are ambiguous (Eidevall 1996: 187). They point to his deceit, though if that was the primary consideration, other instances could have been noted. The encounter at Bethel (12:4) and his serving for a wife (12:12) appear more positive.

Comment
i. Deceit and false confidence (11:12 – 12:1)

12. In the first part of the verse, Ephraim and Israel are parallel, indicating the northern kingdom. *Lies* (cf. 7:3; 10:13) and *deceit* (*mirmâ*) probably relate to the people's double-dealing, both with one another and with Yahweh, as well as to the self-deception of putting trust in other things, rather than in him. These 'surround' Yahweh (cf. 7:2), suggesting that they both pervade the life and worship of the people and separate them from him.

The translation of the second part of the verse is uncertain. A key term, *rād*, is usually related to *rûd* ('to wander, roam'). The NRSV understands this positively: in contrast to Israel, 'Judah still walks with God [*'ēl*] and is faithful to the Holy One [*qĕdôšîm*]' (cf. ESV; Mays 1969: 159–160; Emmerson 1984: 113–116; Sweeney 2000: 118; Dearman 2010: 295–297; Lim and Castelo 2015: 200–201). *Qĕdôšîm* could refer to Yahweh, as a plural of intensity, though may be translated 'holy ones', possibly referring to the religious circles with which Hosea identified (Wolff 1974: 209–210; Achtemeier 1996: 97) or to the divine council (Emmerson 1984: 113–116). This then relates to the current situation, where Israel will fall but Judah will survive. Others view Judah negatively (cf. 12:2) and take *rûd* to imply that Judah wanders away from God (cf. Jer. 2:31). Another suggestion is that *rād* refers instead to seeking to gain mastery over God (Macintosh 1997: 473–474; Moon 2018: 190), which may be related to Jacob, striving with God (12:3). In this case, 'faithful' qualifies *qĕdôšîm* (cf. NIV, *the faithful Holy One*). It is possible, too, that *'ēl* and *qĕdôšîm* refer to other gods, further emphasizing Judah's defection (Andersen and Freedman 1980: 593, 603; Hubbard 1989: 199–200; Garrett 1997: 230–231). On balance, though, the more positive picture of Judah seems preferable.

12:1. This verse refers to seeking foreign alliances, which is an exercise in futility: 'shepherding [*rā'â*] the wind,¹ and pursuing the east wind' (MT). The east wind is associated with the dry desert

---

1. *Rā'â* relates to shepherding. With flock or shepherd as subject, it means, respectively, 'to graze' (cf. NIV) or 'to pasture, tend, shepherd' (cf. NRSV).

heat that brings discomfort (Jon. 4:8) and withers crops (Gen. 41:6, 23, 27) and so may represent divine judgment (13:15; cf. Hab. 1:9). This suggests that the people's futile search is for something that will ultimately do them harm. Sins also include the multiplication (cf. 8:11, 14; 10:1; 12:10) of *lies* (cf. 7:13) and *violence*/'destruction' (*šōd*), which will rebound in corresponding judgment (cf. 7:13; 9:6; 10:14).

The verse again condemns Israel's attempts to secure help from Assyria and Egypt (cf. 7:11). The treaty (*bĕrît*) with Assyria is probably a suzerain–vassal treaty between Shalmaneser V and Hoshea (2 Kgs 17:3), though could relate to an earlier agreement between Tiglath-Pileser III and Menahem (2 Kgs 15:19). The oil sent to Egypt was likely to have been olive oil (cf. NIV), offered by Hoshea to enlist Egyptian support for his rebellion against Assyria (2 Kgs 17:4).

ii. Jacob: past and present (12:2–14)

2. Yahweh again brings a charge (*rîb*; cf. 4:1), which includes Judah. Despite problems with the reference to Judah, it seems reasonable to take it as original.[2] And, while *Jacob* may more specifically refer to Israel, both kingdoms share the failings of their common ancestor. The consequence, which repeats the language of 4:9, will be repayment (*šûb*) in divine punishment for their attitudes and actions.

3–5. Verse 3 notes two significant incidents from the life of Jacob, both linked with name-giving. *Jacob* (*yaʿăqōb*) is associated with *ʿāqab* (Gen. 25:26), which can mean 'to grasp by the heel' (cf. NIV), with the idiomatic sense of 'to cheat, supplant'. Jacob was born grasping his elder brother Esau's heel, and later, *as a man* (literally, 'in his strength [ʾôn]'), he demonstrated the appropriateness of the name by cheating Esau of his birthright and blessing and usurping his place as Isaac's heir (Gen. 27:36). Hosea's many references to *lies* (see on 10:13) suggest that Israel is Jacob's true son. There may also be an allusion to internecine conflict, also a significant issue for Hosea (see comments on 5:8; 6:9; 9:9; 10:10). The

---

2. See the discussion above, pp. 18–19.

second incident is Jacob struggling (*śārâ*) with God (*'ĕlōhîm*) at
Peniel, and being renamed Israel (*yiśrā'ēl*) (Gen. 32:28).

The incident at Peniel is picked up in verse 4, though variations
from the Genesis account suggest that Hosea may have had access
to different Jacob traditions (Good 1966b: 137–151; McKenzie 1986:
311–322; Whitt 1991: 18–43). Differences include Hosea's reference
to an *angel* (*mal'āk*), which parallels *'ĕlōhîm* (v. 3; cf. Gen. 48:15–16).
And, while Jacob insists on receiving a blessing (Gen. 32:26), there
is no specific mention of weeping and seeking favour. Sweeney
(2000: 122) suggests that it is the man defeated by Jacob who pleads
for favour, though that seems unlikely. The language of weeping
and the request for favour is used, though, when Jacob meets Esau
(Gen. 33:4, 8), and it is possible that the four lines in verses 3–4a
have a chiastic structure: the first and last refer to Jacob's relationship with Esau, while the middle two are parallel references to
the encounter at Peniel (Holladay 1966: 53–64; cf. Garrett 1997:
239). Jacob's reunion with Esau may then serve as a model for
the humility required, in Hosea's day, to end the conflict between
north and south.

The MT of verse 4 begins with the expression *yāśar 'el*, which may
deliberately play on the name Israel (*yiśrā'ēl*). It is usually taken to
describe Jacob's struggle (*śārâ*) with the angel. The preposition *'el*
('towards') is used unusually here, and some emend it to *'ēl* ('God'),
providing a closer play on *yiśrā'ēl*. This gives either 'he struggled
with God and overcame the angel' (Andersen and Freedman 1980:
593), or, taking *yāśar* from *śārar* ('to rule, lord it over'; cf. Num. 16:13;
Judg. 9:22; Isa. 32:1; Prov. 8:16), 'he lorded over God and prevailed
with an angel' (Hubbard 1989: 203–204; cf. Ackroyd 1963: 248,
250).[3] While variations are not significantly different, 'he struggled
with the angel and prevailed' seems preferable (Garrett 1997: 237;
Dearman 2010: 295; Moon 2018: 190).

The final part of verse 4 refers to God's encounter with Jacob at
Bethel. It is not clear who found whom, though the verb, *māṣā'*, is

---

3. 'God ruled, and (the angel) prevailed' (Yee 1987: 231–234; cf. Wolff
1974: 206; Macintosh 1997: 483–484) is less probable, as is the view
that 'angel' is a later addition.

the same as in 9:10, where Yahweh is the subject. Genesis records two such incidents: one before Peniel and one after Jacob's meeting with Esau (Gen. 28:10–22; 35:5–14). Hosea's other references to Bethel (or Beth Aven) are condemnatory (4:15; 5:8; 10:5, 15). This suggests that Bethel as a meeting place between God and Jacob is a further example of early promise which now stands in marked contrast to what Bethel has become: the home of the calf-idol (cf. 10:5) and the centre of Baal worship. The term translated *with him* (*ʿimmānû*) generally means 'with us' (ESV). The former is possible, though there may also be an intentional link between Jacob and those descended from him.

In verse 5, the God who appeared to Jacob at Bethel is identified as Yahweh (cf. Gen. 28:13). The divine name *ʾĕlōhê haṣĕbāʾôt* is usually translated 'God of hosts' (cf. NRSV).[4] The LXX frequently translates it 'God Almighty' (cf. NIV), though in English versions that is usually the translation of *ʾēl šadday* (cf. Gen. 35:11). In the second part of the verse, 'Yahweh' is described as a memorial name (*zēker*). This comes from the verb 'to remember' (cf. 8:13; 9:9) and is specifically associated with the revelation of the divine name to Moses (Exod. 3:15; cf. Hos. 12:13). Its similarity to the title in Amos 4:13 suggests that the title 'Yahweh, God of hosts' may be formulaic, possibly a doxology. Significantly, it emphasizes God's power over people and events, and that this is the One with whom Israel has to do.

6. A key element in Jacob's encounter with God at Bethel is the promise that Yahweh will keep (*šāmar*) him and enable him to return (*šûb*) (Gen. 28:15, 20–22). The same terms appear here in 12:6. God's commitment to Jacob offers hope to his descendants. They, though, must respond to the often-repeated call for Israel to *return* (*šûb*) to God (cf. 6:1; 14:1–2).[5] The MT reads, literally, 'return *with* your God', and may include the sense of 'return *with the help of* your God' (Mays 1969: 161; Macintosh 1997: 491; Moon 2018: 190). As part of what it means to *return*, Israel must *maintain* (*šāmar*) (cf. 4:10) *love* (*ḥesed*)[6] and *justice* (*mišpāṭ*). These are both associated with the

---

4. For further discussion, see Seow 1992b.

5. See above, p. 24.

6. See above, pp. 31–32.

covenant, and are currently lacking, but with God's help may be restored (cf. 2:19). The call to *wait for* . . . *God always* implies continuing trust and expectancy (cf. Isa. 25:9; 33:2; 40:31), and so contrasts with putting confidence in other things. This may also be related to Jacob's experience of holding on to God's promises over a significant period (Gen. 49:18).

7–9. These verses return to Ephraim's sin. The first word of verse 7 is *kĕna'an* ('Canaan'), though because Canaanites were noted as traders, the word also came to mean 'merchant' (Andersen and Freedman 1980: 615; Dearman 2010: 309). However, continuing the links with Israel's past, it may carry a double meaning: Israel's dishonesty makes them no different from the Canaanites, whose practices they continue to follow (Macintosh 1997: 494; Moon 2018: 196). *Dishonest [mirmâ] scales* (Prov. 11:1; Amos 8:5; Mic. 6:11) symbolizes fraudulent business practice, while *mirmâ* also provides a link with Jacob (Gen. 27:35). *Loves to defraud* suggests that oppressing and exploiting the weak is something Israel has come to enjoy. Another possibility, 'defrauds a loved one' (cf. Andersen and Freedman 1980: 617; Hubbard 1989: 207), may allude further to the tension between Jacob and Esau.

In verse 8, Ephraim declares that he is rich and has *become wealthy* (literally, 'found [*māṣā'*] wealth [*'ôn*] for myself [*lî*]'). This probably relates historically to Israel's prosperity under Jeroboam II, and further indicates that the people have lost sight of the true source of blessing. It also continues the allusion to Jacob. God *found (māṣā')* Jacob at Bethel (v. 4), and Jacob, 'in his strength [*'ôn*]',[7] struggled with God (v. 3). The remainder of the verse is best understood as a spurious claim that, in the acquisition of wealth,[8] Ephraim has done nothing wrong (*'āwōn*) so as to be guilty of *sin (ḥēṭě')*. This includes a play on words:

I have found [*māṣā'*] wealth [*'ôn*] for myself [*lî*]
They have not found [*māṣā'*] iniquity [*'āwōn*] in me [*lî*]

---

7. The term *'ôn* can mean 'wealth' or 'strength'.

8. The noun *yĕgîa'* suggests something acquired through labour (cf. Gen. 31:42).

Verse 9 gives Yahweh's response to Ephraim's boasting. Everything they have and are has come through him. 'I am the LORD
your God from the land of Egypt' (NRSV; cf. 13:4)⁹ echoes the
frequently repeated statement 'I am the LORD your God, who
brought you out of Egypt' (cf. Exod. 20:2; Lev. 25:38; Deut. 5:6;
Ps. 81:10). This emphasizes the distinctive nature of the relationship between God and his people, established through the Sinaitic
covenant. It was Yahweh who brought the people into Canaan, and
for all their boasting it was he, not they, who enabled them to
prosper there. But they do not acknowledge Yahweh, and have
instead taken on the characteristics of Canaan. As a result, they
will be taken back to a time before the settlement had its adverse
effects. The reference to living in tents points particularly to the
exodus. The 'appointed festival' (NRSV) may be the feast of Tabernacles (cf. 9:5), when the people constructed booths to recall the
days in the desert. The Hebrew expression is 'appointed days' or
'days of the assembly', and this is sometimes taken to refer to the
wider exodus period (Wolff 1974: 215; Andersen and Freedman
1980: 618; Hubbard 1989: 208; Macintosh 1997: 499). In either case,
the return to that time points to a new exodus, which, as noted in
2:14–20, will have a very different outcome.

10. As if to highlight the need for a new start, Hosea resumes
his indictment of Ephraim. The emphasis here, and in verse 13, is
on the divinely appointed role of prophets within the life of the
nation (cf. 9:7–8). While the prophetic word may be challenged,
particularly by those who object to the message, true prophets do
not speak on their own authority. Yahweh speaks to them. He
multiplies their *visions* (*ḥāzôn*);[10] and that is the basis of the parables,
similes and metaphors (*dāmâ*) which are then applied to the life of
the nation.[11]

---

9. This is a literal translation. The NIV is a paraphrase, though conveys
   the correct sense.
10. Visions are important in prophetic revelation (1 Sam. 3:1; Lam. 2:9;
    Ezek. 1:1; Zech. 1:8; cf. Isa. 1:1; Obad. 1:1; Mic. 1:1; Nah. 1:1).
11. *Dāmâ* may mean 'to destroy' (NRSV; cf. 4:5–6; 10:7, 15), though here
    it means 'to compare' and hence 'to speak in parables' (NIV).

11. This may be an example of the prophetic comparisons described in the previous verse (Coote 1971: 397–401; Hubbard 1989: 209; Macintosh 1997: 504) in relation to Gilead and Gilgal. The first part of the verse may be translated, 'if Gilead (is) evil, they have surely become worthless' (Mays 1969: 166; Garrett 1997: 244; Macintosh 1997: 504; Dearman 2010: 296). Gilead's sin (*'āwen*) has already been noted (see on 6:8). Gilgal, too, has been criticized, as a corrupt cultic centre (4:15) and maybe also as a base for political insurrection (see on 9:15). Here the criticism appears to relate to the sacrifice of bulls as part of illicit cultic rites. Some altars were, essentially, piles of stones (*gal*), and Gilgal's altars will become as useless as the piles of stones cleared from the field before ploughing. There is also a possible further allusion to Jacob. After Jacob fled from Laban, Laban caught up with him in Gilead (Gen. 31:23), and the two men made a covenant, and set up a *gal* as a witness (Gen. 31:46–50).

12–13. Hosea now returns explicitly to the story of Jacob fleeing to Aram and working for a wife (v. 12; cf. Gen. 27 – 29), and he links this with the exodus (v. 13). Though some see an abrupt shift in focus here, there are common themes running through these verses, and they can be linked to what precedes as further examples of prophetic comparisons.

Jacob was forced to seek sanctuary in a foreign country. There, he worked to marry Rachel. Although the NIV has only one reference to *wife*, there are two in the MT: 'Israel served for a wife and for a wife he guarded sheep' (NRSV, ESV). This may suggest service for two wives (e.g. Andersen and Freedman 1980: 620). More likely, though, it emphasizes that, having been deceived by Laban, he did double service for Rachel, who has particular significance as Ephraim's grandmother. Nevertheless, God gave Jacob the upper hand, and eventually he brought his bride back to the land of promise. Israel, too, had sought refuge, in Egypt, and also became subject to hard labour. But Yahweh, through Moses his prophet, rescued his people, and Yahweh also brought his bride back to the Promised Land.

While some of the comparisons noted are between Jacob and the nation descended from him, significantly the idea of going into a foreign land to bring back a wife parallels Jacob with Yahweh, and echoes themes in chapters 1–3. That link is reinforced by the double reference to *šāmar*. Most English versions refer to Jacob serving for Rachel by 'tending [*šāmar*] sheep' (v. 12). And Yahweh, through a prophet, *cared for* (*šāmar*) Israel (v. 13). The term for *sheep*, though, is lacking in the MT, and it may be better to take *šāmar* to suggest devotion (cf. 4:10). Macintosh (1997: 508) gives the alternative translation: 'to a wife [i.e. Rachel] he devoted himself', thus paralleling Yahweh's devotion to Israel. The *prophet* on this occasion may again be Moses, who guided the people through the desert, or possibly one more associated with the settlement, maybe Samuel or Elijah. The twofold reference to 'prophet' matches the twofold reference to 'wife' and may further the comparison between Jacob's devotion to Rachel and Yahweh's devotion to Israel. In addition, by omitting the names of key figures, Hosea also emphasizes the role of prophets in general within the life of the nation (cf. 9:8; 12:10).

14. The prophet here returns to condemnation, using ideas that echo verse 2, including a further reference to *šûb* in the context of bringing Ephraim's sin back on him. Despite Yahweh's care, Ephraim has provoked him to bitter anger. The sins noted are *bloodshed* (*dām*; cf. 1:4; 4:2; 6:8) and showing contempt for Yahweh, which includes bringing him dishonour by forgetting him and turning to other gods. Yahweh's authority to judge is emphasized in the description *Lord* (*'ādôn*). This may, more generally, refer to a 'master', but though Hosea uses the term only here, it is related to Yahweh over four hundred times throughout the Old Testament.

Meaning
These verses compare and contrast Ephraim/Israel with Jacob. Israel shares Jacob's deceitfulness: deceiving others, and also deceiving themselves into thinking that they are better than they are, and able to solve their own problems without Yahweh (cf. 11:12 – 12:1; 12:7–8). There are, though, more positive aspects. Despite Jacob's deceitfulness, God met with him at Bethel and entered into a relationship with him there. Bethel has since become a centre of corrupt worship, but things didn't begin that way, and the people may still return to God (12:6) and trust him as Jacob did. The reference to Jacob serving for, and being devoted

to, a wife and bringing her back to the Promised Land is also linked with Yahweh's care for Israel, and recalls the metaphor of Israel as Yahweh's bride in chapters 1–3. And, again, there is the suggestion of a return to the desert (12:9; cf. 2:14–15): Yahweh remains committed to his people and wants to restore the love and commitment of earlier days (cf. Rev. 2:4–5).

One further key element here, which picks up on earlier statements, is the role of God's prophets (12:10, 13) in guarding and guiding the life of the nation. The people have been brought into a covenant relationship with Yahweh, and he continues to care for them, despite their failures. A key role of prophets was to call the people back to their covenant obligations. For Israel in Hosea's day, this emphasizes the importance of listening to God's representatives. For the church, it points to the continuing importance of being open to, and guided by, God's Word.

B. Ephraim's exaltation, sin and judgment (13:1–16)

Context

This begins a new section. However, while introducing some new terms, it also repeats earlier themes, and appears to summarize Ephraim's failure and the devastating effect of divine judgment. There is, too, a possible reprise of the possibility of resurrection (13:14; cf. 6:2). This summary then prepares the way for the call to repent and the further message of hope in chapter 14. As an overview of the sin of the northern kingdom, it is probably set close to the fall of Samaria. However, sin is continuing and judgment is still future, suggesting that the kingdom has not fallen yet.

The passage is framed by references to Ephraim's guilt (*'āšam*) and its consequences (vv. 1, 16), indicating that this is a major emphasis. Themes repeated from earlier passages include worshipping idols (*'āṣāb*, v. 2; cf. 4:17; 8:4; 14:8), and especially the calf-idol (cf. 8:5–6), the failure of kings and leaders (vv. 10–11; cf. 5:1; 7:3–7; 8:4; 10:3), Ephraim's early promise in the days of the exodus, followed by ingratitude (vv. 4–6; cf. 9:10; 11:1–2), and the description of coming judgment as an attack by a wild animal, in particular a lion (*šaḥal*, v. 7; cf. 5:14). Ephraim's transience is also described in the same terms as the people's *ḥesed* (v. 3; cf. 6:4).

Comment

1–3. As in previous sections, the nation's early history is contrasted with what it has become. Mention of Ephraim's significance in Israel (v. 1) may indicate that this refers to the tribe of that name, which was prominent in the north. Ephraim, though, came to represent the whole of the northern kingdom, and that is its primary significance in relation to the coming judgment. The term *rĕtēt* (v. 1) occurs only here in the Old Testament and is usually translated in the sense of 'trembling'.[12] This is usually taken to reinforce the tribe's significance: 'When Ephraim spoke, (there was) trembling' (NRSV, ESV; cf. NIV; Hubbard 1989: 213–214; Moon 2018: 202). In the context, this seems the most likely understanding. There are, though, several suggested variations: 'when Ephraim spoke in agitation' (Dearman 2010: 316); 'when Israel spoke disruption' (Macintosh 1997: 518); or, taking Yahweh as the subject, '[Yahweh] has spoken terror against Ephraim' (Stuart 1987: 186; cf. Andersen and Freedman 1980: 624; Yee 1987: 249). Alongside Ephraim's prominence there may be an indication, too, of his pride (cf. 12:8). The guilt incurred 'through Baal' may be a further reference to Baal Peor (9:10) or to the secession of the northern tribes under Jeroboam I, which led to setting up calves at Dan and Bethel and hence to greater involvement with Baal worship (cf. 2 Kgs 17:16), particularly under Ahab and Jezebel (Macintosh 1997: 520). As a result, the nation *died* (*mût*) – that is, it became as good as dead (Dearman 2010: 319), because of its liability to the judgment that would result in its eventual demise.

Verse 2 notes that Ephraim continues to sin (*ḥāṭāʾ*; cf. 4:7; 8:11; 10:9) through Baal worship, which has persisted and grown. *Idols* translates *massēkâ*, the same term used for the golden calf in the desert (Exod. 32:4, 8). Here it is singular (cf. NRSV) and probably refers to the calf-idol in Bethel (cf. 1 Kgs 12:28; Hos. 10:5). The related term, *images* (*ʿăṣāb*), occurs frequently in Hosea (see *Context* above) and is combined with *silver* in 8:4. Though made by skilled craftsmen (cf. 8:6; Isa. 40:20), these images are still only the work of human hands. The final part of verse 2 is unclear. The NIV and

---

12. It has this sense in 1QH 4.33.

ESV take the expression *zōbḥê 'ādām* ('sacrificers of people') to indicate human sacrifice (Wolff 1974: 219; Andersen and Freedman
1980: 624; Yee 1987: 249–250; Hubbard 1989: 215). However, if
this was practised it would likely have received more direct condemnation (Emmerson 1984: 147–148; see also on 4:2). Another
possibility is to take *ādām* with what follows: 'men kiss calves' (cf.
NRSV; Mays 1969: 171; Emmerson 1984: 148–149; Stuart 1987: 198;
Dearman 2010: 316). It may be better, though, to take the expression
to mean 'people who sacrifice' (Moon 2018: 202; cf. Macintosh 1997:
522): 'they (are) saying to them, "people who sacrifice kiss calves."'
Kissing is a mark of devotion to Baal (1 Kgs 19:18) and may have
accompanied the offering of sacrifices. As with many passages in
Hosea, the precise translation is uncertain. The text does, though,
clearly indicate Ephraim's continuing attachment to Baal.

The consequences of that attachment are emphasized in verse
3. Two pairs of similes emphasize the transience of those who
worship worthless idols (cf. Jer. 2:5).[13] Mist and dew quickly evapor-
ate in the heat of the day (cf. 6:4); chaff and smoke disappear when
caught in a swirling wind. Ephraim's sin means that the nation will
not survive long.

4–6. These verses again recall the exodus. The opening expression of verse 4, which is identical to 12:9a, emphasizes the
relationship between God and his people and his commitment to
them from the time they left Egypt. The next part of the verse
echoes the second commandment (Exod. 20:3). However, consistent
with what is a significant theme for Hosea, it refers to knowing
or acknowledging (*yāda'*),[14] rather than 'having', no other God.
Israel's whole history testifies to there being only one God and one
Saviour (cf. Isa. 43:11; 45:21). Here the reference is probably to the
idealized honeymoon period in the wilderness (cf. 2:15; Jer. 2:2). The
theme continues in verse 5. The MT reads, 'I knew you [*yāda'*] in
the desert' (cf. ESV; Andersen and Freedman 1980: 624; Eidevall 1996:
196; Garrett 1997: 258; Macintosh 1997: 528; Dearman 2010: 316).

---

13. It is less likely that this relates to the idols; however, see Macintosh
1997: 525–526.

14. See above, p. 15 n. 42.

Following the LXX, *yĕdaʿtîkā* ('I knew you') is frequently emended to *rĕʿîtîkā* ('I shepherded/fed you') (NRSV; cf. NIV; Mays 1969: 173; Wolff 1974: 221; Stuart 1987: 198; Moon 2018: 202), though the MT fits the context and continues the marriage metaphor. It also fits with the emphasis on *yādaʿ* ('to know') throughout the book. The sense, though, may not be too different; *yādaʿ* implies a caring relationship, which enabled the people to survive the inhospitable desert.

When I fed them (v. 6) translates literally as 'according to their pasture' and makes the shepherding imagery explicit. There is also the return of a familiar theme. Divine provision led to the people being satisfied, which, in turn, led to complacency and self-reliance (literally, 'they lifted up their heart'). And with that, they *forgot* (*šākaḥ*) Yahweh (cf. 2:13; 8:14), the opposite of acknowledging him as the true source of their blessings (cf. 2:8; 11:2–3).

7–8. Because the people have forgotten Yahweh and failed to acknowledge him as their God and Saviour, they will face judgment. The imagery here, of being torn apart by wild animals, is relentless. Yahweh, who was their Saviour, will become their destroyer; their shepherd will attack the flock as a predator. In this, there appears to be progression (Eidevall 1996: 197–199). The reference to a *lion* (*šaḥal*; cf. 5:14) alerts people to the threat: Yahweh has become their enemy. That threat intensifies with the leopard lurking (*šûr*) by the path, waiting to pounce. Then there is a ferocious attack, this time of a she-bear separated from her cubs, who rips open the chest cavity and exposes the heart. Finally, what is left is devoured by a lioness (*lābîʾ*) and torn apart by wild animals, emphasizing the completeness of the destruction.

9. The MT of verse 9 is terse and has given rise to various translations. Three seem most likely: 'I will destroy you, Israel, for (you were) against me, against your helper' (cf. NIV, ESV; Moon 2018: 203); or, following the LXX, some read: 'I will destroy you, Israel; who will help you?' (cf. NRSV; Mays 1969: 176; Wolff 1974: 221; Stuart 1987: 199); a third possibility reads the verb as a noun: 'your destruction, Israel, is from me, from your helper' (Macintosh 1997: 535; Dearman 2010: 317). All of these continue the theme that the one who was Israel's helper has now become its destroyer. The first makes explicit the people's ingratitude for what God has done, and may fit the context better.

10–11. The prophet returns here to his criticism of the failure of Israel's king and leaders, and their false confidence in their ability to resolve the crisis in the nation. The opening term, *'ĕhî*, is usually translated *Where . . . ?* (see also 13:14) (cf. LXX). *Save* (v. 10) translates *yāša'* and may be an ironic play on the name of Israel's last king, Hoshea (*hôšēa'*), which derives from it. The reference to cities implies a military threat, and the verse emphasizes the impotence of the king and other political leaders, referred to as *rulers* (*šōpēṭ*; cf. 7:7) and *princes* (*śar*; cf. 3:4; 5:10; 7:3, 5, 16; 8:10; 9:15), to avert the coming disaster. These, though, were what the people asked for and on whom they continue to rely.

Verse 11 appears to refer to Israel's request for a king (1 Sam. 8:5, 19–20), which Hosea may have linked with the northern monarchy (see on 9:15). Yahweh viewed this as a rejection of his kingship and symptomatic of Israel's wider failure to acknowledge him (1 Sam. 8:7–8), and it was in *anger* (*'ap*; cf. 8:5; 11:9; 14:4) that he gave them what they wanted. The corresponding removal of the king in *wrath* (cf. 5:10) may refer to Saul's rejection, though while that may be in the background, it more likely points to the imminent demise of Hoshea and of the northern kingdom.

12. Ephraim's sin, referred to as *'āwōn* and *ḥaṭṭā't*, has been catalogued throughout the book.[15] The emphasis here is on the inevitability of judgment. The language may reflect the practice of binding together important documents, or other items of value, and sealing them for secure storage (Isa. 8:16; cf. Jer. 32:14) (Macintosh 1997: 542). In this case, it results in a permanent and inescapable record of Ephraim's culpability.

13. There seems to be two related metaphors here. One portrays Ephraim's desperate situation as that of a woman in labour whose pain in the end is futile and will result in a stillbirth. The second emphasizes Ephraim's foolishness (cf. 7:11). Labour pains indicate that the time for birth is near, but Ephraim is oblivious to the signs and refuses to leave the womb. Consequently, the nation cannot survive (cf. v. 14). The imagery suggests that if the people did heed

---

15. The terms appear together in 4:8; 8:13; 9:9 (see also 12:8); *'āwōn* also occurs in 5:5; 7:1; 9:9; 10:10; 12:8; 14:1–2; and *ḥaṭṭā't* in 10:8 (cf. 13:2).

the warnings and respond to Yahweh, there might be the possibility of new life. But they will not listen.

14. There is here a double reference to 'Sheol' (*šě'ōl*). The NIV usually translates *šě'ōl* as *grave* (Harris 1961), though it is better understood in the sense of 'underworld' (Merrill 1996; Johnston 2002: 74–75; Routledge 2008b: 24) and, more particularly, the place of those who die under divine judgment or outside God's blessing (Johnston 2002: 79–83; Levenson 2006: 67–81; Routledge 2008b: 29–30). Sheol, here, is paralleled with *death* (*māwet*) and is set in the context of Ephraim's imminent demise (cf. 13:1).

Two further parallel terms, 'ransom' (*pādâ*; cf. 7:13) and 'redeem' (*gā'al*) (cf. Hubbard 1996a; 1996b), imply rescuing from need, usually by making a payment, and recall Hosea buying back Gomer. In Isaiah, *gā'al* frequently refers to Yahweh as Israel's Redeemer (e.g. Isa. 41:14; 43:14; 44:6; 48:17) and, like *pādâ*, it is associated with the exodus (Exod. 6:6; 15:13). In 13:14, the MT reads: 'I will ransom them . . . I will redeem them'. However, in the light of the later emphasis on judgment, *I will have no compassion* [*nōḥam*] (NIV), literally: 'Compassion is hidden from my eyes' (NRSV),[16] these are sometimes taken as questions suggesting a negative answer: 'Shall I ransom them . . . shall I redeem them . . . ?' (NRSV; Mays 1969: 178; Wolff 1974: 221; Stuart 1987: 199; Macintosh 1997: 546; Dearman 2010: 317). In that case, the parallel expressions *Where, O death, are your plagues? Where, O [Sheol], is your destruction?* are understood as invitations to these powers to carry out their destructive work.[17] It may be better, though, to see them as a taunt (cf. 13:10; Deut. 32:37; Isa. 36:19; Jer. 2:28), emphasizing the impotence of death and Sheol compared with Yahweh's power to save (Garrett 1997: 264; cf. 1 Cor. 15:55). The earlier expressions are then translated as in the MT: 'I will ransom them . . . I will redeem them' (cf. NIV; Andersen and Freedman 1980: 625; Hubbard 1989: 221–222; Garrett 1997: 264–265; Moon 2018: 210). The sense is, then, that Yahweh wants to deliver his people but is frustrated by their intransigence (cf.

---

16. *Nōḥam* is from the same root as *niḥûmîm* (cf. 11:8).

17. *Plagues* (*deber*) can also mean 'thorn'; *destruction* (*qeṭeb*) may be translated 'sting'.

7:13). This leads to the withdrawal of divine compassion and to further threats of judgment (vv. 15–16). In the light of Israel's impending demise, redemption from death and Sheol should probably be understood as a reference to national resurrection (cf. 6:2).[18]

15. In the first part of the verse there appears to be a play on the words *'eprayim* ('Ephraim') and *pārā'* ('to thrive, be fruitful').[19] The MT *bēn* ('son') is generally emended to *bên* ('among'), and some also emend *'aḥîm* ('brothers') to *'āḥû* ('rushes') (Mays 1969: 179; Stuart 1987: 199; Garrett 1997: 266). This gives either: *even though he thrives among his brothers* (NIV, ESV; Dearman 2010: 317), maybe reflecting Ephraim's pre-eminence (13:1), or 'although he flourishes among the rushes' (cf. NRSV), representing Ephraim as a flourishing plant. However, divine judgment, in the form of the hot east wind that blows from the desert (cf. 12:1), described also as a wind (*rûaḥ*) from Yahweh, will dry up Ephraim's water supply and bring its prosperity to an end. This probably refers metaphorically to Assyria. Plundering the nation's treasury suggests a less-metaphorical reference to impending invasion, which continues in the following verse.

16. This verse, which echoes 13:1, concludes the final section of judgment. Samaria here represents the whole of the northern kingdom. However, references to Samaria are relatively few (cf. 7:1; 8:5–6; 10:5, 7), and its mention here may indicate that the siege of the city by Assyria has already begun. The reason for judgment is that the people have incurred guilt (5:15; 10:2; 13:1), because of their rebellion against God. This is the only reference to rebellion in Hosea, but it aptly characterizes Israel's sin as rejecting divine authority and offering allegiance to, and putting trust in, other things. The rest of the verse describes the horror of the Assyrian invasion, which is characteristic of warfare in the Ancient Near East (cf. 2 Kgs 8:12; 15:16). Hubbard (1989: 224) suggests that, if the east wind in verse 15 is a metaphorical reference to Assyria, the

---

18. Resurrection imagery may derive from Baal's dying and rising (see on 6:2).

19. A link with *pere'* ('wild donkey'; cf. 8:9) (Andersen and Freedman 1980: 625; Macintosh 1997: 550) is less likely.

further reference to Ephraim's spring being dried up may also
point to the deaths of the nation's children (cf. 9:13–14, 16).

Meaning
The passage begins and ends by emphasizing what the nation was
and what it has become because of its failure to acknowledge God.
As we see throughout the book, the people have forgotten him,
and continue to worship false gods and to put their trust in themselves, their leaders and their military strategy. Through his activity
in the nation's history, Yahweh has demonstrated that he alone is
their God and Saviour, but the people do not recognize what he
has done, and compound their guilt by attributing those blessings
to other things. Characterizing this as rebellion emphasizes its
seriousness. The people may claim to be devout, but they are, in
fact, in wilful defiance of God. This failure to properly appreciate
what God has done, and the danger of complacency and self-
reliance, remain, albeit at different levels, issues for God's people
today.

As a result of Ephraim's sin, judgment is inevitable, and will
result, effectively, in the death of the northern kingdom. That,
though, is not the final word. Yahweh can redeem his people even
from death (13:14), opening the possibility of national resurrection
and restoration. This, together with 6:2, probably influenced the
development of the Old Testament hope of resurrection to life
beyond the grave (Levenson 2006: 203–204, 214). It is used in the
New Testament (1 Cor. 15:55) to emphasize Christ's ultimate victory
over death, which he shares with believers who put their trust in
him.

C. Call to return to Yahweh; healing and restoration (14:1–9)

Context
This section concludes the prophecy and picks up on vocabulary
and themes from elsewhere in the book (Dearman 2010: 334; Moon
2018: 218). It is made up of three parts. The first (vv. 1–3) calls Israel
to return (*šûb*) to Yahweh and sets out, in a form resembling a
liturgy, what the people need to say to express true repentance.
The second (vv. 4–8) gives Yahweh's response: repentance opens

the way for national healing and restoration. The postscript (v. 9) contains wisdom themes encouraging the reader to learn from Hosea's message. This is widely viewed as editorial (Mays 1969: 190; Wolff 1974: 239; Macintosh 1997: lxxii, 583; Moon 2018: 221–222).[20] However, it too uses Hosean language[21] and is consistent with the thought of the prophecy, and may have been added by Hosea or a disciple (Stuart 1987: 219; Garrett 1997: 281).

As a summary, this passage is probably relatively late in Hosea's ministry. Some date it after the fall of Samaria (Moon 2018: 207–208; cf. Macintosh 1997: 559). It may be better to place it, like the previous section, just before Samaria fell. However, the judgment announced throughout the prophecy is now inevitable, and the promise of restoration is projected into the more distant future.

Comment

1–3. In verses 1–2a, the repeated call is for Israel to return (*šûb*) to Yahweh (cf. 6:1; 12:6). The result is expressed in two further occurrences of *šûb*: Yahweh's anger will turn away (v. 4) and the people will dwell again in his shade (v. 7).[22] The expression *the LORD your God* also appears in 12:9 and 13:4, where it specifically recalls the exodus, and the covenant relationship may be in view here. *Israel*, then, might refer to the whole nation (cf. 11:1), though the primary focus is still on Ephraim (v. 8). The second part of verse 1 notes the problem. The NIV's *Your sins have been your downfall* is more literally translated, 'you have stumbled [*kāšal*] because of your iniquity [*ʿāwōn*]' (NRSV). The same two terms also appear together in 5:5, again indicting the nation. *Kāšal* points, further, to the failure of the religious leaders in 4:5, and *ʿāwōn* is frequently used to refer to the people's sin.[23]

---

20. Kruger (1988b) also views 14:1–8 as a later redaction.

21. E.g. *stumble* (cf. 4:5; 5:5; 14:1), 'rebel' (cf. 7:13; 8:1), 'know' (*yādaʿ*; cf. p. 15 n. 42), *ways* (cf. 4:9; 10:13). Israel is also described as being without *understanding* (4:14) and *wisdom* (13:13). See Andersen and Freedman 1980: 647–648; Seow 1982; Dearman 2010: 345–346.

22. On *šûb*, see above, p. 24.

23. See above, p. 171 n. 15.

Alongside the call to return, verse 2a includes two further imperatives, *Take* and *Say*. These are now plural, perhaps emphasizing their significance for the whole nation. *Take words with you* may refer to renewed vows of penitence and obedience, some of which is elaborated in the next part of the verse. Worshippers should not come before Yahweh empty-handed (e.g. Exod. 23:15; 34:20; Deut. 16:16), and as the people return, they need to bring an appropriate offering: in this case, an expression of true repentance.

Verses 2b–3 outline what the people's prayer should include. This begins with two imperatives, addressed to Yahweh. The first is an appeal for him to forgive (*nāśā'*; cf. 1:6) *all* their sin (*'āwōn*), or, considering the unusual construction, to forgive their sin 'completely' (Stuart 1987: 210; Garrett 1997: 269). The second, 'accept that which is good' (NRSV), appears to be a recognition that the people need to present what pleases Yahweh rather than the false worship associated with Baal.[24]

The final part of verse 2 is problematic. The MT reads: 'we will offer [*šālēm*] bulls [*pārîm*], our lips'. This is sometimes taken to suggest that that penitential prayer is as effective as the sacrifice of bulls (Macintosh 1997: 563; McComiskey 1998: 228–230). Lim (Lim and Castelo 2015: 219) suggests that it refers to bringing bulls that have been promised. Most, though, following the LXX, read *pĕrî* ('fruit') instead of *pārîm*, and take *the fruit of our lips* as a further reference to the words they will bring (Garrett 1997: 271; Dearman 2010: 335). Taken with *šālēm*, which includes the idea of repayment, this may refer to the fulfilment of vows, including making good on their covenant commitment. Such prayer, though, should not be seen as replacing animal sacrifices where they are offered sincerely and not superficially or as part of a syncretistic cult (cf. 6:6) (Routledge 2009).

Verse 3 picks up the theme of the people's past failure to depend on Yahweh and instead trusting in other things. The prophet has already emphasized Assyria's inability to give Israel the help it needs (5:13). The reference to not riding on horses indicates that

---

24. *Receive us graciously* (NIV) is unlikely.

they will no longer rely on military strength (cf. 1:5, 7; 10:13–14),[25] though there may also be an oblique reference to Egypt, whose support is associated with horses (Isa. 31:1) (Dearman 2010: 339; Moon 2018: 220). The people will also renounce idolatry; they will no longer worship what their hands have made (cf. 8:4; 13:2). The final line refers to Yahweh as the true source of strength. In particular, he is the one in whom *compassion* (*reḥem*) may be found, reversing the name of Gomer's second child, Lo-Ruhamah (1:6; cf. 2:1, 23). Orphans are among the weakest in society and are the object of Yahweh's special care (e.g. Deut. 10:18; Pss 10:18; 68:5). And there is the added sense that Israel, who has become fatherless by rejecting the covenant relationship that brought the nation into Yahweh's family (cf. 11:1), may still know his fatherly compassion.

4. Yahweh will respond to Israel's prayer of repentance in the previous verses. First, he will offer the healing (*rāpāʾ*) they need (cf. 6:1; 7:1; 11:3) and can find nowhere else (cf. 5:13). Israel's *waywardness* (*mĕšûbâ*; cf. 11:7) leads to judgment. This is described as wounding (e.g. 5:14; 6:1; 13:8), and so healing indicates restoration. There may also be the sense that only Yahweh's healing can bring about the spiritual change that will enable Israel to return. Second, he will *love* (*ʾāhab*) Israel, *freely*. Yahweh's love for Israel is noted on several occasions (e.g. 3:1; 11:1, 4).[26] *Freely* translates *nĕdābâ*. This often relates to freewill offerings (e.g. Exod. 35:29; Lev. 22:18) and indicates something given willingly, spontaneously and generously (Exod. 36:3; Ps. 68:9). The final line of verse 4 notes that Yahweh's anger (*ʾap*; cf. 8:5; 11:9; 13:11) has turned away (*šûb*). This is another play on words: as Israel returns (*šûb*) to Yahweh, so his anger turns (*šûb*) from them.

5–7. Restoration will also bring renewed fruitfulness. These verses are held together by the repeated comparison with Lebanon, which was noted for the fertility of its soil and richness of its vegetation (cf. Ps. 72:16). Garrett (1997: 277–278) suggests further that Lebanon's fertility may have been associated with Baal, and

---

25. Horses are specifically noted in relation to Judah in 1:7.

26. See above, p. 13.

that in the future what Israel expected from Baal will come from Yahweh.[27]

In verse 5, Yahweh is likened to the *dew* (*ṭal*) that watered the land during the dry summer. Because the dew evaporated in the heat of the day, it is also used to describe both Israel's fickleness (6:3) and its transience (13:3). Here, though, Yahweh's blessing brings the spiritual and physical refreshment that will enable renewal and restoration. The result is that Israel will blossom like the *lily* (*šûšan*). This may refer to the nation's future glory. However, unlike flowers, and in sharp contrast to the withered roots in 9:16, Israel's roots will become 'like (the trees of) Lebanon' (ESV),[28] ensuring stability and permanence.

The series of similes emphasizing future prosperity continues in verse 6. Fresh shoots indicate life and growth which, again, is in stark contrast to the picture of judgment (cf. 9:11–13; 13:15–16) that threatens to destroy the nation and its progeny and so take away future hope. Instead, Israel's *splendour* (*hôd*) will be like that of the olive tree, which is noted for its foliage and valued for its oil. Again, this contrasts with the 'glory' (*kābôd*) that has been lost (cf. 4:7; 9:11). The verse concludes with a further comparison to Lebanon, whose lush vegetation results in a pleasing *fragrance* (*rêaḥ*; cf. Song 4:11).[29] References to *rêaḥ* are frequent in the Song of Solomon (e.g. Song 2:13; 4:10–11; 7:8) (Yee 1987: 138–139; Hubbard 1989: 230–231; Garrett 1997: 274; Macintosh 1997: 572; Ben Zvi 2005: 297; Dearman 2010: 342), and Hosea's possible allusions to love poetry may further reflect the relationship between Yahweh and his bride.

Verse 7 continues the theme of restoration. The translation, though, is debated. One issue is the referent of *his shade*. It may be Yahweh (Andersen and Freedman 1980: 647; Hubbard 1989: 231; Dearman 2010: 342), who is likened to a tree in verse 8 and is frequently described as providing shade for his people (e.g. Pss 36:7;

---

27. Cf. n. 35 below.

28. The MT here reads 'like Lebanon', though the reference to 'roots' may suggest trees. Though Lebanon was noted for its cedars, the NIV rendering is too specific.

29. The NIV again understands 'cedars', though this is unnecessary.

91:1; 121:5; Isa. 25:4; Lam. 4:20). Because this involves a change from
first person (vv. 4–5) to third (v. 7) and then back to first (v. 8), some
also emend the text to '*my* shade' (NRSV, ESV; Mays 1969: 184; Wolff
1974: 232). This then contrasts with the shade under which the
people have prostituted themselves to Baal (cf. 4:13). Also, there
may be a further allusion to love poetry (cf. Song 2:3). It may be
better, though, to continue the thought of the previous verses and
see a reference to *Israel's* shade (cf. Ps. 80:8–11; Ezek. 17:23) (Stuart
1987: 216; Garrett 1997: 275; Macintosh 1997: 574; Moon 2018: 221).
Under the shade of the restored nation, people will prosper. This
may refer to the regathering of exiles,[30] and might also indicate a
future role for Israel in relation to other nations, who would also
benefit from Israel's renewed blessings (cf. Gen. 12:2–3; Isa. 2:2–4).
The distinction between Israel's and Yahweh's shade is, though,
perhaps not too great, since Israel's restoration is wholly the work
of Yahweh, and any future prosperity comes from him alone. And
Eidevall (1996: 216–218) may be right in suggesting that the ambi-
guity is intentional. *They will flourish like the corn* (NIV) may parallel
they will blossom like the vine, highlighting Israel's renewal (Stuart 1987:
211; Moon 2018: 216; cf. Garrett 1997: 275–276). Or it could be
translated 'they will grow grain' (Mays 1969: 184; Wolff 1974: 232;
Macintosh 1997: 573; Dearman 2010: 335). Both indicate an increase
in produce, reversing the judgment in 8:7. The final line makes a
further comparison with Lebanon. *Fame* translates *zēker* ('memorial';
cf. 12:5), and here suggests renown or reputation. Lebanon was well
known in the ancient world as a wine producer, and Israel's fame
will extend just as widely.

8. Verse 8 continues the theme of Yahweh's provision and forms
an appropriate conclusion to this section and to the book. The
rhetorical question *what more have I to do with idols* [*'āṣāb*]*?* points to
the end of Israel's idolatrous worship (cf. 4:17; 8:4; 13:2; 14:3).[31] The

---

30. *Again* (NIV, NRSV) translates *šûb*, taken as an auxiliary verb. It may also
    suggest a return to Yahweh and/or the land (cf. ESV; Stuart 1987: 211),
    and the double sense may be intentional.

31. Following the LXX, some read 'What more has Ephraim to do with
    idols?' (NRSV mg.; Stuart 1987: 211).

inclusion of *more* (MT, NIV) suggests that, in the future, Yahweh's provision will no longer be associated with Baal (cf. 2:8; 11:2–3), and he himself will no longer be regarded as just another 'baal' (cf. 2:16).[32] In contrast to those idols, Yahweh affirms that he is the one who answers and watches over (*šûr*) them.[33] In 13:7, *šûr* points to Yahweh as a leopard, stalking his prey. The sense here of watchful care (Macintosh 1997: 578–579; Dearman 2010: 343; Moon 2018: 216; contra Garrett 1997: 278–279) indicates another reversal of judgment. Yahweh is further described, uniquely in the Old Testament, as a luxuriant tree, providing Ephraim with fruitfulness.[34] This imagery is frequently associated with fertility cults, and may again contrast Yahweh, the true source of provision, with those on whom the people have previously relied.[35]

9. This directly addresses the readers of the prophecy. Whether or not written by Hosea, it is consistent with the message of the book,[36] and is an appropriate postscript, commending its message as one that will guide the wise and discerning in the ways of Yahweh. The language reflects wisdom traditions.[37] The contrast between those who do and those who do not follow the right path is a common theme in wisdom texts (Prov. 10:29; 16:17; 21:8). It also recalls the choice set before the people in Deuteronomy

---

32. See above, pp. 9–10.

33. The NIV reads the verbs as future (cf. Macintosh 1997: 576), though a present sense seems preferable (NRSV, ESV). Some read *'šr* ('to bless') instead of *šûr* (Mays 1969: 184; Stuart 1987: 211).

34. Continuing the wordplay between Ephraim ('*eprayim*) and *pĕrî* ('fruit'); cf. 9:16.

35. Commentators note Wellhausen's conjecture that 'he answers' (*'ānîtî*) and 'he watches over' (*'ăšûrenû*) refer to the fertility deities Anat and Asherah, suggesting that Yahweh provides what the people previously sought from them. However, reference to them here for the first time seems unlikely. See Hubbard 1989: 232–233; Dearman 2010: 343; Moon 2018: 221.

36. Cf. n. 21 above.

37. E.g. *wise* (*ḥākām*), 'upright' (*ṣaddîq*), 'to understand' (*bîn*), to walk in *ways* (*derek*) that are *right* (*yāšār*); see Hubbard 1989: 233–234.

(e.g. Deut. 30:15). Walking in Yahweh's ways is another closely related Deuteronomic theme (Deut. 30:16; cf. 10:12; 11:22; 28:9), and the verse is also similar to Deuteronomy 32:29. It draws, then, on both wisdom and covenant traditions to encourage the discerning reader to choose the path of obedience to Yahweh, which leads to life. By contrast, those who rebel against him and his words will stumble and fall.

Meaning

The opening chapters of the book emphasize Yahweh's love for his bride, Israel, and that love is affirmed in these closing verses (cf. v. 4), which, apart from the warning in the final line, point to a hopeful future. The people have been unfaithful. They have failed to recognize Yahweh as the true source of life and blessings, and have turned to other things: to Assyria and Egypt; to their own political structures, plans and military strength; and, crucially, to idolatry and the worship of Baal. When Israel recognizes that these are futile and returns to Yahweh, with true repentance and full confession of sin, the way is opened for restoration and renewal, and for the possibility, too, of blessing for other nations.

The continuing relevance of Hosea's message is emphasized in the final verse. The same message of divine love and faithful commitment, even towards those who turn away from God, is for all generations. It is tempting to turn away from God and put trust in other things, but they will fail. However, when we turn to God through Christ, we find that his loving commitment will not let us down. In him alone we can know forgiveness, restoration, blessing, true security and real hope for the future. And those who are wise will follow that path.